THE FILMS
OF
FRED ZINNEMANN

THE SUNY SERIES

CULTURAL STUDIES IN CINEMA/VIDEO

Wheeler Winston Dixon, editor

THE FILMS
OF
FRED ZINNEMANN

Critical
Perspectives

Edited by

ARTHUR
NOLLETTI
JR.

STATE UNIVERSITY OF NEW YORK PRESS

Published by
State University of New York Press, Albany

© 1999 State University of New York

For information, address State University of New York Press,
State University Plaza, Albany, N.Y., 12246

Production by Marilyn P. Semerad
Marketing by Patrick Durocher

Library of Congress Cataloging-in-Publication Data

The films of Fred Zinnemann : critical perspectives / edited by Arthur
    Nolletti, Jr.
        p.   cm. — (The SUNY series, cultural studies in cinema/video)
    Filmography: p.
    Includes bibliographical references and index.
    ISBN 0-7914-4225-X (hc : alk. paper). — ISBN 0-7914-4226-8 (pb :
alk. paper)
    1. Zinnemann, Fred, 1907–   —Criticism and interpretation.
I. Nolletti, Arthur, 1941–   . II. Series.
PN1998.3.Z56F56 1999
791.43′0233′092—dc21   98-43754
                                                                                       CIP

10 9 8 7 6 5 4 3 2 1

CONTENTS

LIST OF
ILLUSTRATIONS

ACKNOWLEDGMENTS

This volume on American director Fred Zinnemann grew out of a Special Double Issue of *Film Criticism* (Spring–Fall 1994). This issue was particularly gratifying to edit, for it not only was on a director whom I had long admired but it gave me the opportunity to meet and interview him. It also gave me the opportunity to work with writers whose knowledge and commitment were exemplary. This issue, however, would never have come into being without Lloyd Michaels, the editor of *Film Criticism*. He not only trusted me with this important task but he was there with unfailing support, good humor, expert advice, and friendship to spare. I also owe a special debt of thanks to Wheeler Winston Dixon. A contributor to the original issue, he was instrumental in the publication of this volume. It was Wheeler who phoned me the day he received his copy of *Film Criticism*, urging me to expand the issue into a book-length study. When he became editor of the State University of New York Cultural Studies Series in Cinema/Video, he invited me to offer the project to SUNY Press. I immediately contacted a group of writers as knowledgeable and committed as the original group and arranged to add five new essays to the existing text, so as to deepen the coverage on Zinnemann. I also seized the opportunity to reexamine the original issue and make it even better. The result is the present anthology.

The following chapters originally appeared as articles in *Film Criticism*, and are reprinted by permission: "Guest Editor's Introduction," by Arthur Nolletti Jr.; "Conversation with Fred Zinnemann," by Arthur Nolletti Jr.; "*Act of Violence* and the Early Films of Fred Zinnemann," by Wheeler Winston Dixon; "The Eyes Have It: Dimensions of Blindness in *Eyes in the Night*," by Martin F. Norden; "Historical Perspective and the

Realist Aesthetic in *High Noon*," by Stephen Prince; "The Women in *High Noon*: A Metanarrative of Difference," by Gwendolyn Foster; "Spirituality and Style in *The Nun's Story*," by Arthur Nolletti Jr.; "Shooting a Melon: The Target Practice Sequence in *The Day of the Jackal*," by Lloyd Michaels; "Real-life References in Four Fred Zinnemann Films," by Claudia Sternberg; "Fred Zinnemann's Actors," by Steve Vineberg; "Mythic Figures: Women and Co-Being in Three Films by Fred Zinnemann," by Joanna E. Rapf; and "Fred Zinnemann Filmography." Minor changes have been made in some of the articles to insure stylistic consistency and clarity and to update the material. The "Guest Editor's Introduction" has been retitled and expanded for this volume.

"Repeat Business: Members of the Wedding," by Louis Giannetti originally appeared in somewhat different form in *Literature/Film Quarterly* 4.1 (Winter 1976): 28–38. Reprinted by permission.

Chapters expressly commissioned for the present volume are: "There Were Good Germans: Fred Zinnemann's *The Seventh Cross*," by Leonard Quart; "*Behold a Pale Horse* and the Spanish Civil War," by Linda C. Ehrlich; "'Do You Understand?' History and Memory in *Julia*," by Stephen Prince; and "Fred Zinnemann, *A Man for All Seasons*, and Documentary Fiction," by Joel N. Super.

Production stills were obtained from the following sources: The Academy of Motion Picture Arts and Sciences, The Museum of Modern Art/Film Stills Archive, Jerry Ohlinger's Movie Material Store, The Larry Edmunds Bookshop, Inc., and Collectors Book Store (Hollywood, Calif.). Still credits are as follows:

Columbia Pictures Corporation: Front Cover and Figures 8.1, 8.2, and 15.4 © 1952; Figures 10.1 and 10.2 © 1964; Figure 11.2 © 1966; Figures 15.1 and 15.3 © 1953.

Department of Fine Arts, Federal Government of Mexico: Figure 11.1.

Loew's Incorporated, Metro-Goldwyn-Mayer: Figure 3.1 © 1949; Figure 4.1 © 1942; Figure 5.1 © 1944; Figure 11.4 © 1951; Figure 14.1 © 1948.

Twentieth Century Fox Film Corporation: Figures 13.1 and 16.1 © 1977.

United Artists: Figures 6.1 and 7.1 © 1952; Figure 11.3 © 1950.

Universal/MCA: Figure 12.1 © 1973.

Warner Bros.: Figure 2.1 © 1982; Figures 2.2, 9.1, and 9.2 © 1959; Figure 15.2 © 1960.

As editor I would like to express my gratitude to all those who facilitated the production of this anthology.

John Fitzpatrick, one of the most perceptive writers on Zinnemann, made sure that I obtained two important but not-easy-to-find essays; Tim Zinnemann, the director's son, kindly sent me a copy of his moving documentary tribute to his father, *As I See It*; and George Zinnemann, the director's brother, not only was a source of unwavering support and graciousness but shared some of his memories with me. This I will always treasure.

The following helped locate stills and offered invaluable advice: Janet Lorenz and Linda Mehr of The Center for Motion Picture Study, Mary Corliss and Terry Geesken of the Museum of Modern Art/Film Stills Archive, Mike Hawks of The Larry Edmunds Bookshop, Inc., Jim Shepard of Collectors Book Store (Hollywood, Calif.), and the staff of Jerry Ohlinger's Movie Material Store.

Among those at SUNY Press who contributed to this book, thanks must go to the three manuscript reviewers and the following individuals: Clay Morgan, Kelli Williams, and Patrick Durocher. Deserving a special nod are Acquisitions Editor James Peltz for his patience and support and Production Manager Marilyn Semerad for her unfailing empathy, wise counsel, and ability to field any query great or small.

And, as always, my thanks to those people who are part of every project I undertake: Mitchell Fields, whose conversations with me about Zinnemann go back to that September day in 1959 when we were freshmen at Ohio University; my parents, Arthur and Vera, who were my first teachers; my daughter, Alexandra, who not only welcomed Zinnemann into her life, but taught me to appreciate Fred Astaire and Ginger Rogers; and my wife, Diana, who besides being my constant collaborator is the best possible in-house computer guru I could ever hope to find.

My special thanks to Fred Zinnemann.

CHAPTER ONE

␣

Introduction

ARTHUR NOLLETTI JR.

One of the most celebrated American directors of the 1950s and 1960s, Vienna-born Fred Zinnemann (April 29, 1907–March 14, 1997), made twenty-two features in a distinguished career that spanned fifty years and includes such films as *The Search* (1948), *The Men* (1950), *High Noon* (1952), *The Member of the Wedding* (1952), *From Here to Eternity* (1953), *The Nun's Story* (1959), *A Man for All Seasons* (1966), and *Julia* (1977). As has been often noted, his films are characterized by an unshakable belief in human dignity; a realist aesthetic; a preoccupation with moral and social issues; a warm and sympathetic treatment of character; an expert handling of actors; a meticulous attention to detail; consummate technical artistry; poetic restraint; and deliberately open endings.

Although Zinnemann acquired the greater part of his technical training in the Hollywood studio system, his political and social views were shaped by his experience as a citizen of two worlds—his Austrian homeland and America—and by such cataclysmic events as World War II and McCarthyism. In Austria, which he left in 1927, he saw a stagnant if polite society in which people faced economic and social hardship. By contrast, he was impressed by the sense of freedom and excitement he found in America, a vitality wholly lacking in Europe.

Zinnemann's career may be divided into roughly three periods: the Early Years (1934–1948); the American Years (1949–1957); and the

International Years (1958–1982). Since Wheeler Winston Dixon surveys the Early Years in this volume, I will confine my remarks to Zinnemann's two maiden films at MGM—*Kid Glove Killer* (1942) and *Eyes in the Night* (1942)—and first two major films—*The Seventh Cross* (1944) and *The Search* (1948). For Zinnemann, these maiden films were strictly studio assignments, necessary obligations under his contract. Nevertheless, as he has said, *Kid Glove Killer,* like *The Day of the Jackal* (1973), offered the challenge of building suspense when the outcome was already known. No less important, its story pits two men against each other in a battle of wits, thereby anticipating *Act of Violence* (1949), *Behold a Pale Horse* (1964), and, once again, *Day of the Jackal.* Zinnemann did not much like *Eyes in the Night,* which is about a blind detective and his guide dog foiling a Nazi plot on American soil. But, as Martin F. Norden points out, its treatment of physical disability and illustration of Zinnemann's emerging directorial style make it far from negligible.

Zinnemann regarded *The Seventh Cross* as the true beginning of his career, no doubt because its story of a political prisoner on the run in prewar Germany allowed him to say something about what was happening in Europe. Told in very compassionate, very human terms, the film presents the first characteristic Zinnemann protagonist: an individual who must stand up for what he or she believes in. It also constitutes Zinnemann's first examination of the trauma of World War II, to which he returned repeatedly throughout his career. *The Search* focuses on that same trauma and came out of Zinnemann's realization that America had no real understanding of the magnitude of the pain and suffering in postwar Europe. In his own words, America was "as on an island of stagnation and claustrophobia in the midst of a rapidly changing world" (*Life* 55). He recognized a need for a new kind of realism on the screen, one that could move and educate audiences like the semidocumentary style of Italian neorealism. Thus in 1947, on leave from MGM, he traveled to Germany and Switzerland to film *The Search* on location with a cast made up in part of displaced children. This story of a young refugee befriended by an American G.I. established Zinnemann's reputation.

Zinnemann's second period (1949–1957) may be seen as the American Period. In a series of eight films, beginning with *Act of Violence* (1949) and ending with *A Hatful of Rain* (1957), Zinnemann turned his attention to postwar American society, representing this expansive, energetic, complex society and its problems in a variety of genres. In the noir thriller *Act of Violence,* postwar prosperity and efforts to deny the past come into conflict with truth and conscience as pillar of the community Van Heflin is terrorized by crippled veteran Robert Ryan. In *The Men* (1950), *Teresa* (1951), and *A Hatful of Rain*, the physical and psychological problems of returning veterans are the central concern, with the latter two films focusing on the additional complication of the dysfunctional family, one of the primary themes of American films in the 1950s. Of this trio, *The Men* is easily the best known, thanks to Brando's powerful screen debut as a paraplegic. By contrast, *A Hatful of Rain*, which deals with a veteran's drug addiction, is forgotten today. So, too, is the uneven but interesting *Teresa*, one of Zinnemann's last films in the social realist style. It concentrates not only on a psychologically troubled young veteran but also on his young Italian war bride, who discovers that life in America is even more difficult than life in war-ravaged Italy. Determined to find a place for herself, she is the first of Zinnemann's strong-willed heroines. *The Member of the Wedding* (1952) also features strong women characters: the young Julie Harris, caught between childhood and adolescence, and Ethel Waters, her family's black housekeeper and her surrogate mother. Adapted from Carson McCullers's novel, this film about belonging also effectively shows what it was like to be black in the fifties' South. *High Noon* (1952) and *From Here to Eternity* (1953), probably Zinnemann's most popular and critically acclaimed films, need little introduction. The former, a quintessentially Zinnemann film about following the dictates of one's own conscience, remains one of the most influential Westerns, while the latter examines the same theme in an army setting on the eve of Pearl Harbor. Zinnemann's adaptation of the Rodgers and Hammerstein musical *Oklahoma!* (1955) would seem a complete change of pace for the director: a pastoral set in the American heartland. But in two respects it is not: it shows Zinnemann's interest in trying new things (in this case, a musical and the Todd-AO widescreen format); it also shows his continued faith in American energy and exuberance.

However that may be, in the third period, the International Years (1958–1982), Zinnemann by and large left behind the American setting for Europe and Australia. (*Julia* [1977] returns to America, but for only part of the time.) Perhaps this shift in setting was prompted by the realization that by the mid-1950s World War II and McCarthyism were, for most Americans, history, and that new times called for a new approach, if not new material. (In the early fifties he had already begun to utilize a more rigorous Hollywood Classical Style.) Whatever the case, his return to Europe was neither a retreat nor an act of nostalgia but a broadening and deepening of the same humanistic concerns that he always held.

Zinnemann's first film in this period was *The Nun's Story* (1959), a masterpiece. In it, Audrey Hepburn's anguished nun comes to realize, after years of spiritual struggle, that she simply cannot give to her convent the unquestioning obedience it demands. Her struggle is not only interior but exterior, and interacts with, and is shaped by, events in the 1930s Belgian Congo and in war-torn Europe. A similar interaction between Zinnemann's uncompromising protagonists and history occurs in *Behold a Pale Horse, A Man for All Seasons* (1966), and *Julia*. However, in these films, three of the protagonists—the exiled freedom fighter of the Spanish Civil War; Sir Thomas More, who refuses to endorse Henry VIII's divorce; and Julia, the committed anti-Fascist friend of the young Lillian Hellman—ultimately sacrifice their lives for what they believe in, rather than bend their will to the state. In this respect, these films are clearly political. No less political is *The Day of the Jackal*, a thriller about an assassination attempt on de Gaulle. Here Zinnemann's concentration on the process by which both sides—killer and state alike—go about their business, works hand-in-hand with the story's rejection of heroism and minimizing of character to underscore the impression that technology has superseded humanity and morality in today's world. It is a chilling film— the most bleak cautionary tale Zinnemann ever made.

By comparison, *The Sundowners* (1960) seems almost idyllic, a sprawling comedy-drama about an Australian family of sheep drovers in the 1920s whose love for one another is their only security. The tone may be lighthearted and the depiction of a *happy* marriage refreshingly honest, but Zinnemann never shies away from showing the price that nomadic life exacts from each of his characters, especially from Kerr, another of his strong, self-reliant heroines. Zinnemann's last film, *Five Days One Summer* (1982), is on the surface a love story about a young woman and her middle-aged uncle on a mountain-climbing vacation, but in actuality it is about moral choice. Set in the Swiss Alps in the 1930s, its mood is meditative; its focus is on memory, obsession, and unspoken passion. The central character is the woman (Betsy Brantley). It is she who must find the inner strength to break off the affair, an act made all the more difficult by the appeal of the Sean Connery character. Though flawed, the film has much in common thematically and stylistically with Zinnemann's other work, especially *Julia*.

In reviewing Zinnemann's career I have not forgotten the distinction that he made between films he directed (such as *High Noon*) and films over which he had artistic control (such as *A Man for All Seasons*). Nor have I forgotten that he always took pains to give his collaborators credit. Even so, his work as a whole is characterized by the repetition and reworking of a number of major themes and concerns. This fact alone makes his dismissal by auteurist critics in the 1960s as an impersonal film-maker especially ironic. (These critics were also unimpressed by Zinne-mann's numerous awards, which include two Oscars, four citations from the New York Film Critics Circle, and the D. W. Griffith Award for Life-time Achievement.) Today Zinnemann is not so much dismissed as neglected by a new generation of influential critics—film academicians. On the whole this group has seemed content to let the auteurist verdict on him stand.

This does not mean, however, that Zinnemann has gone unappre-ciated. On the contrary, in the eighties and nineties he was the recipient of numerous honors for his body of work. There were retrospectives at London's National Film Theatre (1982), the Cinémathèque Française (1983), and the University of Southern California (1988); he was feted at the Barcelona Film Festival (1988); and in May of 1996 the jury of the Berlin Film Festival presented him with "a lifetime achievement award," the first ever bestowed upon a foreign filmmaker. He also was granted an honorary doctorate from the University of Durham, England, which he received in a ceremony from one of the Chancellors, Peter Ustinov.

In addition to these honors Zinnemann earned recognition for his indefatigable support of artists' creative rights. He was one of the first filmmakers to take a public stand against colorization; he testified before a congressional committee to protect films from being bowdlerized on television; and he spoke at the 1993 Cannes Film Festival, urging direc-tors to work together for greater creative control over their films. That same year he received the first John Huston Award from the Directors' Guild of America for his lifelong contribution to film. However, in 1996, the last year of his life, he found himself in the ironic and no doubt galling position of having to defend his own creative rights when Univer-sal announced an updated version of *The Day of the Jackal* that appropri-ated the 1973 film's title. When he and Frederick Forsyth, the author of the novel, protested this appropriation, the studio agreed to change the name, but intimated that the word *Jackal* would most likely be part of the new title. Zinnemann stated that he was "'80 percent happy' with the decision" (Petrikin 6). It was a wry, knowing response, the kind that might well have been made by one of his own protagonists.

Released in the fall of 1997 as *The Jackal*, Michael Caton-Jones's remake starring Bruce Willis was deemed by critics to be inferior to the original. This was the same reception accorded two previous remakes of Zinnemann's films: Buzz Kulik's 1979 TV miniseries of *From Here to Eternity* and Charlton Heston's 1988 made-for-cable production of *A Man for All Seasons*. Kulik's film promised viewers a more steamy and complete version of James Jones's novel than the 1953 classic and was a ratings success no doubt because of the promised steaminess. However, its beach scene proved no threat to the famed Kerr-Lancaster scene, and the film itself suffered from ineffectual casting, particularly in the Clift and Sinatra roles. Critics found Charlton Heston's production, which he directed, a solid, respectable effort, and had praise for him in the title role and Vanessa Redgrave and John Gielgud in supporting roles. But once again, the film could not match the quality of the original, and like Kulik's film, is little seen or remembered today, a fate that *The Jackal* is likely to share. In short, these three remakes have one important thing in common: they serve as testimony to Zinnemann's exceptional ability and achievement.

This volume is the first book-length study on Fred Zinnemann. As such, it continues the reexamination of this major American director's career that began with a special double issue of *Film Criticism* (Spring–Fall 1994). Consisting of fourteen critical essays, an interview, and a detailed filmography, this volume expands the *Film Criticism* issue, offering readers information and analysis that are unavailable elsewhere. The chapters that follow are characterized by a variety of methodological approaches and a range of voices. The ideas expressed both overlap and diverge, resulting in a lively dialogue that not only ensures continuity among the selections but situates Zinnemann in his dual role as creative artist (auteur) and participant in the complex nexus of historical, political, and industrial conditions that shape and constitute filmmaking practices. The first eleven chapters concentrate on individual films and are organized chronologically so as to convey a sense of Zinnemann's development; chapters 12 through 14 each deal with several films or more, and investigate an important aspect of the director's work.

The volume opens with an extensive interview with Zinnemann, in which he looks back over his career. Among the topics he talks about are his views of what film is, his approach to filmmaking, his relationship to the Hollywood industry, his work with actors, and his influence by John Ford. Several films are discussed at length, especially *The Nun's Story*.

Wheeler Winston Dixon chronicles Zinnemann's early years of

apprenticeship to the Hollywood studio system. He sees the director as working within this system while turning away from it to create a personally committed, near-documentary style of realism. Dixon devotes the greater part of his chapter to a close analysis of *Act of Violence* (1949), which he regards as a "sort of 'dress rehearsal'" for the second half of Zinnemann's career.

Martin F. Norden, as previously mentioned, examines Zinnemann's construction of blindness in *Eyes in the Night*. He focuses on Hollywood's tendency to "remasculinize" disabled male figures during wartime; the questions related to the theory of "the gaze" that are raised by the representation of the blind detective's perspective; and last but not least, Zinnemann's emerging directorial strategies.

Leonard Quart finds that *The Seventh Cross*, which is set in prewar Nazi Germany, is about the protagonist's rediscovery of faith in mankind rather than an exploration of Nazism. He explains that while it was one of the few American films made during the war to recognize there were good Germans, it does not distort historical reality. He also sees its themes of human decency and individual conscience as setting the tone for Zinnemann's later work.

Two chapters deal with *High Noon*. Stephen Prince contextualizes the film's design and themes in terms of Zinnemann's life, personality, and social aims as a creative artist. He emphasizes the following factors: Zinnemann's European background, his preference for socially cognizant filmmaking, the resonance of Cooper's character for him, Zinnemann's contributions to the visual design, and the competing views of history that are at the heart of the film and about which Zinnemann cared deeply.

Gwendolyn Foster details how *High Noon*'s complex split narrative elucidates not only the struggles of the male hero but those of the two major women characters, as well. She shows that the film can be read as a criticism of postwar America, gender expectations for both men and women, racism, McCarthyism, and the mentality of the Hollywood movie machine itself.

Louis Giannetti reconsiders *The Member of the Wedding*, which many critics have dismissed as canned theater. He argues that like many films dealing with the theme of confinement, Zinnemann's preserves the sense of spiritual entrapment that the characters experience, and that the director was right not to try and break up static space but to serve it with a sensitive use of close-up, medium shots, and moving camera.

My own piece examines Zinnemann's spiritual style in *The Nun's Story*. My emphasis is twofold: I explore the stylistic means—the subtle interplay between "abundance" (visual sumptuousness) and "austerity" (visual rigor)—by which Zinnemann creates spirituality. I also trace the journey of self-discovery that Hepburn's nun makes, comparing and contrasting the nature of her spirituality with that of the convent, which she ultimately rejects.

Linda C. Ehrlich focuses on Zinnemann's presentation of the aftermath of the Spanish Civil War in *Behold a Pale Horse*. She sees his treatment of the relationship between the protagonist, a former resistance fighter, and two secondary characters as an effort to "resolve visualising a reality that has become highly abstract." In addition, she situates Zinnemann's film alongside other films on the subject, thereby viewing it in a broader context.

Joel N. Super analyzes how *A Man for All Seasons* reflects the documentary aesthetic that Zinnemann developed in early films like *The Wave*, *The Search*, *The Men*, and *Teresa*. Among the topics he examines are the relationship between the play and the film, Zinnemann's interest in the intersection of the political and the personal, and the similar world view held by Zinnemann and More himself in *Utopia*.

Lloyd Michaels discusses the famous target-practice scene in *The Day of the Jackal* as an illustration of both the evanescent nature of human character and the imaginary realm of cinema itself. He points out that the scene satisfies the audience's desire to see, at least in symbolic form, an act of violence denied by history: de Gaulle's assassination.

Stephen Prince examines *Julia* as a demonstration of the continuing importance of Zinnemann's realist aesthetic and the historical perspective that underlies it. Besides focusing on the care that Zinnemann takes in reconstructing different periods and the reasons that this care is significant, Prince considers how the shifting time frame and overlapping voice and images embody Zinnemann's theme of the crisis of conscience.

Claudia Sternberg investigates Zinnemann's use of *etic* references—that is, historical facts, situations, events, characters, institutions, or settings that have a real-life existence outside of the fictional world in which they appear. Concentrating on *The Search, From Here to Eternity, Behold a Pale Horse*, and *Day of the Jackal*, she shows the choices and problems involved in using such material, the various reactions from outside generated by these choices, and Zinnemann's statements with regard to some of these choices.

Steve Vineberg finds Zinnemann to be a consummate director of actors, who in his best movies gets stunning ensemble work out of actors with different approaches and styles. Vineberg analyzes some of the rich performances in *The Member of the Wedding, From Here to Eternity, The Sundowners,* and *The Nun's Story,* and concludes that, "in terms of actors, [Zinnemann] is Hollywood's great democrat."

Joanna E. Rapf discusses mythic women figures in *The Member of the Wedding, The Nun's Story,* and *Julia,* women who struggle to achieve a sense of "co-being"; that is, the discovery of their true place in the community. Acting on their belief in equality, social justice, community, and great leadership, these women reflect Zinnemann himself, a point Rapf corroborates by drawing on her interviews and conversations with two of Zinnemann's writers.

Following the chapters are a filmography and a selected bibliography.

Finally, we hope that this anthology will serve not only as a model for further study but as an invitation to scholars and readers alike to look at Zinnemann's films either again or the first time.

WORKS CITED

Petrikin, Chris. "U Concedes Title Fight to 'Jackal' Helmer." *Variety.* December 2–8, 1996: 6.

Zinnemann, Fred. *A Life in the Movies: An Autobiography.* New York: Scribner's, 1992.

FIGURE 2.1. FIVE DAYS ONE SUMMER (Warner Bros., 1982). Fred Zinnemann on location.

CHAPTER TWO

—————————————— ⊞ ——————————————

Conversation with Fred Zinnemann

ARTHUR NOLLETTI JR.

This interview took place in two forty-five- to sixty-minute sessions at Fred Zinnemann's office in London on March 17 and 18, 1993. A warm and gracious man, Zinnemann did his best to accommodate me and to answer whatever questions I asked. He even made sure that we sat close together, so that we could have a genuine conversation. The only thing between us was a lamp and small table. The interview begins with Zinnemann himself setting the scene.

Zinnemann: Well, first of all, I'd like to say that whatever I talk about is, from the point of view of today, obsolete because the values I grew up with no longer exist to any great extent. But I'll say what I have to say. Now, concerning the position of a film director: in my day the film director was, ideally, the only man who had the central vision of a film. By that I mean he was the one person who, once he had a script to his liking, could really visualize what he was after, what kind of actors would be best for the action, how the picture should look, how it should sound, and what sort of pace it should have. And this would then be tested at a preview to see if the audience went along with it. After that, he had the right to recut or change the film. When it came out, it was that man's picture. It was John Ford's *Stagecoach* or Billy Wilder's *Sunset Boulevard.* It did not matter to the public whether it was a Fox movie or a Paramount movie. Ideally this was the way a director functioned.

Producers, if they were very good, were not only immensely helpful but also usually came up with the original idea, so that they had a function which was secondary to the function of a director and the making of a film. John Ford would not have a producer tell him how to shoot a picture, what kind of set-ups to use, or what kind of actors to use. Creatively, he was the locomotive. There were a number of us who worked like that. Granted, there were many others who weren't so fortunate. And that was based, I think, primarily on boxoffice and secondarily on the caliber and quality of the pictures. There were of course a number of excellent creative producers. And you know the names as well as I do, so I don't need to go into that.

Anyway, to me being a director is comparable to being a chef in a restaurant. Let's say you have a chef who is famous for making a very good soup, and he has associates who supply the various ingredients. The writer invents the recipe, and so forth; but the director is still the only one who creates the soup from the recipe, who brings it to reality. (The French word for "director" is *réalisateur*.) The producer is the owner of the restaurant.

The other people are each authors of their own thing. In other words, the writer is certainly the author of the screenplay, the cameraman is the author of the photography. But all in all, the author of the *film* is the director, the only person who has the *central*, overall vision of it from beginning to end.

It is very regrettable that today in an era of mass production the producing arm has become so strong that a film is now judged only by the bottom line: how much money does it make? And if it makes one hundred million dollars, it's a better picture than if it makes fifty million dollars. It's twice as good. This did not necessarily hold true in my day because producers were showmen. They were very good businessmen, but primarily they were showmen. They were excited about the idea of making an audience feel good because it was the obvious way to make big money at the boxoffice. Today that doesn't matter. You can torture an audience, and if they pay their money, it's still a great picture. On the other hand, today's audiences obviously enjoy being tortured and pay for the privilege. I find this a bit sick. And usually these pictures are wonderfully well made; it's just they are very cold, most of them.

Nolletti: That's because they aren't much interested in humanistic values, unlike your films, Ford's or Wilder's.

Z: That's right. Well, I'd just like to make that very clear because a lot of the things that I may be talking about don't apply any more.

N: I want to hear whatever you have to say. So do the readers.

Z: Well then, I'll go on. . . . I'll continue because I also would like to say [something about] the great difference between the producers of those days and now. If you take Sam Goldwyn—you may have heard this story about him. He was producing a picture that he liked very much, and he said, "I don't give a damn if it makes a nickel, but I want everybody in America to see it." Nowadays it's not that at all. It's a very different kind of business.

And the way most of us [directors] went—subconsciously, I think—was [to follow] the two-thousand-year-old rule that a drama, in order to create real emotional relief, has to have a balance of terror and pity. Today, a great many of the films have a lot of terror but very little pity, or no pity at all. And that's why I say they are cold as stone, so many of them. Well, I think I've given you the introduction to how I see this thing.

N: Let's start with some general questions. As you know, proponents of the *auteur* theory have been highly critical of your work. They say that you maintain a safe middle distance from your material because you don't want to get too involved with it or with your characters. How do you respond to this?

Z: Of course I'm involved with my characters. Ask most actors who have worked with me. Ask Vanessa Redgrave. The "safe middle distance" is nonsense. It's just that I don't like to put people under a microscope and look at them as if they were like so many bugs. As to the *auteur* theory: it has always seemed to me to be little more than a gimmick, creating a completely arbitrary and pedantic set of rules by trying to put everyone's work into "artistically correct" pigeonholes. As Billy Wilder once said to me, people should be judged by the best work they have done. The rest is a sort of sterile bureaucracy.

N: In fact, to pick up on a related point, you've always been interested in allowing audiences to make up their own minds.

Z: Of course. Rather than pushing things down the audiences' throats, I strongly believe in allowing them to use their own imagination.

N: Like the ending of *The Nun's Story* [1959] where you fought not to have Franz Waxman's music—

Z: Yes—

N: —because you felt it imposed an interpretation.

Z: That's right.

N: Don't you think that allowing an audience to make up their minds can actually be a way for a director to express his personality?

Z: I wouldn't know because I don't think in those terms. All I think about is that when I'm very moved by something and very excited about it, I would like to share it and express it in the only way I can. It's that simple.

N: It's been said that your films have a common theme, the struggle of the individual.

Z: Well, it's not, you know—Perhaps I should say this: I work by intuition, by instinct, not by analysis. All I worry about is, Am I moved by the story emotionally, or am I not? If it's just cold logic, if I don't find something in it that is inspiring or exciting, something that makes you feel that the human spirit still exists, then it's not for me. You see? So that's the only way I can go. I can't say I'm doing this because the theme is a noble theme or anything. But I can say that [in *A Man for All Seasons* (1966)] Thomas More standing up for what he believes in, until he gets his head cut off—which in his defeat is really a victory—is to me a celebration of the human spirit. I also feel that this is something that we have been missing a great deal [recently]. There are some films—well, offhand, for instance, *Dead Poet's Society*. I think it's a great picture. *Breaker Morant* is also a great picture. Those are the kind of pictures that leave you with some belief in the human spirit, and you don't feel ashamed to be a member of the human race when you leave the theater.

N: Let's talk about your visual style, how you formulate the visual plan for your films—like, for example, *High Noon* [1952].

Z: Well, that's purely intuitive, you see. It so happens that my imagination starts with the visual end of it so that, after reading the script [for *High Noon*], the first thing I saw in my head were the railroad tracks pointing to the horizon, [which] never allow the audience to see beyond the horizon, except to know that whatever bad news comes, it would come from there. Then it occurred to me that it would be interesting to see *in contrast* the marshal [Gary Cooper] moving about all the time. So we had a static main theme and a dynamic second theme. And that was then accentuated by the urgency of time—the clocks—which gave a strong and growing feeling of time being your enemy. So that's how the visuals came to exist. When it came to what the story was about, as you probably know, it seems to mean different things to different people. To me, it was a simple thing. To me, it's a picture of conscience as against compromise: how far one can follow one's conscience before having to compromise—just that, nothing else. That's a universal theme, and never mind whether it's an allegory on the Korean war, as an *auteur* critic wrote.

N: In terms of your preparation, how extensively do you story-board?

Z: I just do thumbnail sketches. In the book [Zinnemann's autobiography] which you've probably seen, there is a page full of little thumbnail sketches just outlining the action. I normally don't do that anymore. It's just a memorandum for myself, nothing else. Sometimes I explain it to the art director because it looks like a hieroglyph . . . primitive and hard to decipher.

N: One thing that amused me in your book was how John Ford, after seeing your first film, told you to quit moving the camera so much. Did you take that advice to heart?

Z: Very much, very much. I think it's something that Ford had his own reasons for, but when you look back, you can't necessarily go along with it. Ford said to me that he liked to treat the camera like an information booth, meaning that he would move the characters in such a way that when he wanted them in close-up, they would actually be moving into a close-up. Well, I think it's brilliant. And I do feel that if you move the camera there has to be a reason beyond just trying to be brilliant. I don't think you should ever in a film have people be conscious of how brilliant the direction is. If people come out of a film and say, "Wasn't the music good?" or "Wasn't the photography great?" it means that the film is not in balance because all these things have to be blended, like soup, in such a way that there's not too much salt in it, there's not too much pepper in it, and that you're not even aware of which is what; you're just aware that it tastes good.

N: Your moving camera, though, is never just functional. It dramatically heightens emotional feelings.

Z: Yes.

N: Two examples come to mind: in *The Member of the Wedding* [1952] the camera moving toward Brandon de Wilde's room the night he is dying, then pulling back from it on what turns out to be a morning weeks later. And in *The Nun's Story*, the tracking shot from the train that is taking Audrey Hepburn away from her beloved Congo. The moving camera here is—

Z: Very important.

N: Which brings me to another characteristic of your work: the finely toned, often understated, emotional quality—as in the scene in *Julia* [1977] when she [Vanessa Redgrave] and Lillian [Jane Fonda] meet in the Berlin cafe. How do you know the exact tone that a scene should have emotionally? How do you get that tone?

Z: That's a very interesting question. That is part of a director's preparation because you have to visualize a scene, you have to get a feeling of what it is that you want to accomplish. And one of the things I knew was that the scene was played in a public place, so there couldn't be a lot of visible emotion. They would try to guard themselves as far as they could so that people wouldn't pay attention. That was number one. And they [Vanessa Redgrave and Jane Fonda] were both very aware of it because we talked about that. The other thing is that Vanessa is one of the great actresses of the century; she has a brilliant talent of not appearing to be acting. She's just there, just like Spencer Tracy, and so that when she says a line that could be terribly emotional like, "I had a baby," she eats caviar and sounds very casual about it. She plays away from the line, you see. Vanessa is the kind of actress that doesn't need to be told things like that.

N: Also, she's perfectly cast.

Z: First of all, in casting perhaps the most important thing I have to help me is that I have a good instinct for talent. I can spot a talented actor; I can spot the actor who has a facet in his or her character that has not been seen in pictures before, like Deborah [Kerr] in *From Here to Eternity* [1953], where we actually cast against type. And it's very interesting because it has to do with applied psychology, really. So once I find the kind of people that I sense can do the job, provided that they are talented actors, or uninhibited nonactors, we sit down, we talk about the character, talk about how it develops, talk about the relationships, and I tell them how I see it. I don't tell them how to do it because I'm not an actor myself. A man like Kazan, who was an actor himself, can talk to actors almost like a teacher, which I can't do. Nor do I feel I need to. All I do is use my instinct for casting and let the actors feel that I trust them and have respect for them, and encourage them. And then that makes them very free to do things which they normally perhaps wouldn't do. And it's a very happy kind of work. And so I get along with talented people. If by some chance I get a mediocre actor, I get very frustrated.

N: Getting back to the scene in *Julia*, one reason it's so effective is that while Redgrave holds herself back, Fonda does a lot of crying.

Z: Yes.

N: Were you surprised to see her do that?

Z: [*Laughs*] No, of course not. Jane is technically superb. She can cry on demand and in the quantity you want. She can cry a drop or a bucket on cue, depending. It was an actor's performance, and a very, very good one. I was not surprised, of course not, because I knew what was going to happen. But I was pleased to see how well she and Vanessa did it. As a director, you have a sense of what you want. Let's call it 100 percent. Now if you get 80 percent, you are in good shape. If you get 90 percent, it's very good. If you get 100 percent, it's quite rare. But these two were 120 percent, way beyond what I thought could be accomplished. They shared a triumph, I thought.

N: While writing your autobiography, you must have gone back and looked at your films, some that you hadn't seen for awhile.

Z: Yes.

N: Had any of your impressions or opinions changed? Were you surprised by what you saw in any of your films?

Z: Not really, no. I can't say I had much emotion one way or another. Occasionally I thought, "It's pretty good." There were a couple which I hated that I had to do because of the contract, the two Butch Jenkins's pictures, *My Brother Talks to Horses* [1947] and *The Army Brat* (*Little Mister Jim* [1947]). And before I knew how to defend myself, I got in a position where I had to make these two pictures. So I learned my lessons through that.

N: Speaking of lessons, in your book you say that you didn't feel you were in command as a director until *Act of Violence* in 1949. That is almost fifteen years into your career.

Z: Well, I was underplaying it a bit. I knew a few things, but that was probably the first time I really felt comfortable knowing exactly what I wanted and exactly how to get it. But I can't tell you why really. One of the reasons was that the actors were so good, Robert Ryan and Van Heflin. And Janet Leigh was marvelous; it was one of her first pictures. Also, I thought the story was good. I liked the story; I liked the picture. And I felt that my visual imagination was getting liberated more and more.

N: How so?

Z: Well, for instance, one of the earliest shots is a shot of Robert Ryan, who is walking, trying to cross the street. A band comes by with the American flag, and then he keeps walking and goes into a hotel. It was all done in one shot. I got a kick out of that because it wasn't an easy thing to do. And I liked the idea of this man, who was a victim of an inhuman experience in war [he was a prisoner in a German concentration camp], having to step back because a few old guys were walking past him carrying the American flag as though they owned it. There was an irony about that that I liked, although I don't think it was picked up by too many people. There are certain things you like to do for your own pleasure, and some people catch them and others don't—like the judge in *High Noon*, who talks about compromise and at the same time is folding the American flag and sticking it in his pocket. Working the flag the way he does is what makes the scene interesting.

N: Plus, it's ironic that after telling Gary Cooper he doesn't have time to give him a civics lesson, that's exactly what he does.

Z: Yes, yes. The same thing happens later. Another character comes in [to Cooper's office] and is very enthusiastic about joining the posse, but comes back later and finds that he's the only person. And at that point he says, "Well, I'm on your side," and as he says it, he plops down his star, and then he starts backing away and all that. I like touches like that. I like in *High Noon* the shot where Cooper finally comes out of the office and goes up the street all by himself—the boom shot. It gives you a lot of fun. So, in other words, I like individual little spots that give me pleasure, but I can't say that this picture is better than others. As far as I'm concerned, *Member of the Wedding* is very moving because of the actors' performances. I think they [Julie Harris, Ethel Waters, and Brandon de Wilde] are all marvelous, and there was not very much work needed because they had done this play for two years and were very well rehearsed.

N: Many of your films deal with the subject of medicine. Is this a special interest of yours, or has it some relationship to the fact that your father was a doctor?

Z: Probably. But it just sort of happened. I did that short subject on child bed fever ["That Mothers Might Live" (1938)]. With that one having got the Academy Award, I seemed to be the specialist for "doctor's pictures," which pleased me. I enjoyed it. That sort of led to a series of other films about doctors. . . . [W]e did what I thought was a good one on insulin ["They Live Again" (1938)], one on sleeping sickness ["Tracking the Sleeping Death" (1938)], and then two or three others. It was always interesting. And then when I did *The Men* [1950], which had to do with a doctor and a group of paraplegic war veterans, that was because Carl Foreman and Stanley Kramer asked me to direct the film. And I was delighted. At that time the executives at any big studio would have dropped dead if you had come up with a subject like that.

N: I've also noticed that your films are very interested in process, how something is done—for example, the different stages involved in becoming a nun, the step-by-step working out of the assassination plot in *The Day of the Jackal* [1973], and so on. Is this interest related to your work or training in documentary films?

Z: I never thought about it in that way. The thing is, I always like to know why something happened, why so-and-so says this, or why he reacts like that. *Why* is a very, very important word in my dictionary. So "why" is probably the answer to the question you are asking.

N: In other words, a natural curiosity.

Z: Yes. With *Day of the Jackal,* in the book a part of the excitement [had to do with] the fact of how the gun was put together. The idea that excited me was to make a suspense film where everybody knew the end—that de Gaulle was not killed. In spite of knowing the end, would the audience sit still? And it turned out that they did, just as the readers of the book did.

N: That left you free to concentrate on another level of suspense.

Z: What was also interesting was the ironic point that one person could bring the entire country to a stop. The entire government, the entire army, the entire air force—everything stopped dead. And they still couldn't find him [the "Jackal"] [Edward Fox]. Then his whole plot went wrong; it got wiped out at the last instant because de Gaulle bent too far forward [during the formal ceremony] to kiss a soldier who was very short. I thought it was interesting.

N: And ironic, too. Plus, the authorities never learn the Jackal's true identity. There's also another nice irony, which you talk about in your book, regarding Cyril Cusak, the gunsmith. For him, the entire matter is strictly a business transaction.

Z: It's very sinister actually, particularly because Cusak looks sort of bland, you know—a very nice gentleman, a serious businessman, an engineer. Nothing wrong with him. It made me think of our atomic scientists and others.

N: Yes, that idea comes across. You're really making a sly point here about the absence of moral responsibility.

Z: Even when he [the gunsmith] asks if it's going to be a head shot [instead of a chest shot].

N: Nobody ever thinks of Fred Zinnemann as being a director of suspense films, yet that is what a good number of your films basically are, like *The Day of the Jackal, The Seventh Cross* [1944]—

Z: And *Act of Violence.* Well, I don't know why that happened. It probably has to do with pigeonholing. You know, many critics just look at one thing, and they become full of preconceived notions and dismiss everything that doesn't fit in. So that all they seemed to know about me was that I was hammering away at integrity, which is nonsense.

N: It's certainly too narrow a view of your films because you have other concerns, too.

Z: Yes.

N: Since leaving MGM, you've worked as an independent, yet in a previous interview you called yourself a Hollywood director. What did you mean by this?

Z: Yes. What I meant was that [although] I have been independent of major studios since 1948, I learned my trade in Hollywood first in the very tough school of short subjects and then [during] the seven years of being an MGM staff director under contract, and in theory having to accept anything they asked me to shoot, [which was] where I got into trouble. But I did learn my lessons there. And I learned how to organize my thinking, and I learned how to tell a story, or at least I hope I learned—up to a point anyway. Because in short subjects, having ten minutes to tell a story on a subject like, let's say, Dr. Carver, the black scientist, from the cradle to when he was ninety—telling it all in ten minutes was quite a challenge! So you learned economy in the best sense of the word. You learned that you had to get your point across in a minimal amount of time to make the maximum impact. And that training in itself was of incredible value.

N: You learned your craft, and you learned it well. Do you ever feel, however, that when people say, "Fred Zinnemann is a superb crafts-man," the word *craftsman* is almost like a left-handed compliment?

Z: Yes, I do, I do. I think there's more to making films than just the craft because technique is nothing but an instrument. You know, I come from Austria where music is a very important way of life, and they have a tremendous, tremendous respect for musicians, like good violin players. But they don't have much use for a virtuoso. In other words, if there's a violin player whose technique is terrific, and he can do very difficult things, but musically he hasn't got it, then they lose interest. And some of the most amazing, great virtuosos didn't get anywhere in Vienna. And some people with much less technique who really got the meaning and emotion of the music they loved. And that's the same in film. I'm very glad that you picked this up because *craft* to me is a slightly demeaning, a slightly patronizing word. I wouldn't like to call myself an artist because I think that's kind of pretentious . . . that's just overdoing it. But I'm certainly not just a craftsman. To be a good craftsman in itself is a wonderful thing, but it's not the same.

N: As you've said, craft is "an instrument." In *From Here to Eternity*, for example, after Maggio [Frank Sinatra] is murdered, Montgomery Clift plays taps, the tears streaming down his face. He has mastered the craft of playing the bugle, but what's more important is that this is the only way he can show his deepest feelings. Isn't this ideally what craft is all about?

Z: Yes. The thing is . . . I wouldn't want to be misunderstood on the subject. I've enormous respect for craftsmen. To be a good craftsman is a great thing. It's just that it's not quite the exact way to define whatever it is that I do.

⊞

Z: I wanted to mention more about camera because I don't think we went into that fully enough. And I'd like to tell you that when I went to school in Paris, to the Technical School of Cinematography [in 1927], there was sort of a new wave, which was called the "Avant Garde." The directors were all very young people: René Clair, Cavalcanti, Epstein, Man Ray, Germaine Dulac, people like that. And they had an expression called *cinéma pur*—"pure cinema"—which meant that the cinema can do things or get things across emotionally that you cannot express in any other way, not with words, not with music—although film is like music, an art which goes directly to the emotions without passing through intellect or through reason. It really addresses itself to the subconscious to a great extent. Anyway, the camera to me is a means of expression rather than simply a technical means of recording. In very many films the camera is used purely to record the action without enhancing it, without taking advantage of any kind of mood it could create. And it's not only lighting, but it's the camera movement and the composition and all sorts of other things.

N: Are you disagreeing, then, with John Ford, who regards the camera as an "information booth"?

Z: I totally agree with him because as he said, "When I move the camera, there's a reason for it." And when you look at a film like *My*

Darling Clementine, which is practically all straight set-ups without camera movement, there's one moving shot, which is when the new-lyweds Henry Fonda and the girl [Cathy Downs] come around the corner of the barn and start walking. And the camera moves with them and then shows the building, which is about to be raised, with the flag on top of it. And it's a marvelous, emotional moment that is brought about really by the way the camera is handled. So, like any artist, Ford did not establish rigid laws for anything. He used the camera movement when he saw a reason for it, but he didn't move it all over the place. That does not mean that people who move the camera are wrong, because everybody has their own way of telling a story.

N: Like Max Ophüls, for one.

Z: Exactly. So what goes for Ford does not have to go for anybody else. But that was what he thought, and that was what I got a lot out of in making pictures like *High Noon*, which had a camera that didn't move all that much, but when it moved—like in the boom shot—there was a reason for it, and it expressed something. It expressed the loneliness of a man who very probably is going to be killed, with no one else wanting to know anything about helping him.

N: It's interesting to learn about this particular influence that Ford had on you. Now, what I thought we'd do today is talk about some specific films.

Z: Would it upset you if I had one other thing I wanted to tell you?

N: No, of course not.

Z: Which has to do with the studios' tampering with films after the films have been made.

N: Please go ahead.

Z: I can give you one example in my picture *From Here to Eternity*, particularly the scene you were talking about yesterday, the bugle scene. You'll probably be surprised to hear that both Clift and I did not want him [Clift] to cry and that it was an enormous battle between the head of the studio, Harry Cohn, and ourselves. He insisted that Clift should cry. Clift did not feel that he would cry, and I didn't, because Clift and I wanted the audience to cry, not

Clift to cry. And by crying, Clift took it away from the audience, even though he was still very strong, but not as strong as we would have wanted to do it. But that was one battle that we lost; we won a great many others.

N: Were you allowed to film the scene your way, as well?

Z: Yes, we insisted on that. And then there was another battle because we still said, "Well, the one [take] without the tears is better." But he [Cohn] had the final cut, so there was nothing we could do about it. The other thing in the same sequence was that to my mind it was an homage to John Ford, these other soldiers who are saluting the man who has been killed. And it was a very careful build-up of showing more and more people coming out of the cubby holes and listening. And all of that was cut by the studio to make room for advertising. And also the opening scene was cut from what I wanted, again to condense footage so that they could get more advertising in it. In the original scene, if you remember, the platoon is starting to march across camera, and then you see a tiny little figure who keeps walking closer and closer. The way this was cut it was covered over with main titles so that you couldn't see it. And originally that was not what it was. It was first the titles, and then you saw the platoon walking, so that the shot ran much longer. Do you follow?

N: Yes, I do.

Z: The scene should have been played in the clear to show that this is a man who is a loner and who walks against the stream—because the stream was moving left to right and he was coming closer. This is a subconscious thing for the audience. It interests them. They don't know why, and they needn't know why, but there's something about it that's intriguing. So this should have been a relentless, steady moving forward without a lot of interference from a lot of letters. [Pauses] I gave all of my 16mm prints to the Academy [of Motion Picture Arts and Sciences] in Hollywood. They have a large amount of material—all my pictures, all my archives, and everything else. And so there is a 16mm print of *From Here to Eternity*, which is available to anybody who goes there and wants to see it. They let you run it on a Steenbeck.

N: In other words, this is the director's cut.

Z: That is the director's cut, yes. That was the original cut. That 16mm print was taken off the negative after the final preview when the final prints were made for the opening of the film.

N: Did this sort of tampering happen with any of your other pictures?

Z: Yes, it happened with *The Day of the Jackal*. They took out about a good twenty minutes. I think they were right to take out fifteen, but they should have left the five others, which were good. But you sit in London, and they are in Hollywood, and what can you do? Besides, they've got thirty lawyers and you can't fight them.

N: Tell me about *The Nun's Story*. Did you pretty much get your cut on that film?

Z: As far as I can remember. Yes.

N: What about the lunch scene early in the film with Audrey Hepburn and Dean Jagger? A shot from the scene appears in the trailer and also in one of the lobby cards. The scene is even referred to in the opening scene when Jagger says, "Come along, Gaby. I've ordered a table for one o'clock." What took place in the scene, and why was it cut from the finished film?

Z: That scene was cut in my own interest because I felt it was repetitious and covered an area which you already knew about, and also prevented the picture from starting to move. The start was fairly static as it was, and it should not have been burdened with a scene like that, which was meaningless because it told you nothing new.

N: How long was the scene? Do you remember?

Z: It must have been about a minute and a half. But that's an awful lot of time, especially at the early start of a picture. It's like a plane starting off: the first two or three hundred yards are always the toughest and the most dangerous because the audience is trying to grab on to what's going to happen. And if they start getting information they already have, it makes them impatient.

N: Since we're already talking about *The Nun's Story*—which is my favorite of your films—I'd like to concentrate on it a while longer.

Z: Sure, sure.

N: In *American Directors* John Fitzpatrick calls it "a transcendent film, comparable more to Bergman or Bresson than to anything in the American cinema" [p. 384]. When preparing the film, did you look at Bresson's *Diary of a Country Priest* or Dreyer's films to see how these European directors had treated the subject of religion, as opposed to how Hollywood had?

Z: Why should I have done that, do you think?

N: Not that you should have done it. I was just wondering if you had.

Z: Well, I think the last thing I would want to do is to try to imitate anybody . . . to get any help from the outside of that kind. I would prefer to go on my own resources. It's conceivable if I felt helpless or stuck that I might have looked for that kind of help, but thank God I didn't need it. I was very fortunate, and I just did my own work the way I felt.

N: One thing that strikes me is that, unlike most Hollywood films, it does not treat nuns, priests, or religion sentimentally. That's very much an attitude that you see only in European films.

Z: Well, that really comes from the enormous amount of preparation that we were able to do, thanks to the Church actually. As you know, I'm not a Catholic, and the Church at first was very careful because here was the story of a woman who was a professional nun for seventeen years before she left, having discovered that she no longer had the vocation. Secondly, they were worried about what we would do with the implied love story between her and the doctor [Peter Finch]. And it took them a long time to decide that we were okay. Up to that point when we wanted to see a convent, they were always enormously polite, and we would get to see a printing machine or the kitchen, and no more. Later, after there was mutual confidence, they did an enormous amount to let us see what the life of the nuns was like, to the point where the individual actresses who played the main parts—none of whom were Catholics—were allowed to spend about four or five days in a convent. Each one— one person per convent—could then see from the early morning until the Grand Silence at the end of the day what it was like and what happened. They were all in Paris, and I used to make the rounds in a taxi each morning from one convent to another to see how they were doing. All these people—Audrey Hepburn, Edith Evans, Peggy Ashcroft—all these famous actresses were doing it, so that when we finally started to really rehearse, they were already in character and they knew how a nun walked. There was only one who wouldn't do it for personal reasons, and she was the only one who swung her hips! [*laughs*]

N: I'm tempted to ask who, but I won't.

Z: And so all of these people, including Audrey, were all very, very clued in because they had seen it firsthand.

N: Even how nuns dismount from a streetcar.

Z: All of that—the way they held their skirts, how they walked, everything. In fact, at the end Audrey added a touch when she walked out of the convent. She is about to do it [to hold her skirt], and then realizes she no longer has that kind of skirt.

N: She also leaves the door wide open, which, of course, if she were still a nun, she would have had to close.

Z: Yes. She also had to leave it open because we had the camera there [inside the room].

N: The scenes of convent rituals in the first forty or so minutes depend almost entirely on visuals. How much guidance did you actually get from Robert Anderson's script here? In other words, how detailed was the script? Aren't these scenes an example of where the director is really the creative force?

Z: Well, I never take credit for work on a script, but in fact I work very intensely on the second draft, and what I do always is ask the writer to write the first draft by himself unless he really wants to talk to me. On the second draft, we work very closely together. And so the thing you refer to is something I saw with my own eyes and then broke down into scenes. And I could say that I had a lot to do with the writing of it, so the script in that sense was in a small way also my script and was there because I felt that that's what it should be.

We were in Rome for this part of the picture, and the people who were in charge of us, as I told you, were the Dominicans. And the man in charge was the head of the liturgy of the Dominican order worldwide. It was in the Mother House, Santa Sabina, and so we saw all the ceremonies of the Dominicans, we saw ceremonies of the Franciscans, and we saw ceremonies of the Augustinians. Then after awhile, the Franciscans would ask us how the Dominicans were doing, and so forth. And they wound up calling me half-brother. [*Laughs*] I'm also probably the only man who ever had the Dominicans and the Jesuits at the same table for dinner!

Well, we were fortunate because we really did have tremendous help, [especially] from the Jesuits. There was a man whose name is Father Gardiner. He was the editor of the Jesuit magazine *America* and a professor at Georgetown University, and he was very helpful. I'll give you an idea of the thinking we found within the various communities. There was a scene when the postulants come in and prostrate themselves before [the Mother Superior] Edith Evans, who says in the script, "The life of a nun is a life against nature." That is what was in the book [by Kathryn Hulme]. Our Dominican adviser said, "You mustn't say that. You should say, 'It's a life *above* nature.'" And I said, "Well, I thought that the religious life is a struggle. It didn't mean, then, that you were above nature." And so we went on for a couple of hours to no avail. That evening I saw Father Gardiner, who was in Brussels by chance, and I told him about it, and he said, "Why don't you tell her to say, 'in many ways it's a life against nature'?" And that did it. And that seemed to show the difference between the dogmatic, strict approach of the Dominicans and the very flexible ways of the Jesuits' thinking. It's fascinating to talk with these people. They were very much the top echelon and really brilliant.

N: Regarding that line, in the film Edith Evans actually says, "In a way it's a life against nature," so she manages a third rewrite and has the final say.

Z: Yes.

N: How did you happen to cast Edith Evans and Peggy Ashcroft?

Z: Because we had a brilliant casting director, Robert Lennard. What normally happens in casting is that the casting director will give you a list of names of actors he thinks might be right for a given part. Let's say he gives you fifteen names. You go through the names, and some of them you know and some you don't. The ones you don't, you say, "Well, can I see a film? Or can I see that actor in the theater, or in a video, or whatever?" And so you then gauge that actor's talent and personality, and gradually in that way, but mainly with the help from a casting director, you arrive at your decision. And Bob Lennard said, "The two people that you should have in this picture are Peggy Ashcroft and Edith Evans." And they both came on interview to the hotel, as a matter of fact, which was rather unheard of. But that's the small amount of merit I had in casting those two ladies. I had more merit in getting other people, who nobody had ever heard of, which was a different thing.

N: Can you give me some details about how you worked with Audrey Hepburn to shape her role?

Z: We got together and talked about the character, how it develops, and how it reacts to the other characters. It took many hours of going into lots of details. I alway work that way with almost all actors. Then when we are rehearsing, I always want to see what the actor brings to the part, without telling him what to do. And invariably, if the actor is a talented person with imagination, he has already a well-developed idea about how to bring the part to life.

N: Audrey Hepburn's face is so expressive that you can read what she's thinking.

Z: It's probably because she and I talked in great detail about what she [Sister Luke] was thinking, but not on the set. We talked about it months before. So she gradually started to live with that and she gradually started to find it in concrete form in the convent when she saw the nuns. And so when we came to shoot, we didn't waste too much time going through explanations. You can work very fast that way.

N: Because the actor already knows the role.

Z: Yes. But also, you see, working fast is very helpful because it maintains the energy of the performance. If you do a scene very many times, it may get polished, but it also loses energy. And then you get a very polished scene that is dead. For instance, we shot *From Here to Eternity*, which was very complicated, in seven weeks—forty-two days, which is very fast. And *High Noon* in twenty-eight days, which is four weeks, and very quick. But you have to have the actors prepared to a point where they know exactly when, what, where, etcetera. You know? That explains it for Audrey Hepburn, as well as for any other actor I worked with. Does that give you an idea?

N: Yes, but it's still hard to imagine, even with thorough preparation and rehearsal, how an actor—in this case, Audrey Hepburn—can summon the kinds of nuances and richness of feeling required right there on the spot.

Z: Yes. Well, that's my job: to create the surroundings where any actor can concentrate. A good actor concentrates tremendously, anyway. . . . And part of the job is to keep actors encouraged, although that's just my own personal feeling. There are other directors who get tremendous performances in all sorts of other ways. I don't say my method is any better than anybody else's, but I happen to work in that way. . . .

N: How did you work with Walter Thompson, your film editor?

Z: Well, Walter was a marvelous editor. The way I work with editors is that they assemble the film, they cut it as we go. From the first day, we look at the rushes, and then he begins editing the way he sees it. And I never look at it at all until he's got it all completed. By that time the shooting is finished, and he usually has about ten more days to really finish his job. For those ten days I used to go skiing up in the mountains and leave him alone, without pressure. When I came back and he was finished, we'd sit down and look at it. And it would be, let's say, instead of two hours, two-and-a-half hours or whatever. We started then to give it the final shape. And with some editors, it was easier than with others. But Thompson was very good. You were talking about the moving shots when Sister Luke leaves Africa. Well, there was also a moving shot when she first comes to Africa. The first shot is when she sees the station from her point of view. Thompson, a new editor for me—this was the first day on the set—said he wanted to have an establishing shot of the station with the train coming in, and I said, "No way!" because if he had it, he would have used it. And I wanted the shot done from her point of view. That makes a difference. But as Ford said, "If they haven't got it, they can't use it."

N: The editing style changes in the film. The scenes at the end are much more fragmented than those at the beginning.

Z: Well, yes. Partly because of the tension and the war, and partly because the tempo of life intensifies. It's no longer the idyllic Congo.

N: The outside world is falling apart, and so is Sister Luke's own private world. And then the last scene returns to the longer rhythm we've seen in the first half of the film. It's a very beautiful and moving conclusion.

Z: Yes.

N: A scene involving three men trapped in quicksand and rapidly rising water had to be abandoned because nature refused to cooperate. How and where would it have fit into the film?

Z: Toward the end of the Congo story, but I can't tell you exactly, as I have given my script to the Academy in Los Angeles. My memories of those years (1958–1959) are fading now.

N: Let's move on to some films we haven't yet talked about.

Z: Whatever you'd like.

N: You've said that there was a problem in adapting *A Man for All Seasons* for the screen. What was this problem?

Z: Robert Bolt, the author of the play, having delivered the first draft of the film scenario, said it would be a bad idea to keep the character of the Common Man because it was, to quote him, "a theatrical device." I disagreed with him and for several weeks we tried to incorporate the character in the screenplay, but it stopped the flow of the story; it never did work and much to my regret we had to finally give up.

N: Why is Alfred Hayes listed in the credits as one of the writers of *A Hatful of Rain* [1957]?

Z: I have no idea. Alfred Hayes was involved on *Teresa* [1951] because he had written the original book, and I think maybe that he was hired to write the original script for *A Hatful of Rain*. It quite probably wasn't very good because I remember that I asked Carl Foreman to write the script, which he did, but he didn't get credit for it, I don't think.

N: Because he was blacklisted.

Z: Yes.

N: But didn't Michael Vincente Gazzo write the first draft of the screenplay?

Z: No, he wrote the dialogue—some of the dialogue—but it was really Carl Foreman who wrote the script, not Gazzo. Gazzo couldn't write film scripts, not at that time.

N: You didn't like using the CinemaScope format in *A Hatful of Rain*. Did you feel the same way about Todd-AO in *Oklahoma!* [1955]?

Z: Not really, because it was a different format altogether, and it was very exciting because it was something really new [and] experimental. That was part of why I wanted to do the picture. Normally I wouldn't touch a musical because it's not really what I'm good at. But also, the idea of doing the whole thing on location seemed exciting. To have the dance and songs out there in Arizona [where the film was shot] was great. Nobody had ever done that before, to my knowledge.

N: Some critics have said that of all your films *The Sundowners* [1960] looks and feels the most like a John Ford film.

Z: That's interesting.

N: What drew you to Jon Cleary's novel?

Z: I was drawn to it because it showed that there were these three people who had no money and owned nothing except the shirts on their backs and this buggy with the old horse. And nothing could separate them. They were for each other and they were a family, and that was tighter and closer than anything else. And to me that was a celebration of family all the way through, with all the troubles they have. He [Robert Mitchum] doesn't want to settle down, she [Deborah Kerr] wants to settle down, and all that. So that's what it was. Having had a pretty good marriage for fifty-eight years, I'm sort of inclined in that direction, you know. And that's really what I liked about it. That was the whole basic theme, and the book was full of humor and rather sparkling Australian dialogue. I found the Australians at that time [the film was shot in 1959] to be like the Californians in my time thirty years earlier, very simple people with a primitive, very warm sense of humor. You couldn't call them naive, but they were very insular. And they knew what they were about and were very honorable.

N: Speaking of the Australian dialogue, I like when Deborah Kerr says, "The tucker [food] will be up to scratch!"

Z: [*Laughs*] Yes, that's the way they talk! It was a happy kind of an occasion [making the picture]. Also, because Peter Ustinov and Robert Mitchum are very funny people, we had a free show every evening for dinner.

N: Let's talk about Deborah Kerr. The part of Ida Carmody is as much a departure for her as her sultry role was in *From Here to Eternity*.

Z: Well, she's just a very, very good actress. She's very adaptable and able to play almost anything.

N: Isn't this another example of your being able to see a quality in an actor that other people don't seem to have seen?

Z: I was kind of lucky about that. When the agent brought up Deborah to play the part in *From Here to Eternity*, it was rather startling because she had never played that kind of a part. She was always an ice cold Queen of England.

N: In *The Sundowners* she's warm and earthy, and completely believable. The scene in which she watches a wealthy woman on a train powdering her nose is particularly well done.

Z: That was interesting, you know, because I remember the writer was a lady writer [Isobel Lennart]. That scene had two pages of dialogue in it, which I threw out, because I said it could all be done just with looks. And this writer never forgave me because her lovely dialogue was thrown out the window, but it would have just killed the scene.

N: Well, the scene is perfect—we understand exactly what Kerr is feeling.

Z: That's all you need.

N: And then Paddy [Robert Mitchum] comes in, and he asks her what's the matter.

Z: Yes, you then understand that relationship.

N: Can you comment on the ending? It seems to me that the viewer identifies so strongly with Kerr's desire to have a permanent home that when she gives up the chance—which she does rather suddenly and very good-naturedly—we have mixed feelings. We're happy that the family will stay together, but we're troubled because she may never get her home. Isn't this ending at best bittersweet?

Z: Well, it's probably true. I must tell you that I can't remember how the book ended, but I remember that I had a very keen feeling of paying tribute to [John] Huston in *The Treasure of the Sierra Madre* when the gold blew away after all these people had gotten killed, and he [Walter Huston] just looked and started to laugh. I wouldn't say I stole it, but something about the human spirit triumphing over what seems to be a disaster made me feel good. It's a very positive thing, and that's what I liked about it.

N: And so Ida and Paddy laugh, too. They are resilient people.

Z: What good would it be if they got mad and slunk away furiously? It's all negative; it's no good. I think we have too much of that anyway.

N: *Five Days One Summer* [1982], your last film to date, seems to me an intensely personal work. How did you come to make it?

Z: That film was based on a sentimental notion I had of showing mountain climbing in the Alps as it used to be in the 1930s when there were considerably fewer people engaging in this sport, which was considered by many to be suicidal and crazy. Having walked in the mountains in those days, I had a very strong feeling of wanting to recreate the atmosphere of solitude and silence and majesty which has now disappeared from the Alps.

N: The film deserved a much better reception from the public and critics than it got. In one very intriguing episode, the frozen body of a young bridegroom lost in a climbing accident many years earlier is discovered, and a reunion of sorts takes place with his now aged bride. Is this episode intended as a comment on the triangle involving the three main characters [Sean Connery, Betsy Brantley, and Lambert Wilson]?

Z: The intention was to show the contrast in the lives of two women: the philandering city girl and the old peasant woman who had lost her fiancé in a mountain accident and had never thought of another man for the rest of her life. It is shown in a time-warp of sorts, in the reaction of the city girl to seeing the old, old woman confronting her dead bridegroom of sixty years ago, looking miraculously young after being buried in the depths of a glacier. The girl's reaction is, from the point of view of storytelling, the important thing, as it triggers her gradual rejection of her uncle.

N: I can't believe it, but I see that our time is almost up.

Z: Yes, it's getting there. Let's have one more question, and then we'll finish.

N: Well, I have so many questions that it's hard to know which one to pick.

Z: [*Laughs*] Go eenie, meenie, minie, moe!

N: We'll end with *Behold a Pale Horse* [1964]. One motif in the film has to do with the soccer ball that Artiguez [Gregory Peck], the aging guerilla leader, gives Paco, the boy who befriends him. Later, when Artiguez dies, there's a striking subjective shot of the boy kicking the ball in slow motion. What did you have in mind here?

Z: I had in mind the last impressions of a dying man, what he last sees before he dies. And what he sees is the staircase whirling around and then he sees the ball . . . because at the end of that talk that he and the priest [Omar Sharif] had [about why a priest would help an enemy of Franco and the Church], Peck throws the ball out of a window and it bounces down the street. That in itself had a symbolic feeling of some kind, which I can't remember, but a lot of people picked that up. And I felt that this is something that stayed in his mind. Why I couldn't tell you. It's not rational.

N: I thought maybe the ball reminded Artiguez in some way of his own youth. He bought the ball for the boy and at one point he even thinks that the boy hasn't fought—

Z: —Well, with all due respect, you are trying to rationalize something that is subconscious and totally irrational. Film basically is an irrational thing, and this is an irrational thing—just simply the notion I had because when a man dies, there are some images from his life that accidentally go through his brain. And that's what it was. You'll find as you get older that your mind becomes very selective, that certain cells just die off and the information disappears, and some different brain cells obviously retain other things. I can remember phone numbers of sixty years ago, but I can't remember what I had for dinner last night. It's like that. So it's got nothing to do with rational meanings. . . . [It] is not a rational thing at all.

N: This is a good place to stop. Plus, we're at the end of the tape.

Z: Probably if we did this for a week, we'd get even more. But you know, unfortunately, that's the way it goes.

N: Well, we've covered a lot of ground, and there's new material here about your work, too.

Z: Good. And also there are corrections of some beliefs that have been held that are just not so.

FIGURE 2.2. THE NUN'S STORY (Warner Bros., 1959). A lobby card displaying a shot from the edited-out lunch scene.

CHAPTER THREE

Act of Violence *(1949) and the Early Films of Fred Zinnemann*

WHEELER WINSTON DIXON

Fred Zinnemann's early career is one of apprenticeship to the Hollywood studio system. Yet Zinnemann was born in Vienna, Austria, on April 29, 1907. The late film historian Ephraim Katz gives us the best summary of Zinnemann's early years. Katz writes:

> As a child [Zinnemann] studied the violin, hoping to become a musician. Later, inspired by the films of [Erich von] Stroheim and King Vidor, he abandoned plans for a legal career, after receiving a master's degree in law from the University of Vienna, to become an assistant cameraman in Paris and Berlin. Among the films on which he worked was Robert Siodmak's famous documentary *Menschen am Sonntag/People on Sunday* (1929). In 1929 he emigrated to the US and headed directly for Hollywood, where all he could land was an extra part in *All Quiet on the Western Front* (1930). He eventually obtained some work as a cutter and became an assistant to director Berthold Viertel, and in 1931 to Robert Flaherty on an aborted documentary project in Russia. Zinnemann also assisted Busby Berkeley on the dance numbers of *The Kid from Spain* (1932). In 1934–1935 he made his debut as co-director on pro-

ducer-screenwriter Paul Strand's documentary feature *Redes Pesca-dos/The Wave*, which he shot on location in Mexico. In 1937 [Zin-nemann] was signed by MGM as a director of shorts, including, "Pete Smith Specialties" and the "Crime Does Not Pay" series. He won an Oscar for *That Mothers Might Live* (1938), part of the "His-torical Mysteries" series. He was elevated to a feature director in 1941 but was given little opportunity to exercise his craft until 1948, when he was assigned to direct *The Search*, a moving drama of the WWII aftermath, in Europe. He subsequently directed sev-eral other productions noted for their realism and meticulous han-dling but not for their box-office appeal. (1263)

Behind these bare facts lie a number of interesting circumstances. Working with Robert Flaherty, for example, remained one of the richest experiences of Zinnemann's career. In an August 1964 interview in *Show* magazine, Zinnemann noted that of all the people he had worked with,

> Flaherty taught me more than anyone else. Number one was to stick to your guns. I learned the importance of expressing what you want to say, to make a film the way you see it. . . . I also learned from him not to try to make pictures about subjects *you don't* know. . . .
>   If you backlight an object, it stands out more sharply in con-trast to its surroundings. Similarly, if you use a person who is not right for the part physically, he sometimes brings an extra dimen-sion to the role. You have to imagine how an actor will relate to the other actors in a film. That is as important as the choice of individ-ual actors. Then you must create an atmosphere in which they can function, *give them* as much assurance as you possibly can. (as quoted in Leyda 520–21)

Yet Zinnemann was never the industry loner that Flaherty proved to be throughout his long and distinguished career. Zinnemann mixed his altruistic work with the young Robert Siodmak (on *Menschen am Son-ntag*) and the uncompromising Flaherty (on the uncompleted Russian documentary) with bread-and-butter "extra" acting jobs for Lewis Mile-stone (on *All Quiet on the Western Front)* and assistant director work for the resolutely utilitarian Busby Berkeley, who more than any other chore-ographer represented the triumph of the Hollywood Studio mechanism over individual talent. Flaherty may have taught Zinnemann how to "stick to [his] guns," but Zinnemann brought to this quality a skill for dealing effectively with large production organizations (such as MGM), and a willingness to work his way up from the bottom, even after his early work with Flaherty, Siodmak, Viertel, Berkeley, and Paul Strand.

Zinnemann's co-direction of *Redes* in 1934–1935 with Gómez Muriel demonstrated once again that Zinnemann felt a strong sense of social commitment in his work. [Ed. Note: Zinnemann has gone on record that he was the sole director of *Redes*. See *Film Criticism* (Winter 1994–1995).] In view of the director's early accomplishments, one might expect that Zinnemann would hold out for a contract directing features immediately, rather than signing on with MGM's shorts department in 1937. Then, too, MGM's resolutely escapist Republicanism and relatively "faceless" studio style (typified by generally flat white lighting and Cedric Gibbons's museumlike set decorations) would seem to be superficially at odds with Zinnemann's highly personal and socially conscious early efforts. Yet Zinnemann took the plunge into the studio system. In addition to working on the Pete Smith shorts and the *Crime Does Not Pay* series, Zinnemann also worked with MGM's historical revisionist John Nesbitt, creator of the *Passing Parade* series. Nesbitt was also active in the production of the *Historical Mysteries* series and narrated Zinnemann's very last short for MGM, *The Lady or the Tiger?* in 1942.

Zinnemann's MGM shorts, however, rise above the purely industrial in most cases either through Zinnemann's personal commitment to the material at hand, or through the use of a highly stylized application of optical effects and diegetic narrative displacement, as evidenced in *The Lady or the Tiger?* Indeed, *The Lady or the Tiger?* recalls nothing so much as the work of Richard Lester in *The Knack* (1965) and *A Hard Day's Night* (1964), with a relentless use of wipes of every description ("burst" wipes, "flip" wipes, "spiral" wipes, to name but a few optical bench techniques employed in the film). One senses that Zinnemann had little interest in the story material of most of these ten-minute shorts, and sought to attract attention to these films through the same eye-catching devices Lester would employ a quarter-century later. Zinnemann did well for himself with the MGM Shorts, winning for the studio an Academy Award in 1938 with his direction of "the best one-reel short" *That Mothers Might Live* (the award went to MGM as producer, not Zinnemann [see Kearns 806]). All told, Zinnemann directed a total of eighteen short subjects including *A Friend Indeed, The Story of Dr. Carver, That Mothers Might Live, Tracking the*

Sleeping Death, *They Live Again*, all 1938; *Weather Wizards*, *While America Sleeps*, *Help Wanted!*, *One Against the World*, *The Ash Can Fleet*, *Forgotten Victory*, all 1939; *The Old South*, *Stuffie*, *The Way in the Wilderness*, *The Great Meddler*, all 1940; *Forbidden Passage* and *Your Last Act*, both 1941; and his final short film for MGM, *The Lady or the Tiger?*, made in 1942.

All Zinnemann's shorts were slick entertainments, if occasionally nothing more, and Zinnemann proved with this "trial period" that he could work well within an often sympathetic and arbitrary bureaucracy. As a final comment on the short films at MGM, particularly on the studio "trickery" evident in the *Crime Does Not Pay* series and the films with Nesbitt, a 1973 interview with Zinnemann demonstrates that although the director had strong naturalist, documentary roots, he was still intrigued by the numerous technical processes employed in the creation of traditional studio imagery.

> One of the best . . . cameramen that I ever worked with was Eugene Schüfftan. . . . He was responsible for developing some of the trick photographic effects that were widely used at UFA. . . . One trick process involved placing a semitransparent mirror at a 45° angle in front of the camera lens. This reflected the image of a scale model which was out of camera range and made that image blend with the live action that was being photographed in front of the camera. For example, a peasant might be ploughing a field, with a moving windmill in the background. The turning windmill was supplied by the reflection of a scale model. (as quoted in Leyda 521)

Despite his flair for the documentary, it is clear that Zinnemann felt entirely at home in the studio, employing whatever devices were necessary to achieve his desired effect. And these early efforts paid off: Zinnemann was signed to direct features (albeit "B" films) for MGM in late 1941.

In 1942, Zinnemann directed his first feature, *Kid Glove Killer*, a "B" programmer expanded from a two-reel short in the *Crime Does Not Pay* series. The seventy-four-minute film starred Van Heflin and Marsha Hunt, and was a thoughtful police procedural that paved the way for such later films as Alfred Werker's *He Walked by Night* (1948), and led to the production of Zinnemann's first true "A" film in 1944, *The Seventh Cross*. With a superb cast, including Spencer Tracy, Signe Hasso, and Hume Cronyn, this lengthy (112 minute) film dealt with "an anti-Nazi who escapes from a concentration camp in 1936 and attempts to get out of the country" (Scheuer 703), and represented a major advance for Zinnemann's career. Yet it would be two more years before Zinnemann directed his next film, *Little Mr. Jim* (also known as *Army Brat*, Katz 1264), featuring Butch Jenkins, James Craig, and Frances Gifford in the story of a young boy who befriends a Chinese cook "when tragedy strikes his family" (Scheuer 462).

This sentimental film was generally well received, but Zinnemann's next feature, *My Brother Talks to Horses* (1947), with a young Peter Lawford (then an MGM contract player), Edward Arnold, and Butch Jenkins again, seemed a much more forced and formulaic film, the sort of "heartwarming" small-town American fantasy that MGM created in the longrunning *Andy Hardy* series. Zinnemann's career seemed to be in something of a decline, then, when he directed *The Search* (1948), also known as *Die Gezeichneten* a Swiss/U.S. co-production starring Montgomery Clift, Aline MacMahon, Wendell Corey, and Ivan Jandl.

Released through MGM, *The Search* was not, for once, shot on the back lot, but rather produced on location in Europe, and boasted beautifully evocative photography by Emil Berna and a spare, incisive screenplay by Richard Schweizer, David Wechsler, and Paul Jarrico (Kearns 529). *The Search* was also Montgomery Clift's first work on the screen (Sarris 168), and Zinnemann shrewdly let Clift work with a group of lesser-known European actors, including a group of nonprofessionals who essentially played themselves, in the tradition of Jean Renoir's *Toni* (1934) and later Italian neorealists. In a 1991 essay on Zinnemann's career, critic Doris Toumarkine related Zinnemann's work on *The Search* to the director's earlier *Redes*, as well as Zinnemann's 1950 film *The Men*, which was actor Marlon Brando's first appearance on film.

> Zinnemann's penchant for realism and authenticity [was] evident in his first feature *Redes/The Wave* (1935), shot on location in Mexico with mostly non-professional actors recruited among the locals, which [was] one of the earliest examples of realism in narrative film. . . . The filmmaker also used authentic locales and extras in *The Search* (1948), which won an Oscar for screenwriting and secured his position in the Hollywood establishment. Shot in warravaged Germany, the film stars Montgomery Clift in his screen debut as a G.I. who cares for a lost Czech boy traumatized by the war. In the critically acclaimed *The Men* (1950), starring newcomer

Marlon Brando as a paraplegic vet, Zinnemann filmed many scenes in a California hospital where real patients served as extras. (as quoted in Pallot 594)

It was during this formative period of Zinnemann's career that the director became known for his work with younger actors of the "Method" school, as a director who was both sympathetic to their needs and able to coax excellent performances from his players with a combination of tact, suggestion, and discussion. Rather than endlessly retaking a scene, or treating his protagonists as automatons, Zinnemann created his elusively powerful mise en scène in concert with his performers, and the results have a degree of verisimilitude uncommon in Hollywood films of the period.

To cite two examples, Deborah Kerr wrote of working with Zinnemann on *From Here to Eternity* (1953) that she had total confidence in his skills as a director:

You're safe within the realm of what you want to do. You feel that the inner you is being used without you having to be too aware of yourself. . . . [Zinnemann] really brings out of me—in a completely different way—an awful lot that perhaps I'd never have the courage to lay bare, to open up. He just knows how to get you to do it, to bring out some inner quality. I always like to cut out words if I possibly can. Why do I have to say anything? You know, just look at someone and it says it. . . . I thought I'd got such a hell of a nerve to think that maybe I could do [her role in *From Here to Eternity*, 1953)]. But with Zinnemann the guidelines were right. The whole movie was a coming together of parts and personalities that together had a magic. (Interview in *The Times of London*, September 2, 1972, as quoted in Leyda 240)

Similarly, Omar Sharif recalled working with Zinnemann on the under-rated 1964 film *Behold a Pale Horse* with affection and respect. In an interview for *The New York Herald Tribune* of August 9, 1964, Sharif noted that

[Zinnemann] does a scene, then he discusses it with you. He lets you bring out your own ideas which he later incorporates into his final instructions. When it's all over, you realize that he has really

guided you into expressing his own ideas, but he has done it so subtly, and with such respect for his actors, that we think we have done
it ourselves. He has a marvelous rapport. (as quoted in Leyda 429)

Thus, in *The Search*, Zinnemann can be seen turning away from the
traditional MGM mold and the pyrotechnics of his earlier short films and
first features and moving towards a more personal and humanistic style,
which would surface next in Zinnemann's 1949 *Act of Violence*, a curious
and effective mixture of noir stylization, social criticism, and documentary naturalism. Shot for the most part on location, most strikingly at Big
Bear Lake, California (Silver and Ward 10), *Act of Violence* marks a tran-
sitional point in Zinnemann's career. In *Act of Violence*, Zinnemann
would effectively merge the fictive studio-synthesized world of his cinematic version of the musical *Oklahoma!* (1955) with the near-documentary style of his more realistic films, such as *From Here to Eternity* (1953),
A Hatful of Rain (1957), *The Nun's Story* (1959), and *The Sundowners*
(1960). *Act of Violence* is thus a sort of "dress rehearsal" for the second half
of the director's distinguished career.

   Act of Violence is a construct, and an uneasy construct at that, a film
that attempts to capitalize on every aspect of Hollywood's technical professionalism (most notably in the superb cinematography of Robert Surtees), while simultaneously aiming for the gritty realism of Jules Dassin's
Naked City (1948), Henry Hathaway's *The House on 92nd Street* (1945),
and other *March of Time* influenced "docudramas" of the period. Part of
the appeal of *Act of Violence* for the contemporary audiences is this grasp
of the mundane and the brutal within the world of the film—a direct
revolt against everything that Hollywood supposedly valorizes. Mary
Astor, who played the character of Pat, a "poor alley cat" (Astor's words)
of a woman who attempts to shield the film's nominal "hero" Frank Enley
(Van Heflin) from the vengeance of Joe Parkson (Robert Ryan), recalled
in her 1971 autobiography *A Life on Film* how she worked out the details
of Pat's physical and emotional character with Zinnemann's aid and
encouragement.

I worked out the way [Pat] should look, and insisted firmly (with
[Zinnemann's] help) that the one dress in the picture would *not* be
made at the MGM wardrobe, but be found on a rack at the cheap-
est department store. We made the hem uneven, put a few cigarette
burns and some stains on the front. I wore bracelets that rattled and

jangled and stiletto-heeled slippers. I had the heels sanded off at the edges to make walking uncomfortable. I wore a fall, a long unbecoming hairpiece that came to my shoulder. And I put on very dark nail polish and chipped it. I used no foundation makeup, just too much lipstick and too much mascara—both "bled," that is, smeared, just a little. [Zinnemann] said, "You look just right!" And [the] camera [department] helped with "bad" lighting. (as quoted in Leyda 17)

Indeed, this aspect of utilitarian "shabbiness" pervades every aspect of the film's technical execution from the lone card used for the main title of the film (simply reading *Act of Violence* in huge letters, entirely filling the screen), all the way to the bare and unadorned cinematography and sets employed throughout the work.

Act of Violence tells the story of Frank R. Enley (Van Heflin), a post–World War II builder respected by his family and friends, and a solid citizen of the small southern California town of Santa Lisa. Enley, however, has a past. Despite his public record as a war hero, Enley in fact turned in the members of the bomber squadron he commanded to the Nazis, after his squadron had been shot down over Germany and interned in a Nazi prison camp.

The members of Enley's squadron, led by the impetuous Joe Parkson (Robert Ryan), plan to escape the camp through an underground tunnel. Enley advises Parkson and the other members of the squadron to abandon the project, but Parkson remains resolute in his plan. Enley then (for reasons that remain profoundly unclear—perhaps self-preservation, perhaps cowardice, perhaps a sense of defeatism) informs the SS colonel in charge of the camp of Parkson's escape plans, convinced that the Nazis will simply dynamite the clandestine tunnel and overlook the attempted escape.

The Nazi colonel, however, allows the escape to proceed, and then orders the squadron members shot and bayoneted as they leave the end of the tunnel, at their supposed point of "escape." Parkson alone survives. Now, four years later, Parkson has trailed Enley from Syracuse, New York, to California, intent on only one thing: killing Enley to avenge the death of his fellow squadron members. *Act of Violence* is thus a film of pursuit, betrayal, deceptive appearances, and the darker side of the post–World War II dream, a vision not often chronicled by mainstream MGM. Dark and unsentimental, the film operates in a world of doom-laden predestination.

FIGURE 3.1. ACT OF VIOLENCE (MGM, 1949). The world of film noir: a
publicity shot with Van Heflin, Robert Ryan, and Janet Leigh. (Courtesy Jerry
Ohlinger Archives)

Stylistically, *Act of Violence* is a tour de force. The film opens with Joe Parkson doggedly walking the streets of a large and hostile metropolis, painfully climbing a set of stairs, and entering a shabby room, where he pockets a gun with a sadistic grin on his face. Dressed in the standard noir costume of raincoat and snap-brim hat, Parkson is every bit the "angel of death," the unstoppable force of retribution so integral to noir's structural conceits. As the main title appears over Parkson's face, the film dissolves to the next day, as Enley addresses the World War II veterans and their families who comprise the principal inhabitants of Santa Lisa, a housing development where all the model homes look alike: cheaply made, hastily built, prefabricated "boom" houses, constructed to create a sense of instant community. Enley is seen as a Babbitesque hero, a builder for the common man, sharing his vision for a bright future in the dry, clear California sunlight with an adoring throng in attendance.

Immediately after the ceremony, Enley leaves for an idyllic vacation at Big Bear Lake with his fishing companion Fred Finney (Harry Antrim). Almost immediately, however, Zinnemann undercuts the superficiality of this escape with the appearance of Joe Parkson. Parkson arrives at Enley's home and demands of Edith, Frank's wife (Janet Leigh), that she disclose Enley's whereabouts. With surprising naiveté, Edith tells Parkson to go to Big Bear Lake, and Joe (who limps badly throughout the film, ostensibly as a result of his war injuries) takes off in grim pursuit. There follows a beautiful set-piece, as Joe shadows Enley and Fred in a small fishing boat. Zinnemann skillfully intercuts location shots with beautifully composed process work in the studio for close-ups. In contrast to the opening scenes of the film (Parkson retrieving his revolver from the cheap rooming house) where crashing music cues dominate the action, Zinnemann stages this strangely quiet pursuit sequence with natural sound only, cutting back and forth between extreme, near scenic wide-shots and extremely tight close-ups of Ryan, pondering his impending act of execution.

It is important to remark here how much Zinnemann does with the power of "the gaze" in this film. In his portrayal of Joe Parkson, Robert Ryan speaks but little; his eyes do most of the work, controlling both Enley's destiny and the intertwined gaze of the audience. As with Deborah Kerr in *From Here to Eternity*, Zinnemann strips away meaningless dialogue to replace a word with a glance, for far greater emotional (and cinematic) impact. The splendor of Big Bear Lake, the "ideal" vacation resort, also forms a neatly contrasting backdrop for Joe's murderous quest.

Enley and Fred, however, are unaware of Joe's presence, and they dock their boat for a beer. There, the owner of the fishing camp, a man known only as Pop (Will Wright), tells Enley and Fred that "a man with a limp" has been searching for them. Much to Fred's consternation, Enley immediately abandons his vacation plans and flees to Santa Lisa. Now the film is truly set in motion, following Enley's descent into the depths of late forties American society.

When Enley arrives at his house, he immediately draws the curtains, extinguishes the lights and double-locks all the doors. Home, in the world of *Act of Violence*, is no place of safety. Enley refuses to answer the phone or the doorbell, even as Edith attempts to restore some semblance of patriarchal "normalcy" to their house with her offer to "whip up a tomato omelet." The house itself has low-beamed ceilings, which Zinnemann uses to full and crushing effect (in the best Welles/Toland manner), shooting up into the faces of Frank, Edith, and later Joe, when he invades the Enley's home to show all the characters trapped in a world of constricting values and false pretenses. Suddenly, the doorbell rings.

"Don't answer it!" Enley commands. "I don't want to talk to anybody, I don't want to see anybody, I just want to have a quiet evening in our very own home!" he pleads. Parkson, however, has no intention of departing. Joe parks his car in front of the Enley house all night and is only momentarily removed from his position of surveillance by the police. When morning arrives, Parkson has resumed his death watch. Clearly, there can be no appeal to the conventional authority of the police.

Throughout the night, Edith sleeps with a carving knife, the sanctity of her home already violated. She awakes with a start to find her husband fleeing again, leaving a hasty note informing her that he is on his way "to the Builders' Convention in LA." As the morning wears on, Joe boldly appears in Enley's yard, and Edith (in a surprisingly resolute gesture for a female fictional narrative construct in late forties cinema) demands that he leave at once. In response, Joe orders Edith into the house, and momentarily menaces her and her son Georgie (played by twins Larry and Leslie Holt). For a terrible moment, we are sure that Joe means to attack both Edith and the child. But Edith is of no interest to Parkson; his quest is for Enley alone.

As Parkson leaves, Edith demands to know the reason for his relentless pursuit of her husband. Parkson is brutally blunt in his response: "He was a stool pigeon for the Nazis." This information, which has been withheld from the audience up to this point, heightens our interest in the narrative structure of the film, precisely because the purpose of Parkson's quest has remained obscure from the outset of the work. Edith bursts into tears, but Parkson advises her to "Save it. He isn't worth it!" Then he abruptly departs.

At last aware of the danger facing her husband and of the dimensions of his secret treachery, Edith leaves Georgie with a neighbor, Martha (Connie Gilchrist), and tails Frank to the Blake Hotel in Los Angeles. As drunken conventioneers lurch through the lobby and bar of the hotel to the sound of a fifth-rate orchestra playing "Happy Days Are Here Again," Edith finds Frank, drags him onto a secluded landing of the hotel's interior fire stairs, and demands to know the truth.

Here, in a dark secret location, hidden from the rest of the conventioneers, Frank Enley finally tells Edith, and the audience, the full story of his betrayal of the members of his bomber squadron. "I was an *informer!*" he shouts, recalling both John Ford's 1935 film with Victor McLaglen, as well as the then-current HUAC hearings in Washington. "They were dead and I was eating—six widows and ten men dead— maybe I *knew* [the SS commandant] would break his word, but I *didn't care.*"

Edith, in shock, attempts to console Frank, but he will have none of it. "*I made a deal with an SS colonel.*" Frank shouts. "You can't make a deal with the Nazis! They set the dogs on them, they bayoneted them, they left them to die like animals on the [barbed] wire [fence]." Against the backdrop of the conventioneers' barely discernible drunken revelry, Frank Enley reveals what we have feared throughout the film. His entire life is a lie, a construct, an avoidance of responsibility and accountability. Frank realizes that there is no value in pursuing "justice" in the affair through normal channels. He is afraid of "exposure" in his new community, and this prevents him from having Parkson arrested. In shock, Edith leaves Frank and returns to Santa Lisa.

A new subplot develops: returning to his cheap lodgings in Santa Lisa, Parkson is met by his fiancée Ann Sturges (Phyllis Thaxter). Inadvertently tipped off by Edith's neighbor Martha that Frank is in Los Angeles (one of the recurring themes of *Act of Violence* is this blind trust in strangers endemic to MGM's house-policy vision of small-town America), Parkson is about to depart for the builders' convention when Ann intervenes. Ann begs Parkson to abandon his quest but he refuses.

Ann then goes to the Enley house and convinces Edith to help her prevent "Joe from becoming a murderer." Edith, overwhelmed by events, shuffles through her once-cherished home like a zombie. Ann finally convinces Edith to telephone Frank at the hotel, where the noise in the bar and Frank's own inebriation prevents him from understanding the danger he is in. But Edith's warning comes too late; Joe suddenly appears and chases Frank from the hotel.

Here, the film in its final third takes on its most sinister aspect, as Frank leaves the relative safety and social status conferred on him by the Blake Hotel and the convention for a world populated by prostitutes, gunmen, and morally bankrupt attorneys—the "underworld" of Los Angeles. Not insignificantly, Frank's entry into this world is punctuated by an endless series of descents down one staircase after another, interior and/or exterior, until he arrives at one of the seediest bars ever seen in an MGM film, populated only by the slatternly Pat (Mary Astor, in a brilliant performance) and Tim (Ralph Peters), a sullen and taciturn barkeep.

"Looking for kicks?" Pat inquires dryly, and immediately latches on to Frank. Too tired to resist, Frank leaves with Pat, and the final third of the narrative is truly launched. Of all the people Frank encounters in *Act of Violence*, however, it is Pat who (being aware of the duplicitous nature of postwar society and urban life in general) offers Frank some genuine concern and assistance. Taking Frank back to her exceptionally cheap apartment, Pat asks him, "What is it, honey? Love or money? It always boils down to two things—love, or money." As Frank sulks miserably on Pat's bed, she drones on. "What you need is kicks. You've *gotta* have kicks. I couldn't *live* without kicks. Now, it can't be *that* bad. Even if you're unhappy, you can still have *kicks*. Look at me. I'm unhappy, but I still get my *kicks*."

Pat leans closer to Frank, who now seems bereft of any shred of self-respect or hope, a broken shell lit in a deathly glow from the cheap lightbulb dangling from the ceiling of the apartment. "Do you have money?" Pat continues. "If you have money, you have freedom. You can get outta town." At this, for the first time, Enley brightens. Pat advises Frank to offer his entire building business to Joe in exchange for Parkson's "disappearance" ("it's worth twenty thousand dollars," Frank tells Pat). At Frank's urging, Pat even telephones Parkson as a go-between to arrange the deal. On the other end of the phone, Parkson merely laughs. Money, in this instance, will purchase neither freedom nor escape.

But the worst is yet to come. Pat, now thoroughly frightened for Frank's welfare, takes him to see an unscrupulous lawyer named Gavery (Nicholas Joy), who advises Frank to employ the services of Johnny (Barry

Kroeger) to "eliminate the problem" of Parkson. The meeting with Gavery marks Frank's complete descent into Hell; even Pat is appalled at what Gavery suggests. "You're going to make him a murderer!" she objects, to which Gavery replies, more to Frank than to her, "What's the difference? You sent ten men off, what's one more?" During this interview, which is conducted in the closet of an even dingier bar than the one in which Frank first met Pat, Gavery continues to ply Frank with liquor until he appears to agree to anything.

Pat finally helps Frank from the bar, but loses him momentarily on the street outside. In a chillingly realistic sequence, made all the more so by the complete lack of process work in its staging, Frank wanders through a railroad tunnel as the voices of his fallen comrades and the duplicitous SS colonel resound in his mind in a nightmarish noir voice-over. Sick to death of what he has done, unable to run any longer, Frank suddenly looks up and sees a train approaching. Slowly, inexorably, he crosses the tracks to stand in front of the train, fully intending to commit suicide. Zinnemann stages the sequence in a skillful series of intercut shots, keeping the oncoming train mostly in wide-shot compositions with extreme close-ups of Frank's anguished countenance. At the last possible moment, Frank dives out of the way of the oncoming engine, lacking even the fortitude to kill himself. It is the film's most genuinely despairing moment. Pat, seeing this from a distance, runs to comfort Frank, and the two stagger back to Pat's apartment.

At Pat's, Johnny barges in and proposes flatly to murder Parkson for $10,000, approximately half the value of Frank's building business. "You see the rest of these guys hangin' on to you? They're chiselers. Not me. I'm going to earn my dough. I'm going to take care of your problem. Let's do it someplace nice and quiet . . . not the hotel. How about that hick town you live in? Nice and quiet. Small town, with them hick cops. It'll be easy." Pat tries to intervene, but Johnny throws a drink in her face.

The murder is set for nine the following night at the Santa Lisa train station. Convinced that Frank will go along with his idea, Johnny leaves, as Frank passes out on Pat's beat-up sofa. Across town, at the Blake Hotel, Ann has located Joe and makes one last attempt to reason with him. This time, however, and rather unconvincingly at that, Joe begins to waver. Of all the sequences in the film, Zinnemann stages this confrontation with the least assurance or interest, covering Ann and Joe's dialogue in a few wide-shots that frame them within the confines of the hotel room, yet suggest little of the emotional content of the scene.

The following morning Pat wakes Frank from his stupor and demands that he write her a check for $100. "It's all filled in; I found your checkbook. You can spare a hundred. All you have to do is sign." But Frank, regaining his senses, remembers his "deal" with Johnny (slightly reminiscent of the "deal" struck between Bruno Anthony [Robert Walker] and Guy Haines [Farley Granger] in Hitchcock's *Strangers on a Train* [1951]), and races to Santa Lisa to prevent the killing. Arriving at the station that evening shortly before the appointed hour, Frank (seen in the distance in a sweepingly vacant wide-shot) is met by Parkson (seen in a similarly composed opposing set-up), as Johnny hides, his gun at the ready, in a large black sedan parked directly between them.

Deciding that his life will be worthless unless he finally faces up to Joe, Frank starts to walk towards him, ready to be killed. Zinnemann stages this sequence in the tradition of the Western-genre "standoff," with strategically intercut shots of increasing tightness as the two men approach each other. However, at the last moment, Frank sees that Johnny is poised to fire at Joe and jumps in front of Johnny's car, taking the bullet himself. Joe, taken aback, watches as Frank, mortally wounded, jumps on the running board of Johnny's car. Johnny and Frank struggle over control of the steering wheel as the car careens through the streets of Santa Lisa.

The car crashes into a light post. Frank is thrown from the wreck and instantly killed. Johnny, plunging through the windshield of the car, also perishes. Joe runs up, conveniently met by Ann, shouting, "I didn't do it, Ann! I didn't do it!" as if this fact represented some sort of internal moral victory (as, no doubt, MGM wished it to be). Seeing that Frank is dead, Joe vows to the police that "I'll tell his wife" of Frank's death, in a moment rather artificially designed to suggest that in his abandonment of violence, capped with Frank's heroic death, Parkson has achieved a sort of atonement for his actions, and release from his epic binge of (justified) hatred. Joe Parkson can now rejoin postwar society and get on with marriage to Ann, two kids, and a heavily mortgaged prefabricated house.

If the conclusion of *Act of Violence* is less impressive than the scenes that lead up to it, we can allot a good portion of the blame in this matter to the exigencies of MGM's script supervisors and the Hays/Breen Office. For the first four-fifths of the film, there is hardly a false step in the proceedings. Zinnemann deals in images, and lets his visual compositions carry the narrative. When Frank flees the Blake Hotel for his first meeting with Pat, we do not need to be told that Pat makes her living as a prostitute; everything about her suggests complete moral collapse. As Frank speaks with Pat in the rundown bar, we *see* every last vestige of human self-respect wash away from Frank's face, which is lit now in a halo of deathlike illumination, coming from nowhere, revealing the complete internal spiritual backruptcy of Frank's life and the collapse of his superficially (and falsely) constructed public image, made to order for the "model" citizens of Santa Lisa.

It is not a coincidence that Frank is a builder; he has built a new life for himself in Santa Lisa. Yet the life Frank has built, like the shabbily built houses he touts near the beginning of the film, is a lie, and has no foundation. Frank's "new life" must and will collapse (as will the lies about his "heroic war record," played up in the Santa Lisa newspapers as part of his "success story" as a postwar building contractor). As an informer to the Nazis, Frank carries a legacy of betrayal into the democratic state that can only be balanced by his own martyrdom. Only Frank's death will preserve his "heroic" image.

In view of the tragedy of the 1947 HUAC hearings, are we too far off the mark to consider the tragedy of Frank R. Enley as the plight of the informer unmasked, of a person who makes a deal with those with whom a deal cannot be made? In *Act of Violence*, Fred Zinnemann suggests (until the final minutes of the film) that we can never escape the moral consequences of our actions; that the one-family home of the 1940s is no refuge from the world, but rather a self-imposed prison; that World War II and the social hatred it engendered have scarred us all; and that the surfaces of any community (as in Hitchcock's *Shadow of a Doubt* [1943], set in the deceptively idyllic community of Santa Rosa, California) hide a wealth of corruption, violence, and false fronts. One of the central conceits of noir is that no one can be trusted, that every surface hides a corrupt interior. Zinnemann's *Act of Violence* demonstrates that precisely those who are the most "boosterish" (in Sinclair Lewis's term) are those who are most suspect. They will hide, until they are discovered, in plain sight.

WORKS CITED

Katz, Ephraim. *The Film Encyclopedia.* New York: Cromwell, 1979.

Kearns, Audrey, ed. *Motion Picture Production Encyclopedia, 1950 Edition.* Hollywood: The Hollywood Reporter Press, 1950.

Leyda, Jay, ed. *Voices of Film Experience: 1894 to the Present.* New York: Macmillan, 1977.

Pallot, James, ed. *The Encyclopedia of Film.* New York: Putnam, 1991.

Sarris, Andrew. *The American Cinema: Directors and Directions, 1929–1968.* New York: E. P. Dutton, 1968.

Scheuer, Steven S., ed. *Movies on TV and Videocassette 1990.* New York: Bantam, 1989.

Silver, Alain, and Elizabeth Ward, eds. *Film Noir: An Encyclopedic Reference to the American Style.* New York: Overlook Press, 1989.

CHAPTER FOUR

▟

The Eyes Have It:
Dimensions of Blindness
in Eyes in the Night *(1942)*

MARTIN F. NORDEN

A seldom-explored aspect of Fred Zinnemann's multifaceted career has been his movie construction of physical disability. The Vienna-born film-maker turned repeatedly to the world of physical disability for source material, and unlike the handful of other Hollywood directors who have done so as well, he transformed that material into films that for the most part are commendable portrayals of people with disabilities.[1] Influenced to some extent by movies of the 1920s and 1930s that dealt prominently with wartime disablement—he was in his words "enthralled" by King Vidor's *The Big Parade* as a teenager (*Life* 8) and later served as an extra on *All Quiet on the Western Front*—Zinnemann went on to create not only the justly famous *The Men* (1950) but also such films as *Eyes in the Night* (1942), *Act of Violence* (1949), the documentary short *Benjy* (1951), and *Julia* (1977). Populated with strong-willed characters who desire to get on with their postdisablement lives and who often engage in acts that have little if nothing to do with "overcoming" disabilities, these films (with the notable exception of *Act of Violence*) typically do not position the audience to regard the characters in terms of pity, awe, or fear.[2]

As a means of gaining a better sense of Zinnemann's generally positive contributions to the Hollywood image of disabled people and also his emerging directorial strategies, I propose to examine his construction of blindness in *Eyes in the Night*, a rarely screened "B" feature he directed early in his career for Metro-Goldwyn-Mayer. The literal blindness of the film's lead character, the figurative blindness of others who surround him, and the concept of blindness as symbolic castration are among the dimensions of sightlessness that I will consider here. Though Zinnemann professed little interest in *Eyes* ("I didn't like it much and remember very little about it," he wrote in his 1992 autobiography),[3] I hope to show that this film is quite worthy of study in that it demonstrates a sensitivity to disability issues seldom found in mainstream narrative movies and also exhibits the early Hollywood tendency to "remasculinize" disabled male figures during wartime. In addition, its problematic representation of a blind character's perspective raises tantalizing questions related to the theory-laden issue of "the gaze"—questions that I shall address in this chapter.

The topic of literal blindness, revealed through *Eyes in the Night*'s surface story, is intimately bound up with the film's literary genesis, production history, and critical reception, and it is worth examining these considerations, however briefly. *Eyes in the Night* was based on a book published in early 1941 called *The Odor of Violets*, one in a series of mystery novels written by Baynard Kendrick that centered on a character who had been left totally blind by a World War I injury. Kendrick, who had served in World War I with the First Canadian Battalion, first encountered blinded veterans while in Europe and was so inspired by them and their abilities (such as one fellow's skill at detailing the military careers of others by running his fingers over their insignia) that after the war he wrote several novels featuring a blind shamus named Duncan Maclain, who made efficient use of his other senses to solve crimes.[4]

Among the appreciative readers of Kendrick's detective novels was Edward Arnold, a Hollywood actor whose own father had been blind for the last twenty-five years of his life. Intrigued by Kendrick's treatment of the impaired detective and well versed on the subject of movie crime-busters (among Arnold's many movie roles were Inspector Porfiry Petrovich in 1935's *Meet Nero Wolfe*), he approached MGM about making several films based on the novelist's works with him in the lead. He found a receptive audience in the form of Dore Schary, the studio's newly appointed B-film executive producer who before assuming that position had blended disability and strength of character himself in the 1940 films *Young Tom Edison* and *Edison, the Man.*⁵ Schary readily agreed to the proposal and with the advice of B-film producer Jack Chertok turned the assignment over to a thirty-five-year-old director showing considerable promise with mysteries: Fred Zinnemann, just coming off his well-received first feature *Kid Glove Killer* (1942), whose *That Mothers Might Live* (1938), an installment in MGM's "Historical Mysteries" series, had won an Oscar for best live-action one-reeler.

Though Zinnemann was less than enthusiastic about the new project—he grumbled in retrospect that it was "not very promising material" and that he "hated the script but liked the writer, Guy Trosper, who also hated the script" (48)—*Eyes in the Night* turned out to be a reasonably well-crafted thriller about blind sleuth Duncan Maclain and his run-in with a nest of Nazi spies in Connecticut. The film's main narrative begins when Maclain's old friend Norma Lawry (Ann Harding) shows up to ask his advice about Barbara Lawry (Donna Reed), her stepdaughter by way of her marriage to a brilliant Allied scientist. It seems Barbara is dating a much older man named Paul Gerente (John Emery), a Barrymoresque ham who happens to be Norma's former paramour, and though Norma regards him as too much of a heart-breaking rogue for her stepdaughter, the feisty Barbara clearly relishes defying her and continues to see him. Things turn more serious after Gerente turns up dead in his apartment, and Barbara, finding Norma nearby, accuses her of the crime. Called in to investigate, Maclain and his seeing-eye dog "Friday" run afoul of a contingent of enemy agents, some of whom use a local playhouse as their front while others pose as Lawry household servants. He learns the spies are bent on extracting a secret document developed by Norma's husband that, according to one of the agents, is "worth ten armored divisions to us." Engaging in a deception himself (he pretends to be a tippling Lawry uncle), Maclain relies on quick wits, a keen intelligence, and a few judo moves to solve the mystery and expose the spy ring.

Critics found quite a bit to praise about this eighty-minute low-budgeted affair, with virtually all of them underscoring its unusual premise. Writing for the *New York Times*, Theodore Strauss noted that "by exploiting the neatest trick of the week, [Zinnemann and Chertok] have converted a basically humdrum yarn of spies and an inventor's precious formulas into a tidy and tingling little thriller. Their central character, the sleuth, is blind. And on that depends every ounce of the film's suspense. . . . Credit the Messrs. Zinnemann and Chertok with another

FIGURE 4.1. EYES IN THE NIGHT (MGM, 1942). Ann Harding asks blind detective Edward Arnold for advice. (Courtesy Museum of Modern Art/Film Stills Archive)

hectic little pulse-quickener." Philip Hartung of *Commonweal* noted that "violence is only incidental in the film. Its most unusual note is that its detective is blind: and half of the fun and excitement of the picture is provided through following the sleuthing, scenting and methods of this crafty blind man. . . . Even when the plot is not entirely credible, the suspense, the blind man's maneuvers and the outstanding performance of 'Friday,' Arnold's dog who is his seeing eye, will keep you absorbed." Calling it "strong supporting fodder," a *Variety* reviewer suggested that the "yarn moves at a fast clip, with plenty of suspenseful, though stereotyped, sequences, making it a strong bet for secondary bookings." Latter-day reviewers such as Don Miller, Jay Nash, and Stanley Ross praised the film as well. Miller, for example, stated that "as a mystery thriller, *Eyes in the Night* held interest from the beginning to the end, which was action-packed in a way not customarily provided by the rather staid MGM script department. Zinnemann paced the last quarter of the film in near serial fashion as the blind detective is held captive by the culprits and manages an escape and last-minute rescue aided by his trusty seeing-eye dog. Too, the sequences dealing with the sightless sleuth and his method of working held a fascination of its own."[6]

In general, Zinnemann and his colleagues dealt with Maclain's blindness in a refreshingly understated way. The other characters tend not to make a big deal of his visual impairment and seldom subject him to the alternating rounds of bigotry, paternalism, and indifference that have so often characterized mainstream society's treatment of its disabled minority. Occasionally they do utter lines that could be interpreted as oblique slurs. For example, one of the spies, realizing that the fellow who has just subdued him has a seeing-eye dog, incredulously asks a Maclain friend named Marty, "Is that guy blind?" With the implication that the spy has been taken down by a lesser human being, Marty replies, "Demoralizing, ain't it?" Such mildly insulting instances, however, are rare.

The cause of Maclain's blindness constitutes one of *Eyes in the Night's* most conspicuous departures from the novel. In *The Odor of Violets*, Kendrick explicitly identifies Maclain as a World War I veteran who had lost his sight as a result of a wartime injury. As the detective tells his canine companion, "You're lucky to be a dog in days like these. You're living in a world that's blind. Blind, as the last war blinded me!" (23). The movie, however, does not specify Maclain's participation in that war or relate his impairment to it. In fact, it makes no mention of the reason for his blindness at all. In addition, Kendrick, as well as the characters in his novel frequently refer to Maclain as "the Captain" (indeed, the nickname appears on almost every other page of the scenes in which the detective appears), but this label barely comes up in the movie: only two or three passing references and with no war-related context. For all the audience members could have known (at least those unfamiliar with Kendrick's novels), Maclain could have served in the merchant marine, skippered a tugboat or a yacht, or even sailed toy boats in his bathtub. Since *Eyes in the Night* began playing in theaters almost a year after Pearl Harbor, we can only surmise that Zinnemann and his MGM colleagues chose to deemphasize Maclain's veteran status because they did not want to dwell on anything that could possibly be construed as a downbeat effect of war. With superpatriotic productions such as Frank Capra's *Why We Fight* films on the rise, movie studios showed little inclination at the time to imply that lifelong disabilities could happen to "good" soldiers, regardless of which good fight they were fighting. Despite its glossing over of this issue and the typical socioeconomic circumstances that surround blind people then and now (the filmmakers took an easy way out by following the novel's lead and making Maclain wealthy), *Eyes in the Night* remains a positive and forthright portrayal of a visually impaired person.[7]

Literal blindness is not the only variant of sightlessness to appear in the book and movie. Indeed, the topic of figurative blindness crops up often in *The Odor of Violets* through both specific movements (e.g., Maclain's "a world that's blind" comment, noted above) and overriding theme. Receiving its first printing in January 1941, the book was essentially a plea to prewar America not to be blind to the presence of Axis spies on its soil. Since this was a dated message by late 1942, however, *Eyes in the Night's* use of figurative blindness is not as pronounced as the novel's. Still, it does play a role in the form of the movie's suggestion of dangerous "blind" allegiances to foreign powers and Maclain's frequently demonstrated ability to "see" (i.e., understand) things that others do not.

It is worth noting that on this latter point Maclain bears some resemblance to a stereotype of blind people that figured in a number of other Hollywood movies, particularly during the early 1930s and early 1940s: the so-called Saintly Sage.[8] Appearing in such otherwise diverse films as *Bride of Frankenstein* (1935), *The Devil-Doll* (1936), *Heidi* (1937), *Saboteur* (1942), and *The Enchanted Cottage* (1943), the Saintly Sage is a pious older person with blindness who serves as a voice of reason and conscience in a chaotic world. A sedentary supporting character, the Saintly Sage is sensible, charitable, and above all wise. Without the slightest trace of bitterness, the Cassandralike sage freely dispenses his/her wisdom to the surrounding able-bodied protagonists, who ignore it at their peril.

Though Maclain differs from typical Sages in some important respects (he is neither particularly spiritual nor as old as they and as a lead character is far more proactive), it is clear he and they share a kinship based on perspectives traceable to the earliest stages of the medium. Consider, for example, the following opinion of blind people issued by a movie publicist during the medium's salad days:

> We, of course, assume that being most unfortunate over whose sight Fate has drawn the mantle of darkness, and it is reasonable so to do, but Divine Providence is sure to compensate those so afflicted with ameliorating gifts that help them bear their ills with fortitude, and not only that, their powers of discernment are far more acute than those endowed with sight. There is the sight of the soul, which sees farther than the eyes. This may be called intuition; but whatever it may be, it is a rare gift. (*MPW* 696)

Though this statement was penned more than thirty years before the appearance of *Eyes in the Night* (it was written by Lee Dougherty to promote D. W. Griffith's 1909 Biograph film, *The Light That Came*), it aptly characterizes Maclain, the sages, and their stereotyped "second sight" abilities. As with the classic Saintly Sage films noted above, *Eyes in the Night* duly heightens its sense of figurative blindness among sighted people by posing a wise and insightful character's literal sightlessness as an ironic foil.

Eyes in the Night's use of literal and figurative blindness, associated largely with its surface narrative, obscures a third dimension to blindness that exists on the film's subtextual level: its symbolic function, or more specifically its representation of sexual disempowerment. As argued elsewhere, the first forty years' worth of mainstream narrative movies tended to position nonelderly disabled males as symbolically castrated and filled with aberrant lusts. Concocting elaborate schemes to "get even" with the patriarchal figures they held accountable for their disabilities and/or other moral-code violations, these embittered souls were almost always doomed to failure and often died as a result of their Oedipal quests. By the late 1930s, however, filmmakers working within the context of the new overseas war and America's leadership as provided by the wheelchair-using Franklin

Roosevelt had begun significantly modifying the image of disabled males; they were now casting them in more of a heroic mold. Though Zinnemann and his co-workers were in some ways hedging their bets on *Eyes in the Night* (as noted above, they went out of their way to avoid associating Maclain with wartime trauma), their film establishes him as the main figure who courageously battles the Nazi spies. As I suggested in a previous work, characters such as Maclain "embodied what for Hollywood was initially a paradoxical construct: symbolically castrated, 'feminized' males simultaneously imbued with the heavily masculinized notion of heroism."[9]

Consciously or not, Zinnemann and his contemporaries often reconciled these conflicting concepts by mandating a resexualization of their disabled male figures to show that patriarchal values had not been permanently weakened. The *Eyes in the Night* filmmakers followed Kendrick's lead by making Maclain's main antagonist a woman—Cheli Scott (Katherine Emery), the spy ringleader who masquerades as a theatrical director—and in so doing suggested that hero and villain are on relatively equal footing at first; that is, both are "weakened" characters from a Freudian perspective. Maclain eventually gains the upper hand, however, by way of the entity that serves as the first of his remasculinizing agents: Friday, the young German shepherd who serves as his seeing-eye dog.

Zinnemann's representation of Friday, Maclain, and the symbolic dimension of the latter's blindness hinges on the director's strategy for creating these characters' points of view, and it is worth examining this theoretically thorny issue more closely at this point. If we accept Laura Mulvey's position, offered in her landmark essay on visual pleasure, that "it is the place of the look that defines cinema" (17), what defines *Eyes in the Night* with its sightless protagonist? Or, as Edward Branigan rhetorically queried, what "is the status of a POV shot when the character is asleep, blindfolded, blind, or dead?" (108). These are questions central to this film, and Zinnemann chose to answer them in a provocative way: by photographing much of the film from the seeing-eye dog's perspective. Consider, for example, the series of shots in the scene that immediately follows the film's opening credits:

1. medium shot of Friday looking off-screen Right, which changes as the camera pans Right, tilts up, and backs away slightly to become a long shot of Maclain and Marty as they wrestle on a mat while two other men watch in the background
2. close-up of Friday looking off Right

3. long shot of Maclain spinning around with Marty on his shoulders
4. close-up of Friday looking off Right
5. long shot of Maclain as he drops Marty on the mat
6. medium shot of Marty as he lands on his head
7. close-up of Friday looking off Right

This scene, in which Shots 4 and 7 are simple continuations of Shot 2, and 3 and 5 are continuations of Shot 1, follows the classic style of Hollywood editing, but with a twist: a canine, not a human, does the looking. Indeed, Friday enjoys more close-ups by far than any other character in the movie, and Zinnemann endowed him with the power of the look throughout much of it.

Though not writing on this particular film, theorist Branigan considered such a cinematic construction of perspective while discussing the relationship of character and point of view. "There is a subtle but important distinction here between a character, and the presence or awareness of a character," he wrote. "We may want to say that 'character' is a more complex effect of the text . . . and that much less is needed to found a POV shot; for instance, the presence of an animal can give rise to a POV shot" (120). Labeling such shots "metaphorical POVs" (105), Branigan suggested further that "strictly speaking, it is not character (which is a rather complex notion), but a mere presence or awareness that is required" to motivate such point-of-view shots (108).

As may be inferred from Branigan's commentary, the directorial decision to allow animals the look from time to time is not terribly unusual. (Indeed, Branigan notes that even inanimate objects such as statuary and portraits are occasionally so endowed.) Yet *Eyes in the Night*'s use of nonhuman point of view is considerably more involved than the simple form suggested by Branigan. A sense of its complexity may be found in a cluster of shots that occurs after Maclain, searching inside Paul Gerente's bedroom for clues to the latter's murder, hears a noise and hides in a closet while Friday ducks under the bed:

1. long shot of Gabriel Hoffman (a Nazi stooge) as he enters the bedroom from Right, switches on a light, and turns Right to make a phone call, with Friday visible to the audience (but not to Gabriel) under the bed
2. close-up of Maclain facing Right inside the darkened closet, a streak of light crossing his face
3. close-up of Friday facing Right

4. medium shot of Gabriel on the phone facing Right
5. close-up of Friday facing Right
6. medium shot of Gabriel on the phone facing Right
7. medium shot of Maclain facing Right as he knocks over something in the closet, making a noise
8. medium shot of Gabriel on the phone as he turns from Right to Center in reaction to the noise
9. from Gabriel's POV, a medium shot of the bottom half of the closet door as several beads roll out from underneath it into the room
10. medium shot of Gabriel as he hangs up the phone
11. medium shot of Maclain facing Right
12. medium shot of Gabriel as he walks Left toward closet door
13. close-up of Friday facing Right, turning his head to Center to face the camera
14. medium shot of Gabriel, framed by the edges of the door and the door frame, as he walks toward (and looks at) the camera and pulls out a pistol from inside his jacket
15. close-up of Friday facing Left as he jumps left out from under the bed
16. long shot of Friday as he runs Left (camera follows) to Gabriel at the closet door and grabs his arm with his mouth

Shots 13, 14, and 15 are the most interesting in this rather lengthy excerpt from the bedroom scene in that Friday appears to see Gabriel *from Maclain's perspective*. It is a curious series of shots, to say the least. Shot 14 is unmistakably from the detective's point of view inside the closet even though, as a blind person, he could not possibly have seen Gabriel. Within the context of surrounding Shots 13 and 15, however, Shot 14 appears to be from Friday's perspective even though it would have been impossible for him to see Gabriel from that angle.

What are we to make of these apparently conflicting shots, and how do they relate to the symbolic side of Maclain's blindness? Given the existence of these and other constructions in *Eyes in the Night*, it is fair to argue that Zinnemann designed Friday to be much more than just the servant suggested by the allusion to Robinson Crusoe's "Man Friday"; the canine is a veritable extension of Maclain himself. He is a seeing-eye dog in several senses: not only in the usual way but also cinematically—his gaze becomes Maclain's gaze. In other words, his perspective is at times a surrogate for his master's. From this standpoint, the film takes on something of a narcissistic quality in that Maclain is occasionally the object of his own "gaze" (i.e., he is both the wielder of the gaze by way of Friday's vision and the recipient of it), as suggested in the first scene detailed above. This powerful strategy has the effect of pulling all of the audience's attention toward Maclain and his canine extension.

Friday represents not only Maclain's vision but also its symbolic connotations. With his animal strength, long and pointed snout, and sharp teeth, Friday suggests Maclain's sexual potency, phallus, and castration threat to others all rolled into one. (Maclain engages in heroic deeds on his own through punches and judo tosses, of course, but he cannot match Friday in sheer animal power.) Friday's embodiment of Maclain's libido is avidly illustrated in several scenes in the film that involve a second dog. While out searching for Maclain's friend Marty, Friday encounters a female French poodle, who at one point actually waggles her rear end toward him. Clearly tempted by her canine charms, Friday pauses at considerable length before continuing his rescue mission. After the conclusion of the main narrative, she reappears and Friday runs off with her on a "date." In somewhat of an unnerving development that coincides with the poodle's return, Barbara Lawry reveals a hitherto unexpressed interest in Maclain that has sexual masochism written all over it; she cites with relish a line that Maclain had uttered earlier about "paddling her canoe" if she does not shape up and now actively seeks the prospect of being with this hard-handed male, one who happens to be about three times her age (Edward Arnold, then fifty-two, essentially played his own years, while Donna Reed's character is supposed to be seventeen). She thus becomes a second remasculinizing agent for Maclain, a kind of affirmation of the Maclain-Friday combination and the potent "whole male" it has produced.[10]

These measures, which Kendrick did not suggest in the novel (Barbara does not come on to Maclain in *The Odor of Violets* and the German shepherd, far from representing Maclain's libido, is a relatively passive female named Schnucke who lacks Friday's oft-represented perspective and does not come close to matching his prominence),[11] work against the movie's resonant portrayal of the blind experience. Its patriarchal subtext notwithstanding, however, *Eyes in the Night* remains a vivid and cogent representation of a disabled person's life and, as such, provided a solid basis for several of Zinnemann's later films. Since *Eyes in the Night* served as a major learning experience for the director (Zinnemann regarded the difficult production as "most useful training for future occasions" [48]),[12] it is more than a little ironic that he should have been so "blind" to its many thought-provoking qualities.

NOTES

1. D.W. Griffith, Tod Browning, Alfred Hitchcock, Frank Capra, Stanley Kubrick, and John Cromwell are among the few others who have directed three or more films with disabled characters. For a discussion of their work as it relates to disability issues, see Martin F. Norden, *The Cinema of Isolation: A History of Physical Disability in the Movies* (New Brunswick, N.J.: Rutgers University Press, 1994).

2. Robert Ryan's *Act of Violence* character—a physically impaired veteran named Joe Parkson, who relentlessly pursues another American vet for betraying their comrades during WWII—is a conspicuous departure from Zinnemann's other disability-related constructions and indeed bears little resemblance to other Hollywood disabled-vet characters of the time. An embittered and threatening figure, Parkson is a throwback to a Hollywood stereotype of the silent and early sound eras that I call the "Obsessive Avenger": a symbolically disempowered male who, Ahablike, seeks revenge on the person he holds responsible for disabling him and/or violating his moral code in some other way. For further discussion of this general image, see Martin F. Norden, "Victims, Villains, Saints, and Heroes: Movie Portrayals of People with Physical Disabilities," in *Beyond the Stars: Stock Characters in American Popular Film*, ed. Paul Loukides and Linda K. Fuller (Bowling Green, Ohio: Bowling Green State University Popular Press, 1990), pp. 224–25.

3. *A Life in the Movies: An Autobiography* (New York: Scribner's, 1992), p. 48. His view of this film has apparently changed little over the decades; when asked in 1953 about his MGM work, he said, "only two features pleased me, some of *Act of Violence* and *The Seventh Cross*" (Howard Thompson, "Directed by Fred Zinnemann," *New York Times* 25 Jan. 1953, Sec. 2, p. 5).

4. *The Odor of Violets* and the other Maclain novels served a purpose beyond providing the basis for Zinnemann's film. Officials at the Library of Congress found Kendrick's books so realistic and attentive to detail that they recommended him to the War Department, which had been seeking writers who could ease the rehabilitation process for newly blinded veterans. Kendrick agreed to help and began writing a novel about a blinded WWII vet and his eventual readjustment to civilian life. Titled *Lights Out*, the 1945 novel served as the source for the Universal-International film *Bright Victory* (1951), directed by Mark Robson and starring Arthur Kennedy. See Thomas M. Pryor, "Happy, Happy Author," *New York Times*, 28 Jan. 1951, Sec. 2 p. 5.

5. Schary served as a screenwriter on the former film and story contributor on the latter. It is difficult to determine the extent of Schary's involvement in *Eyes in the Night*, but given his association with other films before and after *Eyes* that featured strong characters with disabilities—the Edison films, a number of the "Dr. Kildare" movies, *Till the End of Time* (1946), *Bad Day at Black Rock* (1955), *Sunrise at Campobello* (1960)—it certainly coincided with his interests. He had already departed MGM, however, by the time the studio made its second film based on a Duncan Maclain novel: *The Hidden Eye* (1945), directed by Richard Whorf and again starring Arnold.

6. See *New York Times*, 16 Oct. 1942, p. 23; *Commonweal*, 30 Oct. 1942, p. 44; *Variety*, 9 Sept. 1942, p. 14; Don Miller, *"B" Movies: An Informal Survey of the American Low-Budget Film 1933–1945* (New York: Curtis Books, 1973), p. 228. See also Jay Robert Nash and Stanley Ralph Ross, *The Motion Picture Guide, 1927–1984* (Chicago: Cinebooks, 1987), p. 795.

7. Zinnemann did not hesitate to underscore characters' veteran status in films made after the war, such as *Act of Violence*, *A Hatful of Rain* (1957), and of course *The Men*. In the case of this latter film, however, the decision did come back to haunt him; *The Men* premiered two weeks after the outbreak of the Korean War. "Designed as a post-war picture it was suddenly facing a pre-war mentality," he wrote. "No wonder that people whose sons, husbands and fathers were going to fight could not bear to watch a movie such as ours. It folded in two weeks." See Zinnemann, p. 85.

8. See Norden, "Victims," p. 226.

9. "Movie Constructions of Gender and Physical Disability: Some Historical and Theoretical Intersections," University Film and Video Association Conference, Philadelphia, Pa., Aug. 1993, p. 8. Kendrick also tapped into this spirit of the times. In an exchange in *The Odor of Violets* that did not make it into the film, a character likens Maclain to FDR and the detective responds, "At least you've compared me with a remarkably able man."

10. Given Barbara's frequent sparring with the maternal Norma over a much older man with whom both had been romantically involved (a bickering greatly understated in the novel, by the way) and her new found attraction to Maclain, *Eyes in the Night* invites a reading as a female Oedipal drama. Such a reading is, alas, beyond the scope of this chapter.

11. In what might have been Kendrick's oblique commentary on the relationship of Maclain and his dog, "Schnucke" is a German colloquialism for a pet dog, a man's "darling," or a wife.

12. The problems Zinnemann encountered on this film included a very tight four-week production schedule, a dog who would often run away and hide

after the first take, and Arnold's lack of preparation. Zinnemann so disliked working with Arnold that he refused to mention him by name in his autobiography; he simply referred to him, twice, as the "blind detective" who kept blowing his lines, necessitating multiple takes. See Zinnemann, pp. 48, 124. As fellow director Frank Capra makes clear in *his* autobiography, this was typical of Arnold. For Capra's account of working with the often unprepared actor, see *The Name Above the Title: An Autobiography* (New York: Macmillan, 1971), pp. 243–44.

WORKS CITED

Branigan, Edward. *Point of View in the Cinema: A Theory of Narration and Subjectivity in Classical Film.* New York: Mouton, 1984.

Kendrick, Baynard. *The Odor of Violets.* Boston: Little, Brown, 1941.

Moving Picture World, 13 Nov. 1909: 696.

Mulvey, Laura. "Visual Pleasure and Narrative Cinema." *Screen* 16 (Autumn 1975): 6–18.

Zinnemann, Fred. *A Life in the Movies: An Autobiography.* New York: Scribner's, 1992.

CHAPTER FIVE

—————————————— ⊞ ——————————————

There Were Good Germans:
Fred Zinnemann's
The Seventh Cross *(1944)*

LEONARD QUART

The Seventh Cross (1944) was Austrian-born Fred Zinnemann's first major "A" production for MGM, and his first film dealing with the trauma of the events leading up to World War II and its aftermath (e.g., *The Search* [1948], *The Men* [1950], *Julia* [1977]). The film was based on a novel by Anna Seghers, who had escaped from Nazi Germany to Mexico, and produced on the studio sound stages and back lots. It was a well-mounted, skillfully directed, low-key work, centering on a prisoner, George Heisler (Spencer Tracy), who escapes a concentration camp in prewar Nazi Germany and struggles to elude his murderous pursuers and resurrect his shattered faith in human beings.

Heisler, a political dissident, is the respected leader among seven men who escape Westhofen concentration camp in a frantic attempt to get to the Dutch border and freedom. The Nazis quickly capture six of the men, hanging them on crosses nailed to stunted, stripped trees in Westhofen's yard, but one cross, the seventh, remains portentously empty. That cross is meant for Heisler.

The Seventh Cross is about the disillusioned Heisler's rediscovery of his faith in mankind, rather than an exploration of either the nature of

Nazism or Heisler's political beliefs. The film tells us little about Heisler's political commitments except that he is anti-Nazi and believes in freedom. We never know if he is a socialist, communist, liberal, or conservative, though, of course, in most Hollywood films ideological and political distinctions of this sort are never developed or demarcated and are essentially seen as beside the point. The historical context for these early Nazi concentration camps for communists, socialists, political dissenters, writers, and intellectuals (many of them Jews) is also barely touched on. What suffices in a classical Hollywood film is that the audience understand that Heisler is a good man on the side of the angels, and that the Nazis, who are sketchily delineated as no more than stock figures, are brutal oppressors and murderers. It is the audience's identification with the virtuous hero's travails that is primary here, not a complex understanding of the political institutions, ideology, or dynamics of prewar Nazi Germany.

The film's narrative centers on Heisler's flight from the camp. Exhausted, despairing, and emptyhearted, he's a man whom we first see with a glowering, dark, suspicious look on his face, the gaze of someone who has lost all faith in human nature. (Tracy's scowl here is just like the one that he wears as the unjustly victimized character he played in Fritz Lang's *Fury* [1936]—a man who sets out to destroy a mob that tried to burn him alive for a crime he didn't commit.) The film depicts his encounters with a wide range of ordinary Germans, who ultimately and predictably resurrect his belief in human virtue and dignity. There are a few Germans who behave badly and either repudiate or betray him, but the majority of people he meets extend a helping hand despite the mortal danger they face.

Heisler's first encounter after his escape is with a too-cute, apple-eating moppet (Shirley Temple redux), who innocently takes his hand as they walk down a road. Luckily, nothing develops from this meeting (Zinnemann avoiding the patent sentimentality the scene suggests), since Heisler has to leave her abruptly and climb over a wall topped with shards of glass and hide from the Gestapo. Some of his early encounters only reinforce his sense of futility. There's a truck driver who gives him a lift, but dumps him when he discovers that he has escaped from Westhofen. And there is his old girlfriend, Leni, whom Heisler first conjures up in flashback, looking like a vivacious, golden-haired dream girl. When he returns to her for help, however, the now-married, domesticated, severe-looking German hausfrau is utterly unsympathetic, threatening to inform on him if he doesn't leave. There is also a brief appearance of the Hitler

Youth. Streaming through the streets of a village, filled with adolescent glee, they help the Gestapo look for the escaped prisoners as if they were Boy Scouts playing a game of hide-and-seek. Finally, there is the mass of ordinary Germans who both cheer the capture of one Jewish escapee and gather in the city square to garner vicarious pleasure from the Gestapo's pursuit of another escaped prisoner/acrobat as he clambers over the pitched roofs of houses, until he calmly surrenders to his fate and takes a suicidal swan dive into the street. In these scenes most of the German people totally identify with and cheer on the hunters, and express only derision for their prey.

Of course, if those were the only Germans Heisler had come across he would have ultimately surrendered to the Gestapo like a fellow escapee who feels devoid of hope because the German people don't care what happens to them and cannot be trusted. He advises Heisler to give up—for it's better to be dead than rotting in an evil world. Zinnemann, however, constructs the narrative so that Heisler meets the kind of ordinary Germans who are gradually able to renew his faith in human beings. For every janitor who informs the Gestapo about Heisler's presence in an apartment there is: a Jewish doctor who cleans up his badly cut hand, and, though suspicious, does not report him to the police, as the law requires; a Madame Marelli (Agnes Moorehead), who owns a costume shop and provides him with clothes, leaving a wad of money in his pocket to help him survive; a Sauer (George Macready), a wealthy, sophisticated architect, who, though terrified of losing his comfortable home and position, is finally goaded by his anti-Nazi wife's scathing contempt to take a risk and go to the resistance to help his old friend, Heisler; and ordinary workers named Fiedler and Schlamm (Felix Bressart), who, without hesitation, do their brave bit to help Heisler escape. Schlamm, in fact, delivers an optimistic, populist parable—along with delicatessen sandwiches—about how people like him are ants who not only do their necessary, little jobs for the cause, but exist in such great numbers that they cannot all be eliminated.

Most importantly for the film's thesis, there are Paul and Liasel Roeder (Hume Cronyn and Jessica Tandy), a working-class couple who are old friends of Heisler. The Roeders have three cute children, and their home is redolent with domestic warmth and marital love and devotion. Paul Roeder is a boyish, pipe-smoking, sweet-natured man, who approves of what the Nazis have done for ordinary people. He is an apolitical, unreflective man who doesn't listen to the radio or read newspapers, but likes the better pay, free diapers, and greater material comfort the Nazis have provided.

It is the Roeders, however, whose innate dignity and warmth move Heisler to renew his sense of hope. Though Paul may have never thought about politics—his prime interest being bread and sausages, not political pamphlets and ideas—his loyalty to Heisler transcends self-interest. After Heisler informs him that he has escaped from a camp, Roeder insists on putting him up for the evening and helping him escape. As a result, Paul is arrested and interrogated by the Gestapo, but gives them no information about Heisler and is released. Afterwards, Zinnemann has Roeder critically reflect on the nature of Nazism. Paul informs his wife that he finally understands the Nazis' capacity for evil, and that it is the Gestapo, not a man like George, who is the real threat to their home.

For Heisler "there's no better man than Paul Roeder," and Hume Cronyn's natural, Oscar-nominated performance convincingly turns him into the incarnation of a human sweetness and concern that still survives amidst Nazi persecution and barbarism. Roeder is a nicely calibrated character, and Zinnemann avoids transforming him into an outsized, heroic figure. The night Roeder returns from Gestapo headquarters with his new understanding of the Nazis, he does not sit declaiming against their barbarism, but takes his wife out to a restaurant. What is most important to Roeder is his family, not public or political life, and the film suggests that he will continue to live his life in this manner.

Still, Zinnemann or the studio is unable to stop on this authentic moment. They tack on a conventional love interest at the film's conclusion—a sympathetic waitress, Toni (Signe Hasso), who hides Heisler from the Gestapo in her room. She is simple, pretty, and kind, and instantly rekindles Heisler's capacity for romantic feeling, complete with lush movie music underlining their passionate embrace. It's a love without a future, for Heisler is off on a freighter to Holland at dawn to repay the debt he owes people like Toni who helped by "healing" him. Their meeting ends the film on a sentimental, upbeat note, leaving the audience with Heisler's belief in love, as well as humanity, restored.

For those in the audience who are so dim they could miss what the film is saying, *The Seventh Cross* uses the voice-over of an omniscient narrator, Heisler's close friend and fellow escapee, Wallau (Ray Collins). Wallau is caught and executed by the Nazis in the opening scenes, but his narration (from heaven?) runs throughout the film. Acting as Heisler's conscience and goad, he informs the audience and Heisler that the world

FIGURE 5.1. THE SEVENTH CROSS (MGM, 1944). Political dissident Spencer Tracy and common man Hume Cronyn. (Courtesy Collectors Book Store, Hollywood, Calif.)

may be cruel, but there are good men to be found. Therefore, one shouldn't give in to despair. Wallau's narration is portentous, hyperbolic, and intrusive, intoning purple, vaporous prose about "the flashes of a small flame that has not gone out in this land." Satisfied that Heisler has been fully regenerated, his spirit leaves the film. Most of the narration is excessive and self-evident, except one surprisingly trenchant and pessimistic statement. When Heisler takes refuge in a church, the narrator declares that the German people were too engaged in slaughter to adhere to the Church's tenets.

The Germany evoked in *The Seventh Cross* looks like any sanitized studio set that was used by Hollywood during the thirties and forties to represent European villages and cities. The charming village depicted in the film has cobblestone streets, chickens wandering about, and stone walls; the city of Mainz, where Heisler hides out, contains a cathedral, a small formal park, and a fountain in the city square. It is all patently artificial, too neat and artfully designed to provide a genuine sense of the ominous texture of fear and oppression that permeated the streets of Nazi Germany in the thirties.

The film is shot primarily in close-up and medium shot with the emphasis on close-ups of Heisler to convey his anguish and sense of isolation. This is a thesis film, however, and, like all the other characters, Heisler is completely at the service of the earnest, repetitious message the film delivers. *The Seventh Cross* is not interested in Heisler's idiosyncrasies, behavioral tics, or interiority except in relation to the inner turmoil he undergoes as he struggles to renew his former belief in human beings. It is Heisler the anti-Nazi, not Heisler the three-dimensional, nuanced character, that the film portrays.

Zinnemann skillfully uses light and shadow, low-key lighting, and noirish, wet, mist-shrouded streets to build tension in a couple of scenes where Heisler is in danger of being caught. The scenes set in the concentration camp are enveloped in fog with shadowy, isolated figures and barking dogs. They evoke an almost abstract vision of the nightmare of the camps, but without even a shred of the vividness and power of postwar Polish films like Wanda Jakubowska's *The Last Stage* (aka *The Last Stop*; *Ostatni etap*, 1948) or the harrowingly authentic portraits of Auschwitz in Andrzej Wajda's *Landscape After Battle* (*Krajobraz po bitwie*, 1970).

The Seventh Cross contains one scene in Sauer's luxuriant house that strikingly uses a mirror image to evoke a split-screen effect and catch the essence of Sauer's anxiety about becoming involved with the resistance. Zinnemann, however, is an austere director who rarely indulges in virtuoso effects. There are few dazzling camera angles and movements, little imaginative editing or innovative sound. *The Seventh Cross* is a classic Hollywood studio film (MGM), built on realistic artifice and big-budget glossiness rather than social realism or verisimilitude. Zinnemann shot it on the studio backlots, but in his World War II film about displaced children, *The Search*, he emphasized the authenticity which characterized most of his films from then on. In *The Search* he used location shooting, some nonprofessional performers, and documentary footage of war orphans, much as he did in his film about paraplegic veterans, *The Men*.

In *The Seventh Cross*, however, it is the depiction of Heisler's spiritual journey that is central, and every camera set-up and movement, and the film's mise en scène and editing are committed to driving home its message. This is an airless, carefully shaped film. It has little room for casually constructed, incidental scenes filled with the type of peripheral detail that evokes the full fabric of German life.

What is clearly of most interest to a viewer about *The Seventh Cross* is not its virtues and defects as a work of art, but what it conveys about Hollywood's treatment of Nazi Germany. The film is true enough to the historical situation that it avoids making it seem that the resistance was a powerful organization enlisting the support of a large number of German citizens. Instead, in *The Seventh Cross* most of the resistance members have been arrested, and there are only a handful left to carry on. The reality was that the Nazis were quick to repress or push into exile most of their political opposition in the thirties, arresting and putting into camps many active Communists, Social Democrats, and trade unionists. The small political underground mainly limited itelf to pamphleteering, and the most effective and organized resistance came from a small number of conservative and nationalist Army officers and a few officials in the foreign office who saw Hitler as leading the country to destruction.

In German society, where self-esteem did not grow out of a sense of autonomy but from one's familial and professional roles, the Nazis reinforced the conformity of the public by threatening both their livelihood and lives. Of course, the Nazis were generally popular with most Germans, whose interest was primarily in a strong and efficient government rather than in a democratic one. With the help of informers, who embodied the will of the German majority, the Nazis created an atmosphere of fear and terror for anyone whose loyalty to the regime was suspect.

Consequently, it's amazing that acts of political and moral courage did occur. Hundreds of thousands of Germans listened to foreign broadcasts, read and distributed illegal literature, discussed taboo political subjects, and even sheltered Jews and political outlaws like Heisler (Gill 24). Still, one doesn't want to overstate the extent of these acts of resistance, for those hundreds of thousands were no more than a pebble in a sea of seventy million Germans, who, whatever their private feelings, passively accommodated or actively supported the Nazis and were generally indifferent to the plight of the regime's victims.

The Seventh Cross does not indulge in the kind of heroics that would distort historical reality. Besides the people who play an active role in aiding Heisler's escape, there are two other minor characters who, in a line or two of dialogue, articulate some passing disenchantment with Nazism. In the too-precious, Hollywood-style German village Heisler first escapes to, a pipe-smoking teacher murmurs ironically about the Nazis' murderousness, and a housewife becomes annoyed that her husband has allowed their private life to be consumed by political activity. Zinnemann's Germany, however, is not filled with people who abhor Hitler, or are ready to engage in bold actions against the Nazis. It's a country basically united behind Nazi policies and practices.

Nevertheless, the film was one of the few American films made during World War II that recognized there were good Germans (though, significantly, the film is set in the prewar era). This view made some people consider the film as "dangerous to American morale" (Furhammar and Isaksson 67). The usual Hollywood treatment of Germany during the war often envisioned the Nazis as maniacs (*Underground* [1941]) or thugs (*The Hitler Gang* [1944]). There were black comic films like Lubitsch's stylish *To Be or Not To Be* (1942), which saw the Nazis as ridiculous and boorish. That artful film, however, was attacked in a *New York Times* editorial as presenting "a fool's paradise" which subverted the war effort (Doherty 127). Afterwards Hollywood film studiously avoided turning the Nazis into comic foils or an indomitable enemy, seeing them as chillingly murderous figures who were "deadly not dumb" (Doherty 133), a serious enemy but one that could be ultimately defeated.

Zinnemann's parents died in the concentration camps in the early forties, but it was only when the war was over that he learned about it. Still, *The Seventh Cross*, like almost all American films of the time, avoided directly confronting the dire situation Jews faced in Nazi Germany during the thirties. A couple of minor Jewish characters make an appearance in the film, but it barely touches on the murderous ferocity of Nazi victimization of the Jews.

Given that the Hollywood moguls were uneasy about their Jewishness and apprehensive about alienating the mass, Gentile audience, it follows that they were hesitant about dealing with anti-Semitism and Jewish victimization. They especially wished to avoid being accused of engaging in special pleading for the Jews. World War II gave them permission to attack the Nazis. They could now do it in the name of patriotism and American unity, not Jewish survival. War films depicted Jewish characters as integral parts of melting-pot U.S. army platoons, but there was no sign in these films of the horrors faced by European Jewry, whose prime option by then was annihilation.

In its commitment to human decency, dignity, and individual conscience, *The Seventh Cross* set the tone for the body of Zinnemann's later concerns and motifs. Tracy's Heisler is the simple embodiment of Zinnemann's vision of individual integrity and heroism—those men like Will Kane (Gary Cooper) in *High Noon* (1952) and Robert E. Prewitt (Montgomery Clift) in *From Here to Eternity* (1953) and women like Julia (Vanessa Redgrave) in *Julia*, who, in more complex ways, steadfastly stood for moral principle against criminality, institutional corruption, and political totalitarianism.

WORKS CITED

Doherty, Thomas. *Projections of War: Hollywood, American Culture, and World War II*. New York: Columbia University Press, 1993.

Furhammar, Leif, and Folke Isaksson. *Politics and Film*. Trans. Kersti French. New York: Praeger, 1971.

Gill, Anton. *An Honourable Defeat: A History of German Resistance to Hitler, 1933–1945*. New York: Henry Holt, 1994.

CHAPTER SIX

⊞

Historical Perspective and the
Realist Aesthetic in High Noon (1952)

STEPHEN PRINCE

Though *High Noon* is generally regarded as one of the classic Westerns, like *Shane*, its respect is hard won and, at times, grudgingly bestowed. In his encyclopedia *The Western*, Phil Hardy dismisses it as a film that "has a certain obviousness about it" (215). John Wayne and Howard Hawks's reputed antipathy toward the picture is well known, culminating in *Rio Bravo*, allegedly intended as an antidote to *High Noon*'s portrait of a marshal anxiously seeking help from townspeople before confronting an armed gang.[1] A seminal work of the genre, *High Noon* carries a lot of cultural baggage, as in the McCarthy-period symbolism to which it is frequently attached, and the film's resonance remains very potent, as evidenced by the practice of cartoonists and political artists of recycling the film's images and title to describe political crises ranging from the 1956 Suez Canal invasions to the national elections in Poland in 1987 (Zinnemann, *Life* 110).[2]

As a product of the American film industry, *High Noon* is clearly the result of a collaborative effort. Director Fred Zinnemann has been especially forthcoming in crediting the contributions of editor Elmo Williams, cinematographer Floyd Crosby, producer Stanley Kramer, screenwriter Carl Foreman, and composer Dimitri Tiomkin. Zinnemann has said that *High Noon* is "a good example of a team effort" (Phillips 25) and has added, modestly, that "it would be unfair to say that I made it— I directed it" (Buckley 26), drawing a distinction between pictures he has directed but over which others have had final control and those which he has, more properly, controlled and made.

But despite the important qualifications we must keep in mind when considering the control the Hollywood director has over what is essentially a collaborative enterprise, a strong case can be made for contextualizing the design and themes of *High Noon* in terms of Zinnemann's own history and outlook as a citizen and as a creative artist. Let me be very careful here. Zinnemann did not have control over the final cut of the film, nor did he do the final edit. Stanley Kramer's ideas about the musical style of the movie included using a theme song at a time when this was not standard practice, and Zinnemann found Kramer's ideas "brilliant" and "original" (*Life* 108). Carl Foreman claimed that his script was a conscious polemic deliberately based in, and responding to, the blacklist atmosphere of the period (Buckley 34).[3] Clearly, the film is one that has multiple authors, each of whom has a claim upon selected aspects of its design. As director, Zinnemann's task was to integrate the work of these multiple originators, yet a series of clear and compelling correspondences exists between the material of the film, and its mounting, and Zinnemann's own life, personality, and social aims as a filmmaker. If we cannot call Zinnemann the author or "auteur" of this film, we can nevertheless supply some very interesting answers to the question of what emotionally drew Zinnemann to this material and why he chose to give the film the visual design it does have in those areas that he claims as his own contribution.

In describing Zinnemann's relationship to this film, I will emphasize the following factors: his European background and influences, his emphasis upon socially cognizant filmmaking, the resonance of the Will Kane character for Zinnemann, the significance of his contributions to the film's visual design, and the competing views of history which are at the heart of the film and about which Zinnemann cared deeply.

The first two factors are closely conjoined. Zinnemann was born in Austria, studied film in Paris, and began his career in Germany. He subsequently came to Hollywood, but shot several of his Hollywood films in Europe (*The Search, Teresa*). The Austrian stage and film director Berthold Viertel was an early mentor, during which time Zinnemann attended the famous coffee sessions hosted by Viertel's wife, Salka, and which were a hub for the European colony in Hollywood.

Zinnemann's European background, of course, does not make him unique in Hollywood. Many of the industry's personnel were émigrés, yet, unlike such directors as Lubitsch, Ford, and Capra, Zinnemann charted his own course in, and out of, the industry, training at MGM, but soon deciding to break with the studio in favor of independent productions and greater personal autonomy. "I decided I had had enough of the factory system and asked to be released from MGM" (*Life* 77). He signed a three-picture deal with independent producer Stanley Kramer, under which *High Noon* was the second production.

Zinnemann valued the connection he found between independent production and social realism. Realism, as understood by Zinnemann, entailed an avoidance of elaborate visual or technical gimmickry and an interest in grounding the image in the ongoing social history which surrounds the filmmaker and the audience and which provides a kind of world stage from which their dramas might be presented. For Zinnemann, realism contained both an ethic and aesthetic—the images were to be honestly obtained by abstaining from elaborate and self-conscious formal manipulations and were to be grounded in real, lived human experience. Formulaic studio productions, he quickly concluded, in their melodrama and sentimentalism, were disconnected from the kinds of issues he felt compelled to make films about. Working independently, he found it easier to make films which might address contemporary history. He noted, "There seems to be a close connection between authenticity and economy; the realistic story can be told without help of large studios, expensive stars and elaborate wardrobes" (Zinnemann, "Different Perspective" 113).

Zinnemann looked toward the most important model of unembellished, antistudio-gloss filmmaking then in existence, neorealism. Zinnemann gave several of his American pictures a neorealist flavor by filming on location and using nonprofessional actors in supporting roles. Both *The Search* and *Teresa* were shot in war-ravaged Europe in the locales called for by the story. Zinnemann claimed that he was working close to the tradition pioneered by Rossellini in *Open City* and De Sica in *Shoeshine* but was newly applying it to the American market. Above all, for Zinnemann, this was an approach that sought to document history. He wrote, "Stated in its simplest terms this approach consists of using the raw material of history in order to make a dramatic document" ("Different Perspective" 113). Stories must be conceived on the spot, in their real locales, and must not be deformed by being tailored to stars or popular formulas.

Stated in these terms, Zinnemann's proximity to neorealism seems much stronger than it really is. Zinnemann's work in the late 1940s and early 1950s is strongly indebted to European models of filmmaking, is particularly inflected with some of the aesthetic of neorealism, but it never embraces the neorealist aesthetic with the kind of fervor and thoroughness of a De Sica or a Rossellini. Zinnemann was, however strong his European background, trained in the American studio system and learned the imperatives and conventions of filmmaking for a popular audience. Indeed, he has described his function as a director in terms of providing entertainment for a large audience (Phillips 28). We should not, therefore, make too much of Zinnemann's break with the studios because it was only a limited break, not one with radical implications for style or politics. A comparison with Carl Dreyer is instructive here. Dreyer is a filmmaker for whom Zinnemann professes great admiration, and he has cited Dreyer's *Passion of Joan of Arc* as one of the great influences on his own work. Like Dreyer, Zinnemann has found internal psychological crises to be very cinematic and has used these "interior dramas" as the basis of a film's action. However—and this is the key point—Zinnemann never became the kind of journeyman director that Dreyer did, driven further and further toward a purity of visual style as he renounced ever more deeply the imperatives of studio style and popular taste.

Zinnemann's aesthetic, grounded in a conception of social and psychological realism, occupies a distinctive niche neither within the orbit of studio filmmaking nor very far from it. *High Noon*, for example, has a big star and is a genre picture, yet its social themes correspond very closely with Zinnemann's own realist aesthetic and with the anxieties he felt about events on the national and world stages and, especially, about the political complacency of American culture. Before coming to the United States, Zinnemann perceived an Austrian brand of fascism beginning to take root in his homeland. Moreover, inside the studio factory system and in American culture he found "blissful ignorance" of the shattering effects of World War II upon Europe. The escapism and sentimentality of Hollywood films appalled him in contrast to the direct social content of postwar European films. "In America there was no clear awareness of what had happened to countless human beings in the rest of the world. . . . We were as on an island of stagnation and claustrophobia in the midst of a rapidly changing world" (*Life* 55).

Within this immediate postwar context, Zinnemann saw his goal as an artist in these terms: "Our primary concern was not to attempt an artistic achievement, but to dramatize contemporary history for the large American audience and to make them understand in emotional terms what the world outside looks like today" ("Different Perspective" 113). This formulation shows both the distance from, and the propinquity to, Hollywood norms which characterize Zinnemann's distinctive niche. He backed off from the purity of the neorealist aesthetic and also distanced himself from the radical self-consciousness of a Godard ("I find all these intellectual arguments [about film style] quite fascinating, but also quite brittle and hollow" [Stang D13]) in favor of reaching viewers emotionally and dealing with issues of oppression, not in a didactically political way, but, as he says, "in a human way" ("Fred Zinnemann" 13), that is, implicitly and indirectly. For Zinnemann, the studio factory system was inimical to his goal of using film in a realistic fashion to dramatize contemporary history in emotional terms, yet he shared the Hollywood system's goal of placing an unobtrusive technique in the service of story and emotion.

Zinnemann's socially informed artistic sensibilities, then, led him away from MGM to independent production, where he would direct *High Noon* for Stanley Kramer. Although Zinnemann did not write the story, he could find resonance in its general shape and moral inflection. Foreman's script details the efforts of Marshal Will Kane (Gary Cooper) to enlist help from the citizens of his community when he learns that Frank Miller, a man he arrested and sent to prison for murder, is returning to town on the noon train. Miller has sworn to kill Kane, and three members of his old gang await his arrival at the station. Kane is deserted by all his former friends in town, even by his Quaker wife, Amy (Grace Kelly in her first substantial film role), and is left alone to face Miller and his gang.

As noted, Foreman felt the script, with its vision of an apathetic community turning on an honorable man, reflected his own political persecution with the blacklist in 1950s Hollywood. Zinnemann felt this was a narrow point of view, yet he found Will Kane an extraordinarily attractive figure. He found Kane's conflict of conscience—whether to stay and fight as he alone believes is necessary or leave town and run as everyone, including Amy, urges him to do—to be central to the film. For Zinnemann, *High Noon* was an interior drama, centered upon Kane's tortured visage and choice. As with the films of Carl Dreyer, Zinnemann has been drawn in drama to the interior crisis of conscience within the heart and

mind of his characters. "I always find questions of conscience very photogenic. That kind of interior drama is to me very, very exciting . . ."
("Fred Zinnemann" 62). He sought to spotlight this interior drama by
exteriorizing it through visual design. One of the principles of the film's
visual style which Zinnemann worked to perfect emphasized the contrast
between Cooper's black-clad marshal and the bleached, barren white sky
beneath which he is in constant motion. Low-angle shots position Cooper
against this barren sky and accentuate the anguish on his face by placing
it within an utterly blank, heartlessly empty, cloudless expanse.[4]

While these images of a frightened and anxious marshal have been
controversial within the genre (e.g., the reaction of Howard Hawks), it
must be affirmed that they possess an extraordinary iconic power. Cooper
is magnificent, dressed in black, lines of worry etched into his aging face
(generally shot without soft-focus filters), moving beneath the pitiless sky
with an eloquent economy of gesture, all of this made more striking by
our memories of a younger star in earlier Western roles. Zinnemann's han-
dling of Cooper's relationship with the camera is so shrewd and intelligent
that the interior drama that so fascinated the director is communicated
with a sharp and lasting power.

This cinematic power is evidence of the importance the Will Kane
character had for Zinnemann. Kane had become an outcast among his
neighbors. He refused to conform to their wishes and appreciated the
importance of standing up to the threat that would shortly arrive in their
insular town. Kane's situation corresponds to Zinnemann's conflicts with
the insularity of American culture on the world stage. In the film, only
Kane can look beyond the horizon (as Zinnemann wished American society to do in the postwar period), discern the true importance of the threat
due to arrive on those rails that stretch to infinity, and prepare to act. Like
Kane, too, Zinnemann realized he would never be "a company man" (*Life*
44) and, professionally, would need to go his own way, ultimately by leaving what he termed the "factory system." Politically, Zinnemann went his
own way as well, resisting attempts in 1950 by Cecil B. DeMille's right-
wing faction in the Directors' Guild to force a signed-ballot vote by
members on instituting an anticommunist loyalty oath.[5]

More profoundly, Zinnemann's experiences as a Jew in Austria may
have made him exceptionally keen to the agonizing dilemma faced by
Kane, deserted and made a scapegoat by his community and by people he
believed were his friends. Like Kane in the town of Hadleyville, Zinnemann, too, encountered social oppression and felt the stigma of being cast

out. "In Austria, discrimination had been part of life since time immemorial. It was always there—oppressive, often snide, sometimes hostile, seldom violent. It was in the air and one sensed it at all levels, in school, at work, and in society. A Jew was an outsider, a threat to the country's culture. Born in Austria, and raised as an Austrian, he would still never truly belong" (*Life* 11).

These factors—political, professional, personal—help us to understand why the interior drama of *High Noon*, and its visual stylization through the images of Kane alone in the street, possess such importance for the filmmaker that he has rendered them so eloquently for the viewer. This interior drama, and these images, are overdetermined.

These factors also help us appreciate the power that the film's engagement with history had for Zinnemann, an engagement manifest both in the film's story and in the external political climate in which it was made. Although he has dismissed Foreman's view of the film as a political allegory of McCarthyism, we cannot completely discount the political context of the period during which it was made, and Zinnemann, too, in his autobiography prefaces his discussion of *High Noon* by sketching the blacklist period in Hollywood and discussing his involvement in the loyalty oath controversy that seized the Directors' Guild shortly before the film was produced.

But, while acknowledging the relevance of the blacklist period for an understanding of *High Noon*'s dynamics, neither should we make too much of it. Zinnemann has always insisted that, for him, the meaningful issues posed by the film are broader than, and go considerably beyond, McCarthyism. We have already noted the extent to which he has defined *High Noon* as a film about conscience and the extent to which he identified with Will Kane as a figure who refused compromise and who, as Zinnemann has said, "then goes back, and takes the consequences, right up to the end" ("Fred Zinnemann" 67). Zinnemann personally has identified with this anticompromising stance, noting that he asked to be released from the MGM contract because he felt independent production would force fewer compromises upon him, and he has described documentary filmmaker Robert Flaherty, one of the mentors who exercised a powerful influence on his own work and life, as a man who refused to compromise and who, therefore, only made a handful of films (a price Zinnemann was willing to risk by exercising great care over his own choice of projects).

Zinnemann has, in fact, gone so far as to insist that, for him, *High Noon* is "not a Western, as far as I'm concerned; it just happens to be set in the Old West" ("Fred Zinnemann" 67). By this, he means that the issues it poses are contemporary ones, and that the presentation of a vulnerable, anxious, vacillating marshal has a certain demythifying effect. We shall see, however, that there are clear limits on the deconstruction of genre in this picture. *High Noon* both is and is not a Western. At this point, though, it should be emphasized that one of the elements that permits the film's social relevance to transcend genre is a dialogue within the narration between competing views of history which Zinnemann may have experienced with some urgency. The railroad tracks in the film, to which the camera repeatedly returns in a series of ground-level framings, stretch, as Zinnemann has noted, into infinity and bring with them the threat of primitive violence, in the person of Frank Miller, to Hadleyville. Within the film, the tracks go north, to the land of business and banks, to the investment capital that entrepreneurs in development-hungry Hadleyville are anxious to secure for themselves, and, therefore, within the genre's logic, the tracks go toward the future, as embodied by an expanding industrial and capital-based economy. Will Kane acts in the most responsible fashion possible because he not only understands that the tracks bring threat to the community but that, metaphorically, by connecting the town to its future, they must always do so, once we accept that the social compact, ever fragile, must be constantly renewed with vigilance and commitment. Like Kane, Zinnemann saw threat on the historical horizon in Austria, both in terms of his own status as a Jew and, more severely, in the rise of an incipient fascism. Zinnemann would later lose both of his parents to the Holocaust, and he has spoken of the general context in which he places his work: "One of the crucial things today [is] trying to preserve our civilization" ("Fred Zinnemann" 12).

This context is emphasized in the film through Will Kane's decision to return to Hadleyville, after initially leaving town with Amy. It is stated with the typical laconicness of the Western hero: "I've got to [go back], that's the whole thing." Kane's decision to return is not just a matter of personal honor (i.e., he'd rather fight than run). It also entails a social commitment and broader political stance that goes beyond his own individuality, and it is here that we may locate the historical perspective with which Zinnemann allies himself in the film. Will's decision to return isn't just a matter of personal courage, of fighting rather than running, but is also an attempt to reclaim his social membership within a community. By going back, Kane chooses to make the social space of the town the arena for his fight rather than become a man without a society. He chooses fra-

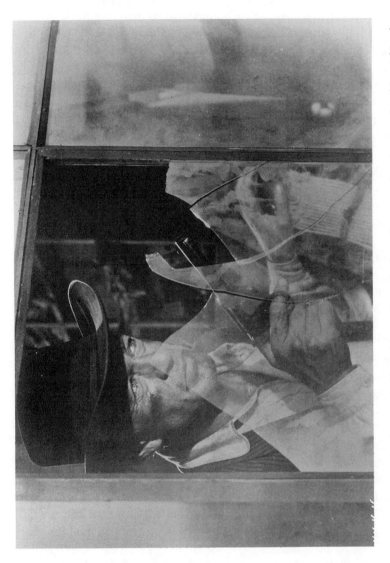

FIGURE 6.1. HIGH NOON (United Artists, 1952). Gary Cooper reclaiming membership within the community. (Courtesy Jerry Ohlinger Archives)

ternity over isolation, and it is the narrative irony which entails that the community will not honor the choice he has made.

His friends in the town refuse to help him for a range of motives. Harvey (Lloyd Bridges), his deputy, is jealous at being passed over for the job as Kane's replacement. (Kane resigned when marrying Amy, who is a Quaker. Thus, when he returns to town and pins on his badge again, it is an emblematic gesture expressing the social, as opposed to the purely personal, component of his decision, especially since he is no longer really the town's marshal.) Sam Fuller (Harry Morgan), a friend and town citizen, is simply afraid. Amy threatens to leave him because, as a Quaker, she wants no violence in their lives, and his former lover, Helen Ramirez (Katy Jurado), declines to enlist help for Kane because of personal bitterness.

Beyond such personal motives, however, other characters offer rationalizations for refusing Kane aid that incorporate social and political dimensions that become part of the historical dialogue the film develops in order to offer its warning about the need, as Zinnemann has phrased it, to "preserve civilization." During the scene where Kane appeals for help to the congregation in the town church,[6] some of the parishioners completely deny the personal-social connection which Kane has decided to honor. One man writes the threat off as a personal quarrel for which the town has no responsibility: "Ain't it true that Kane ain't no longer marshal? And ain't it true that there's personal trouble between him and Miller?" Another views the law as a commodity: "We've been paying good money right along for a marshal and deputies. Now the first time there's any trouble we're supposed to take care of it ourselves. Well, what have we been paying for all this time?"

Kane's close friend and town councilman, Jonas Henderson (Thomas Mitchell), betrays Kane and would sacrifice him on the altar of capitalism. Noting that the town is hoping to attract investment capital from the north to build factories to expand its businesses, Jonas points out that the spectacle of violence in the town streets will be bad for development. It will scare away the northern investors. "Everything we worked for will be wiped out. In one day, this town will be set back five years." Kane should leave town, he concludes. "It's better for you, and it's better for us."

Each of these speeches offered in the church denies the close connection of personal behavior with the social and political health of a community, which Kane has intuitively grasped. Despite Zinnemann's insistence that he doesn't see *High Noon* primarily as a Western, it must be acknowledged that this church scene, with its explicitly philosophical debates about the nature of law and historical progress, is precisely the kind of scene the genre has traditionally included and been well equipped to handle. (One can think of analogous scenes in *Shane, The Man Who Shot Liberty Valance,* and countless other Westerns.) Furthermore, the Western was a good genre for Foreman and Zinnemann to use in mounting their cautionary fable about what happens when democracy goes soft because the populist outlook of the genre, its antipathy for big business, provides the context within which Jonas's speech is understood as callous and opportunistic, and the genre's traditional skepticism about the merits of settled town life provides an inherent structural inclination in the direction of Foreman's critique. Zinnemann couldn't completely deflect or demythologize the conventions of the genre (the social isolation of Kane at the end, when he throws his badge in the dirt and leaves town, is, to give another example, deeply congruent with the genre's portrait of its archetypal hero). *High Noon* is, rather, best understood as an expanded and idiosyncratically modulated (e.g., the stress on Kane's anxiety and human vulnerability) genre film.

To return to the film's historical dialogue, each of the church members denies the social grounding of personal behavior that Kane sees as essential to democratic life. They would deny the social compact upon which their community rests and, with it, the community's origin and history. But it is through encounters with two other characters to whom Kane turns for help that the dimensions of the film's engagement with history are most explicitly set out. Kane initially turns to the judge who passed sentence on Frank Miller only to find him hurriedly packing his things to leave town. The judge's demeanor is full of quiet contempt for Kane. He says Will is "stupid" for coming back and then gives him a civics lesson by pointing out that, in the fifth century B.C., the citizens of Athens suffered under a tyrant but managed to depose him only to welcome him back when he returned with a mercenary army. Furthermore, those same citizens watched while he executed members of the legal government. The judge adds that a similar thing happened eight years ago in a town called Indian Falls, from which he managed to escape, as he is now doing again. As the judge relates this history, he takes down the American flag from his office and packs up his scales of justice and law books, emblematic of the collapse of democracy. The judge leaves Kane with a cynical admonition: to stay is simply a waste. "Look, this is just a dirty little village in the middle of nowhere. Nothing that happens here is really important." The judge's views are repeated by Mark (Lon Chaney, Jr.), the old, retired marshal who has been Kane's friend and mentor. Mark renounces the life of a lawman as meaningless. "You risk your skin catching killers, and the juries turn them loose so they can come back and shoot at you again. If you're honest, you're poor your whole life, and in the end you wind up dying all alone on some dirty street. For what? For nothing, for a tin star."

This is a nihilistic view, and Mark goes farther. Echoing the judge, Mark notes that "People got to talk themselves into law and order before they'll do anything, maybe because down deep they don't care, they just don't care," and, again like the judge, he concludes, "It's all for nothing, Will, it's all for nothing."

The views of Mark and the judge entail the abolition of history. Meaningless events occur in inconsequential places that no one will remember. By contrast, Kane's stance, with which Zinnemann's perspective is clearly allied here as in his other films, is to answer that history does matter and that individual decisions and behavior are important because they are the register of a state's health. The micro and the macro levels are linked. The antithesis of Kane's position results in either opportunism or nihilism, and in either respect culture and civilization are voided.

The film's moral perspective is clearly allied with Kane, but there is real political bitterness in this film, honed by Foreman's acute sense of political crisis and informed (if not acceded to) by Zinnemann's own experiences with fascism and consequent appreciation of how readily democracy may yield to its opposite. The events in the narrative, the failure of the town to rally around Kane, would seem to bear out as truth the views of Mark and the judge. Kane, too, seems to repudiate the town at the end when he throws his star in the dirt, but it would be wrong to conclude that he has been driven to their nihilism and disillusionment. Instead, he repudiates *this* community, as the film's conclusion sounds a note of warning, but not of cynicism. A delicate balance is maintained throughout the film between political bitterness and cynicism (Foreman's perhaps) and an urgent but more balanced and hopeful understanding of history as a dialectic incorporating the responses of opportunism and disillusionment, on the one hand, and, on the other, courage and commitment.

The emphatic nature of the historical debates within the narrative is a clear index of the film's close connection to the political turmoil of the period in which it was made but also of a longer view, of the philosophical basis that might underlie an aesthetic of social realism. History matters because people matter, and their behavior carries clear social consequences. It is the task of the artist, as Zinnemann has often understood it, to dramatize these connections. In this respect, we can see how *High Noon*, in its didactic seriousness of purpose, achieves some distance from the entertainment formulas of studio filmmaking. *High Noon*, shot in only twenty-eight days and produced outside the constraints of the major studios, enabled Zinnemann to realize another application of his socially grounded aesthetic. If the collaborative nature of the film's production, with key inputs coming from Foreman, Stanley Kramer, Floyd Crosby, Elmo Williams, and Dimitri Tiomkin, prevents the strict application of an auteur perspective, we have nevertheless seen how Zinnemann's realist aesthetic, social outlook, and historically engaged brand of filmmaking made him singularly well equipped to direct Foreman's script and, furthermore, how these factors ensured that the images he helped create would have a powerful resonance both for him and the film's viewers.

NOTES

1. Zinnemann has, of course, denied that his film debased the genre by presenting a hero who vacillates. "I'm told that Howard Hawks has said on various occasions that he made *Rio Bravo* as a kind of answer to *High Noon* because he didn't believe that a good sheriff would go running around town asking for other people's help to do his job. I'm rather surprised at this kind of thinking. Sheriffs are people and no two people are alike . . . respect for the Western has not been diminished by *High Noon*" (Phillips 26).

2. Zinnemann (*Life* 110) discusses these appropriations of the film.

3. Foreman stated, "It's the only time I consciously wrote a polemic. It was my story of a community corrupted by fear—the end of Hollywood. When I was in England (after being blacklisted, which coincided with the start of production on *High Noon*), I was very pleased to get letters from people who said they could see it was about Hollywood. I never said that to anyone. I couldn't even say it to my associates because then the film would not have been made" (Buckley 34).

4. By shooting without filters and using flat front light, Zinnemann was aiming to achieve the look of a period newsreel, had newsreels existed in the 1870s. His incorporation of a newsreel aesthetic is further evidence of his

documentary training (in MGM's shorts department) and realist style. Newsreels are also incorporated into *From Here to Eternity* and *Behold a Pale Horse.*

5. See Zinnemann (*Life* 97–99) and Parrish (201–10) for accounts of the incident.

6. *High Noon* was shot radically out of continuity, and this was the first scene filmed.

WORKS CITED

Buckley, Michael. "Fred Zinnemann." *Films in Review* 34.1 (1983): 25–40.

Hardy, Phil. *The Western.* London: Aurum Press, 1983.

Parrish, Robert. *Growing Up in Hollywood.* New York: Harcourt, Brace, Jovanovich, 1976.

Phillips, Gene. "Fred Zinnemann Talking to Gene Phillips." *Focus on Film* 14 (1973): 21–32.

Stang, Joanne. "'Tis the Season to Be Zinnemann." *New York Times* 5 March 1967: D13.

Zinnemann, Fred. "Different Perspective." *Sight and Sound* 17.67 (1948): 113.

———. "Fred Zinnemann." *American Film* 11.4 (1986): 12–13, 62, 66–67.

———. *A Life in the Movies: An Autobiography.* New York: Scribner's 1992.

CHAPTER SEVEN

⊞

The Women in High Noon *(1952)*: A Metanarrative of Difference

GWENDOLYN FOSTER

Classical Hollywood Westerns usually exemplify the homogenizing practices of dominant societal values, particularly as these values are applied to the marginalized "other" of American patriarchy: women, people of diverse sexual orientations, and all people of color. As Vivian Sobchack has noted, this tendency has left the modern critic a major task; that is, to locate the place from which the other has been "elided or marginalized within the homogenizing rhetoric of culturally dominant discourses" (147).

Fred Zinnemann's *High Noon* (1952) illustrates a site in which a seemingly classic Western narrative of the male heroic quest is apparently subverted by the inclusion of a metanarrative of the other. The surprising element of the movie, which has been overwhelmingly praised as a male quest narrative, is that it is ultimately a complex split narrative that elucidates the struggle of a white Quaker woman and a Mexican American woman, who, in turn, fully represent the struggle of the difference of the other. Theirs is a heroic struggle that is perhaps far more interesting than that of the central hero, Will Kane, played by Gary Cooper.

In many ways, the women in *High Noon* overturn the codified, expected gendered, and radically troped behavior of the Hollywood Western. Katy Jurado who plays Helen Ramirez, a Mexican American businesswoman, shares the metanarrative with Grace Kelly, who plays Amy Fowler Kane, a woman whose Quaker pacifism clearly places her oppositionally in face of a violent, brutal, patriarchal power structure. Both women surprise the viewer with their ability to survive in the narrative. Both are mature women with principles, and neither fits the mold of the classical good-girl, bad-girl scenario. In fact, Zinnemann plays off these clichés of female Western types.

While Amy is introduced into the narrative in the classically submissive posture expected of a wedding sequence, she subsequently disrupts our expectations and continually threatens to leave her good man, as well as the narrative. She argues aggressively with her partner, rather than listening passively, yet she does not adopt the mother role of guidance and temperance. Instead, she forms a bond with Helen Ramirez, whom she learns from, and in turn guides. Though Helen Ramirez is dressed in the classical bad-girl garb, dark haired and black bodiced, and Amy Fowler is dutifully white skinned, white bonneted, and classically beautiful, neither character corresponds with the codified behavior of the dichotomized female of the Hollywood Western.

The viewer expects to learn that the nonwhite Helen Ramirez is a prostitute bent on the destruction of the good girl who takes her man. Instead, Ramirez is a businesswoman, we learn, who must protect her investment when the town is disrupted by evil forces. One also expects Amy Fowler and Helen Ramirez to become polarized by their skin color and by the fact that they are both emotionally involved with the hero. Instead of the expected catfights, Zinnemann treats us to female bonding across racial lines. In a few key scenes which the women share, Zinnemann's women criticize the patriarchal system and recognize their racial difference, even as they find common ground for speaking to one another as women.

In addition, both women take action in the narrative and power over their bodies, and neither is sacrificed in the film. Zinnemann does not take the usual route of killing off the nonwhite other as a sacrificial tribute to her acceptability to hegemonic discourse; nor does he pander to audience expectations with a lengthy heroic rescue scene of the white woman by her man. Instead, Amy Fowler tries to scratch out the eyes of the antihero, and only after freeing herself does Zinnemann allow the hero to shoot Frank Miller.

High Noon is significant as an example of a film that includes a dual positional narrative of male and female perspective. Vivian Sobchack has

FIGURE 7.1. HIGH NOON (United Artists, 1952). Katy Jurado and Grace Kelly taking action and taking power. (Courtesy Jerry Ohlinger Archives)

identified films that share such a "paranoia of split vision," in which the filmmaker desires "not only to describe the structure of cinematic signification but also to critique the hegemony of classical cinematic practice" (262). *High Noon* engages in a multilayered narrative in order to criticize cinema, societal codes, and expectations from a safe perspective. *High Noon* fulfills the requirements of the heroic narrative on the most basic level.

But as Dana Polan has demonstrated, some Westerns stray from the monologic form and follow a "two-part structure," in which "there is no longer a place for the individual western spirit" (256). These Westerns schizophrenically attach pastoral values to spaces that "represent the unproductive places left behind in modernity's expansion" (267). *High Noon* fits a pattern of the Western of dystopia. The hero's quest is viewed as futile, and the quest of the other is marked as that of the women characters within Zinnemann's narrative.

High Noon, as many critics have noted, is centrally consumed with the cynicism of the postwar years. Zinnemann anticipates the modern narrative of the repressed and the disenfranchised. The question is why he weaves his hero's quest into the metanarrative of the female other, or, as Mary Ann Doane puts it, "why must the woman always carry the burden of philosophical demonstration, why must she be the one to figure truth, dissimulation, untruth, the abyss, etc. . . ?" (74). The answer is to be found in an analysis of Zinnemann's women as representations of difference, rather than gender. "Because the female is the repressed it is, in this fabric of understanding, the silenced, the unexpressable" (93).

Thus, Helen Ramirez and Amy Fowler speak of the repressed anger of the other in American postwar society. Amy Fowler's line of dialogue, "I don't understand any of this," in response to her husband Will Kane, who feels he must go back to face his opponent, is the voice of pacifist America that still refuses to "understand" acts of war. The comment may be taken as stereotypically female, as a woman who cannot understand a man's world, but within the metanarrative of the repressed, it is calculatedly a rupture of the discourse of warmongering and blind patriotism. This is a fine example of Zinnemann's articulation of a fifties' "paranoia of split vision," as used by Sobchack.

The inherent multivalency of Amy's measured response is later revealed in a scene in which Amy Fowler discusses with Helen Ramirez how she came to be a pacifist. Amy explains that she watched her nineteen-year-old brother and father die from bullet wounds. Helen Ramirez's reaction to Amy Fowler's tale is to bond with her and to explain why she must leave town: "I hate this town, I've always hated it. To be a Mexican woman in a town like this. . . ."

Amy Fowler responds, "I understand," as if a white woman can easily come to grips with racial hatred as a compound to gender-based discrimination. Surprisingly, Helen responds, "You do? That's good. I don't understand you." In this moment, it seems that the two women will not be able to overcome their racial otherness. But Zinnemann allows for the difference to exist between the women's world views, and Helen and Amy form a union continually reinforced visually through the inscription of shots of the women together, watching and waiting, until the climactic male killing spree is over.

Zinnemann's inclusion of such a strong nonwhite character as Helen Ramirez in the metanarrative may be an early example of a "deflection" of the suffering of the other, as defined by bell hooks, in which the dominant culture is continually "reenacting and reritualizing in different ways the imperialist, colonizing journey as narrative fantasy of power and desire" (25), but Zinnemann does not choose the characteristically racist route of "seduction by the other" (25), typical of the scenario painted by hooks. Helen Ramirez as a character subverts this expectation; she seduces neither the hero Will Kane nor the criminal Frank Miller.

Edward Said notes that imperialist American culture often evokes a centrality that works in "preventing counter-narratives from emerging" (324). *High Noon* is a Hollywood Western that seeks to disrupt centrality, both in the male heroic narrative, which one character, played by Lon Chaney, Jr., describes as "All for nothin,'" and in the counternarrative of the women as others. The reading of the female metanarrative is certainly against the grain of criticism that perpetuates the centrality of the heroic male narrative in *High Noon*.

But, as Judith Mayne reminds us, "If feminist criticism seeks to demystify the classical cinema, a reading against the grain encourages us to assume that cinema does not 'reflect' as much as it signifies, and that narrative is a complex and multileveled system" (25). Zinnemann's choice of interweaving an early feminist and socially conscious metanarrative through the voice of the female is subtly effective precisely because women are, as Lois McNay notes, "engendered across a vast number of subject positions" (67) and are therefore more capable of fully articulating the gaps, ruptures, and silences enforced upon a culture of domination, such as the one in which Zinnemann was immersed.

Rereading *High Noon* with an eye open to the possibilities of multiple narratives and multiple female subject positions allows for a fuller dialogic reading of the carefully woven texts critical of postwar America, of war, of gender expectations for both men and women, of racism in America, of McCarthyism, of commercialism, of hero worship, and of the mentality of the Hollywood movie machine itself. Ironically, the film's incessantly recurring theme song, "High Noon," written by Dimitri Tiomkin and Ned Washington and sung by Tex Ritter, only adds to the criticisms of the multifaceted narrative. The lyrics are heard so many times throughout the film that they become almost humorous:

> Do not forsake me, oh my darlin'
> You made that promise when we wed.
> Do not forsake me, oh my darlin'
> Although you're grieving.
> I can't be leavin'
> Until I shoot Frank Miller dead.

The song would seem to suggest that Will Kane's quest in *High Noon* is the stereotypical desire to please and then possess the female within the narrative. But, in fact, the song foreshadows that it is the men in the film, the hero's best friends, who will forsake him, and not Amy Kane. It is his supposed comrades and constituents who will refuse to help him in his "heroic" quest. Some lines in the song specifically raise the issue of the idiocy of masculine hero role playing:

> If I'm a man I must be brave.
> And I must face that deadly killer . . .
> or lie a coward in my grave.

Zinnemann interweaves a subtle attack on these gender expectations throughout both narratives. As these words are sung, an old, presumably wise woman who has no other place in the film is shown crossing herself as she looks upon the three bad men who ride into town. The figure of the old woman foreshadows the senseless violence in a grave manner, but in other sites in the film, Zinnemann includes women laughing at the stupidity of stereotypical male roles.

Helen Ramirez, in particular, ridicules the masculine domain of senseless brutality. As a nonwhite figure, she apparently has the privileged subject position of being able to see and know the foolishness of the violence of patriarchal western culture. When Harvey (Lloyd Bridges), Ramirez's boyfriend, makes fun of the Kanes' initial flight from town, away from the oncoming violence, Helen regards him with a look of revulsion, which turns into a grave laugh. Kane himself makes an utterance that establishes a strong undercurrent against hero worship and expectations of men: "If you think I like this, you're crazy," he says to Amy, even as he is compelled into turning around to return to town to fight his enemy.

But the most revealing criticisms are offered by Helen Ramirez, who voices a strong subtext against male power and violence against women. Not only does Zinnemann create in Helen a nonwhite central character of nonstereotypical significance within the narrative of *High Noon*, he allows her to speak on equal terms with Will Kane, Amy Kane, and others within the narrative. And in her world-weary presence, Helen embodies the violent and reductive truth of the location they all share more than any other single character in the film. In a pivotal scene, Kane suggests that Ramirez leave town because of the impending return of Frank Miller. "You know how he is," says Kane.

Helen gazes at him for a moment, then responds wearily, "I know how he is." That Zinnemann would include such allusions to male violence against women, especially in a recognition across gendered lines in the Western, is atypical. That he would contextualize a criticism against it is remarkable. In a later scene, in which Helen explains to Harvey why she must leave, Helen Ramirez restates her revulsion to male violence and power over her body:

> I'm all alone in the world. . . . I have to make a living . . . and as for you . . . I don't like anybody to put his hands on me unless I want him to, and I don't like you to, anymore.

As if to totally reverse our gender expectations, Helen delivers these lines and immediately slaps Harvey out of the frame as a seeming answer to male violence. The possibility of male violence against women is continually, if subtly, referred to throughout the film. In the church meeting hall scene, for example, an older woman gets up in defense of Kane and says, "Don't you remember when it wasn't safe for women and children?"

Metaphorically, Zinnemann adds touches that remind us of the omnipresence of brutal violence in American western society. One sequence, for example, highlights the villains carefully oiling and cleaning their phallic weaponry in anticipation of the upcoming violence. Another scene suggests the probability of the rape of women in the future, if Kane does not succeed in eliminating the violent male figures. In this scene, one of the men breaks a window, steals a bonnet, and attaches it to his belt, in a metaphoric equivalent of rape. Seeing this action, another member of the gang comments, "Can't you wait?"

The violence itself erupts methodically when it finally arrives in *High Noon*, after a montage sequence. The montage sequence foregrounds the faces of the women, Amy Fowler and Helen Ramirez, who are seen in tighter close-ups as the tension builds. In this way, Zinnemann plays up the importance of the female metanarrative. Zinnemann firmly establishes the bond between the women with several shots of them riding in a wagon together.

With a final look over her shoulder, Helen Ramirez leaves the film's narrative, as if to remind the viewer that this is, after all, a white struggle. In the final shootout, Amy Fowler Kane is the central viewer of the male violence. Surprisingly for the period, Zinnemann then turns the female narrative into the central narrative. The white woman is the silent but omniscient presence that carries the filmmaker's social criticism to the end of the film. When Amy views a slain man in the street, we identify with her quest for nonviolence and pacifism, instead of the machismo of the conventional male hero.

Rather than foregrounding the traditionally inviolate nature of the stereotypical Western hero, Zinnemann shows us Will Kane's humanity, as well as the pain he bears as the standard-bearer of "justice" within a patriarchical society. As critic Stuart Kaminsky notes in his essay on the narrative structure of *High Noon*:

> At one point Kane, alone in his office, puts his head down on his desk, possibly to weep, and then wearily pulls himself up again. In the final confrontation with Miller and his gang, Kane does stand alone until the last moment, when Amy saves his life by shooting down Frank Miller (387).

As Joanna Rapf notes, the script for *High Noon* went even further in its description of the unusual character of Amy Kane than the finished film was allowed to. Rapf writes that "the unique, indeed revolutionary position of the two main women in *High Noon*, and in particular, of the seemingly conventional Amy, is supported not only by character descriptions in the script, but by a significant piece of dialogue that, unfortunately, was cut from the final film. In Amy's conversation with Helen just before the two of them leave for the train station at noon [Amy says in the script, but *not* in the finished film] . . . 'Back home they think I'm very strange. I'm a feminist. You know, women's rights—things like that . . .' (Script 95)" (78).

Thus Zinnemann's intent throughout the film is clear; he wishes to foreground the voices of Helen and Amy within the cinema/text of the film, and this sequence in the script makes the centrality of this intent unquestionable. Rapf suggests the lines were cut because "to have included them would have been anachronistic" (78). Perhaps this is true, but whatever the reason for the deletion of these lines of dialogue, the other textual evidence grounded within the work is more than sufficient to support a feminist interpretation of the film.

In the final analysis, Fred Zinnemann's women in *High Noon* are presented to the viewer in a charitable progression toward reclamation of the female body, and the individual in society by extension. Amy Fowler's final act of attempting to tear the eyes out of Frank Miller can be compared with Fred Zinnemann's ability as a filmmaker to tear the eyes out of passive onlookers, and make them work on the material of this problematic film. Produced as it was in the 1950s, what surprises us in retrospect is how much the film questions the values that make up the supposed fabric of American society, a fabric that can be ripped asunder with unsettling ease.

Zinnemann presents us with a paranoid and dual set of narratives which, in the end, denies the viewer the comfort and distance of a passive spectatorial gaze. The well-developed female characters, who display the disenfranchisement of America—the Mexican American worker and the pacifist Quaker—disrupt the expectations and limitations of classical Hollywood Western stereotypes. Their action speaks as loudly as their words. These mature women introduce dangerously regarded subject matter into what may have been wrongly regarded as a monologic, patriarchal discourse.

In addition, Zinnemann further subverts Hollywood generic convention by continuing his dystopic vision into a reversal of the wedding trope. Instead of ending with a happy wedding, the film begins with a wedding, and the trouble begins. In this way Zinnemann displaces the notion of the female as commodity, a usually sacrosanct notion in Hollywood filmmaking, particularly in the 1940s and 1950s. Though the white couple does ride off into the sunset, it is less with a sense of jubilation than grave acceptance of the current state of American values, and of the false lip service these values are given within society. It seems that Zinnemann is saying that no one will be emancipated from this thoroughly corrupt and valueless system unless women and men are willing to work together to bring about effective change.

WORKS CITED

de Lauretis, Teresa. "Through the Looking Glass." *Narrative, Apparatus, Ideology: A Film Theory Reader.* Philip Rosen, ed. New York: Columbia University Press, 1986. 360–72.

Doane, Mary Ann. *Femmes Fatales: Feminism, Film Theory, Psychoanalysis.* New York: Routledge, 1991.

Gordon, Linda. "On 'Difference.'" *Genders* 10 (Spring 1991): 91–111.

hooks, bell. *Black Looks: Race and Representation.* Boston: South End Press, 1992.

Kaminsky, Stuart. "*High Noon.*" *The International Dictionary of Films and Filmmakers, Vol. 1.* Nicholas Thomas, ed. Chicago: St. James Press, 1990. 385–87.

McNay, Lois. *Foucault and Feminism: Power, Gender and the Self.* Cornwall: Polity, 1992.

Polan, Dana. *Power and Paranoia: History, Narrative and the American Cinema, 1940–1950.* New York: Columbia University Press, 1986.

Rapf, Joanna. "Myth, Ideology, and Feminism in *High Noon.*" *Journal of Popular Culture* 23.4 (Spring 1990): 75–80.

Said, Edward W. *Culture and Imperialism.* New York: Knopf, 1993.

Sobchack, Vivian. *The Address of the Eye: A Phenomenology of Film Experience.* Princeton, N.J.: Princeton University Press, 1992.

Todd, Janet. *Women and Film.* New York: Holmes and Meier, 1988.

CHAPTER EIGHT

Repeat Business:
Members of the Wedding

LOUIS GIANNETTI

It [*The Member of the Wedding*] has always been my favorite
picture, perhaps because it is not entirely my own.

—Fred Zinnemann, *A Life in the Movies: An Autobiography*

The Member of the Wedding enjoys the unusual distinction of masterpiece
status in three different mediums. Carson McCullers's novel, originally
published in 1946, was hailed by critics as an extraordinary achievement,
and she was even compared to Hemingway and Faulkner by French and
British literary critics. McCullers's friend and fellow Southerner Tennessee
Williams persuaded the young author to convert the novel into a play.
Williams even helped her in matters of dramatic structure and dramatur-
gical conventions, such as building a scene toward a precurtain climax.
The stage play, which was directed by the great Harold Clurman, opened
on Broadway in 1950 and ran for nearly two years. It featured the same
principal actors as the movie version: Julie Harris, Ethel Waters, and the
juvenile, Brandon de Wilde. The stage drama also won the prestigious
New York Drama Critics Award as Best American Play of 1950. It is still
regarded as a classic of the American theater.

The movie version was less lucky. In fact, director Fred Zinnemann described the film as "a resounding flop, declared by the establishment to be fit only for 'art-house' cinemas" (*Life* 115). Of course the irony is that today the movie *would* be classified as an art film, and would be shown in the same kind of theaters that specialize in foreign, classic, and independent movies: that is, the most original and artistically significant films of the contemporary cinema. But in 1952, when Zinnemann's movie was released, there were only a handful of such theaters, and motion picture exhibition was still dominated by the slick products of the big Hollywood studios. The film version of *The Member of the Wedding* just slipped through the cracks. Most critics ignored it. Of the major film commentators, only Pauline Kael championed the movie. In his gentlemanly autobiography, Zinnemann sadly concludes that "the audience was not ready for it" (112). It was their loss. Compared to the soulless drivel that dominated movie screens of that era, *The Member of the Wedding* still shines, a small masterpiece of poignancy.

The original commercial failure of the movie isn't surprising, for its cast was unknown at the time, there was very little physical action in the film, and the dialogue probably struck many audiences as too "literary." There was also the problem of genre. The story revolves around two female characters, a middle-aged African American maid (Waters) and a precocious, prepubescent tomboy (Harris). But the movie isn't a "women's picture" in the conventional sense of the term. Most examples of this popular studio-era genre featured a glamorous female star, glossy production values, and a strong emphasis on romantic or melodramatic plots. *The Member of the Wedding* does not remotely resemble the conventional Hollywood women's picture. That was probably the problem: Columbia Pictures, which distributed the movie, hardly bothered with a promotion campaign. Nor, in this era of Jim Crow, would any major studio permit a black actress to carry one of their own pictures, to serve as the main attraction. The film was produced and financed by Stanley Kramer, a progressive and risk-taking independent, who later became a director. Columbia merely distributed the picture, in its own fashion.

The reaction of those few critics who bothered to write about the movie was surprisingly insensitive. They complained that the film was too talky, that it was too restricted spatially and ought to have been "opened up"—a critical cliché that is still commonly applied to stage adaptations. Presumably the opening up of a play makes it instantly more "cinematic," for what is cinema if not wide open spaces, sweeping crane shots, and all the other extravagant techniques that are supposed to differentiate movies from the live theater?

France's greatest critic, André Bazin, demolished these simplistic notions, insisting that great movies need not be less verbal, more kinetic, and "open" than the stage. And was it not Hitchcock, arguably the most cinematic filmmaker since Eisenstein, who warned of the aesthetic dangers of opening up plays when adapted to film? With characteristic shrewdness, Hitchock pointed out that works written for the theater are *designed* for a limited area of presentation, which is part of the meaning of these works (Hitchcock 41). That is, the idea of entrapment—or at least temporary confinement—is symbolically inherent in most stage plays. By opening up such works, the film director runs the risk of releasing all the spatial and psychological tensions created by the restricted space of the original stage play.

Some very great films deal with the theme of entrapment, and for the most part they are deliberately not opened up. Movies like Bresson's *A Man Escaped* and Hitchcock's *Rear Window* take place in a single setting and are suffocatingly claustrophobic in their effects. The power of these movies is due in large part to their very rigor, to the fact that we feel as trapped as the protagonists.

A film like George Stevens's *The Diary of Anne Frank*, based on the stage play, was similarly confined to a single setting, but because Stevens unwisely chose to shoot the movie in a wide-screen format, he dissipated much of his tension. The sense of constriction that is inherent in the work is counteracted by the spaciousness of the mise en scène. Zinnemann's *The Member of the Wedding* was shot in a conventional aspect ratio rather than the then-new wide-screen format. Hence, the video version of the film includes virtually all of his original mise en scène, though of course vastly reduced in size, not to speak of emotional impact. However, because Zinnemann confined himself mostly to medium shots and close-ups, the movie suffers less than, say, *Citizen Kane*, with its bravura long shots and richly textured images, which are sadly impoverished by the diminutive video screen.

Most of Zinnemann's films might aptly be entitled *No Exit*. The director referred to the kitchen setting of *The Member of the Wedding* as a "prison," and noted that McCullers told him that her story was about "the great American disease, loneliness" (112). Of course the movie doesn't deal with literal imprisonment, but with various forms of symbolic entrapment. The housekeeper Berenice and the other black characters are trapped by their race in a sleepy Georgia town during the early 1940s. Frankie, the main character, is trapped by her age. A gawky twelve year old, she's neither a child, like her seven-year-old cousin John Henry (Brandon de Wilde), nor an adult, like her older brother Jarvis (Arthur Franz), who is in the army. She's not even an adolescent yet, merely on the threshold of adolescence, and hence, an "unjoined person."

Like *High Noon, The Member of the Wedding* preserves the unities of time and place, though not so rigorously, for the final scene of the film occurs "several months later." Zinnemann also takes us out of the immediate environs of the Addams house twice: when Frankie goes out on her bicycle to announce to various townspeople that she will be leaving town, and when she actually runs away from home. She gets only so far as the shabby downtown section, however, before she's frightened into returning home, her tail between her legs.

When Zinnemann read the novel, he was enchanted with its literary style, which he described as "sheer magic" (112). He wanted to preserve that luminous prose as much as possible. When McCullers expressed anxiety that her story would be trashed by the Hollywood slicksters, Zinnemann assured her that he would do everything in his power to protect her work. In fact, no one interfered with the production. It wasn't considered important enough to bother.

Originally, Zinnemann wanted to use the novel, not the play, as the source material for the movie. But the budget was too small, and eventually Kramer and Zinnemann hired the respected team of Edward and Edna Anhalt to adapt the play into a film script. The Anhalts managed to salvage a few details from the novel, but roughly 90 percent of their script is based on the play. The screenwriters pruned a few lines here and there, added even fewer. They dramatized the two scenes in which Frankie leaves home. In the play, she verbally recounts her off-stage actions to Berenice. In the movie, we see them.

All three versions of the story preserve the themes of entrapment, loneliness, and frustration. What is extraordinary is that each version explores these ideas in ways that are totally organic to each medium. Each version has a three-part structure, though this is less evident in the movie than in the novel and stage play. Part One in each form deals with Frankie's restless dissatisfaction with her life, her sense of purposelessness. She doesn't seem to "belong" to anyone or anything. Her mother died when Frankie was born, her father is busy with his work, her bother Jarvis is in the military and away from home, and Berenice goes to her own home each night.

Part Two deals with Frankie's romantic infatuation with her brother's wedding. She decides that after Janice and Jarvis get married she will go with the couple and join them in what she imagines will be a life of constant excitement and glamor. Part Three of the story deals with her bitter disillusionment when she is not allowed to be a "member" of the wedding, and she believes that she will remain "captured" in the same town and house with the same tiresome companions. Each version of the story ends with a scene of reconciliation that takes place several months after the main action. Frankie is somewhat wiser now, and because she has found new friends her age, her prospects for the future seem more promising.

In the novel, which is told in the third person from Frankie's perspective, these various stages of her emotional development are conveyed by the nuances in her point of view. In Part One, she is called "Frankie," an appropriate name for a tomboy just leaving childhood. In Part Two, she is called "F. Jasmine," a name she selects because it sounds more mysterious and exotic. It also begins with Ja, like Janice and Jarvis, and hence reinforces her belief that she "belongs" with her brother and his bride. In Part Three, she is called "Frances," a more suitable name for a young Southern girl just entering adolescence. In the stage version of the story, these sections are logically converted into three acts of about the same duration. The movie version resembles the play, though of course the three acts are given no demarcation.

All three versions of the story preserve the same sense of constriction in time and place. The Addams's kitchen is the major setting in each version, and the same period of time is covered. In the novel we are permitted to enter the heroine's consciousness, while in the play we are always objective observers. The movie opens with a brief off-camera third-person narration (spoken by Julie Harris), but most of the film preserves the same external objectivity as the stage play. The novel is the least tightly constructed. It contains more characters and events than the play, which in turn contains more than the film. The movie version focuses almost exclusively on the three entrapped kitchen dwellers: Frankie, Berenice, and John Henry.

Time as well as place is a prison. John Henry, like most children, is concerned only with enjoying himself in the present. The future is too abstract for him, and he's too young to recall much of a past. Frankie feels imprisoned by the present, despises her past, which she considers childishly irrelevant, and lives only for the future, which she fervently hopes will be filled with extraordinary people, places, and events. The middle-aged Berenice is preoccupied with the past, especially with her happy, youthful marriage to Ludie Freeman, her dead first husband. At the conclusion of the story, her future looks bleak, for she has lost both her step-brother Honey and her spiritual son John Henry, who during the course of the action suddenly becomes ill and dies. She also loses her job at the end of the story, for her services will no longer be required after Mr. Addams and his sister (John Henry's mother) move into a new house together.

Almost everything in the story tends to fall naturally into threes. At one point Frankie expresses the fear that she may grow up to be a "freak" because of her exceptional tallness. But in a sense, all three of the major characters are freaks: John Henry, with his gnomic mannerisms, and his weird habit of dressing up in women's clothes; Frankie, with her high-flown literary affectations and imaginative flights of fancy; and Berenice, with her grotesque blue glass eye, which she alternates wearing with a black eye-patch. In some ways, these highly individualized characters are also three aspects of a single personality: romantic, lonely, and frustrated, trapped in bodies that somehow don't seem to fit them, or fit what they wish to be. John Henry embodies the childhood innocence of this personality; Frankie represents the hopeful yearning of youth; and Berenice, the sadly chastened wisdom and resignation of maturity.

Most of the action of the movie takes place in the kitchen and its adjoining areas. This static setting presented Zinnemann with some considerable challenges: "The great thing was that in the stifling claustrophobia of that kitchen nothing ever happened. There was hardly any action: everything important took place in the souls of these people" (*Life* 112). Had he been a less gifted craftsman, the movie might have merited those shallow accusations of talkiness that were originally leveled at the work by some reviewers. But Zinnemann had a lot going for him, including one of the best written plays of the American repertory, and three principals who are never less than excellent.

Indeed, in Julie Harris's case, the acting is brilliant, one of the finest three or four performers he had ever worked with, according to Zinnemann, who, it must be recalled, worked with such superlative actors as Marlon Brando, Montgomery Clift, Deborah Kerr, Jane Fonda, Paul Scofield, and Vanessa Redgrave. When one considers that Harris was twenty-five when she played this twelve-year-old character, her performance is all the more astonishing. We are never once allowed to see the

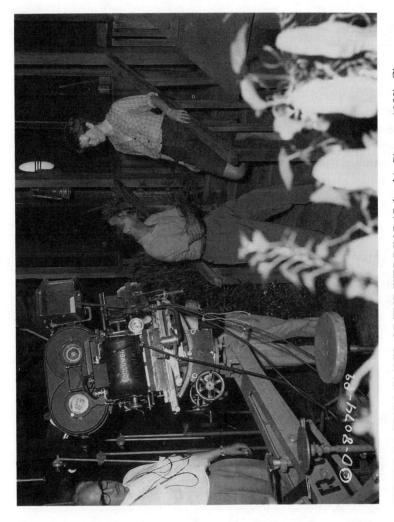

FIGURE 8.1. THE MEMBER OF THE WEDDING (Columbia Pictures, 1952). Cinematographer Hal C. Mohr (far left) stands beside the camera while Zinnemann confers with Julie Harris.

mature, sophisticated actress beneath the role. She never condescends to the part, never adds "adorable" little knowing touches to differentiate herself from the character. Her passionately intense performance, so sincere and consistently believable, is a fine example of the quality of "being" (as opposed to "acting") which distinguished the best Method actors from their more "techniquey" predecessors. Like Zinnemann's direction, Julie Harris's artistry consists primarily of her ability to conceal her art.

Zinnemann's techniques are always subordinated to the needs of the script and the performers. Precisely because he is a recessive artist whose "effects" are usually concealed, we are likely to minimize his extraordinary technical achievement in this film. Rather than pretending that the kitchen is not a confining area, the director emphasizes its constrictiveness. He often uses lengthy takes, in which Frankie is trapped in both space (the edges of the frame) and time (the duration of the take). Many scenes are photographed in deep focus (by the great Hal Mohr, who used new lenses, by Garutso, which allowed an unprecedented depth of field), and with the speaker in medium close-up range dominating the frame, and the listener in the "rear" of the image in long-shot range. In those instances in which Zinnemann is more concerned with the reaction of the close-up figure, the character in the rear does most of the talking. In shots such as these, the figure in the rear—generally Berenice—is engaged in some kind of physical motion, while the foreground figure remains stationary.

Most of Zinnemann's oeuvre is character based; hence the heavy reliance on close-ups in the majority of his movies. In this film he typically uses many close shots, but not to "break up" the static space—a technique that would have been as mechanical as "opening up" the play with arbitrary exterior locations. Characteristically, Zinnemann uses his close-ups to emphasize moments of spiritual isolation. Though the three major characters spend most of their time confined in the same room, they are often miles apart in terms of psychic space. Zinnemann's editing and use of space are almost musical in their quasi-abstract joinings and separations. During much of the action, the characters inhabit their own isolated space cubicles, but in those instinctive moments of unity, the characters are brought together in medium-long shots, in which they temporarily share the same spiritual as well as physical space. In such brilliantly edited movies as *High Noon* and *The Day of the Jackal*, Zinnemann's cutting style is conspicuously virtuosic, but in *The Member of the Wedding*, the cutting is more subtle precisely because the editing strategy is primarily psychological rather than physical.

Zinnemann isn't afraid of talk—provided it's good talk. When the dialogue is exceptionally rich, he avoids any excessive technical distraction and shoots the scene without visual flourishes. In this respect, the self-effacing style of Zinnemann is preferable in many ways to some of the shots in the stage adaptations of Orson Welles. In movies like *Othello* and *Macbeth*, Welles's baroque visual extravagance too often overwhelms rather than enhances Shakespeare's lines. One feels that there is a competition rather than a collaboration between artists. Notwithstanding Welles's disclaimers to the contrary, his Shakespearean adaptations are not truly collaborative enterprises, and unlike Zinnemann, one instinctively feels that Welles doesn't always trust his actors. In adaptations like *The Member of the Wedding*, on the other hand, we never get the impression that the director is "dressing up" the script with fancy visuals: The actors and writers participate fully with the director in creating a unified aesthetic effect.

The writing and acting in *The Member of the Wedding* are so fine it would have been artistically criminal to drown them with "cinematic" trumperies. Frankie is in love with language, and though she is often ungrammatical, she's fond of punctuating her talk with precocious "literary" affectations, like "I am sick to death . . ." and "It was one of the ironies of Fate . . . " and "If it's one thing I mortally despise. . . ." She likes the exotic flavor of certain proper nouns like "Winter Hill" and "Rachmaninoff." Occasionally she is not totally sure of the pronunciation—not to speak of the meaning—of certain favorite expressions, like "candy opinion" instead of "candid opinion." She's particularly fond of squelching John Henry with condescending hauteur, like "It is immaterial to me," and "He's entirely too young." At one point she expresses her "adult" exasperation by exclaiming to Berenice: "See? He's nothing but a child. It's hopeless. (She bangs her fist on the table.) Hopeless!" On the other hand, she is still mostly a child herself, and in moments of anger, her expressions are more direct, as when she chases John Henry around the kitchen table with a flyswatter, screaming, "Get out of here, you little midget!"

The Member of the Wedding is easily Zinnemann's funniest film, but it's also one of his most poignant—often simultaneously. For example, in the scene in which Frankie is rejected for membership in the local girls' club (the girls are two or three years older than she), her reaction is both comic and moving. "Why didn't you elect me? Why can't I be a member?" she screams at them in anguish, the camera at an extreme close-up range. Then, tomboy fashion, she chases the "ladylike" girls out of her yard,

John Henry shaking his fist at them in an absurdly comic gesture of soli-
darity. When Berenice suggests that Frankie ought to form her own club
with all the youngsters of the neighborhood, she replies contemptuously:
"I don't want to be president of all those little left-over young people!"
The movie is also filled with sly bits of comic business, as when John
Henry casually peeks up the dress of a doll, and when Frankie tries to
remove a tiny splinter from her foot with an enormous kitchen knife.

Frankie also has some lyrical speeches of heartbreaking fervor, as in
the scene in which she suddenly realizes how she will escape her entrapment. In the novel, most of this speech is "thought" by Frankie when she is
alone. In the play and movie, she recites it aloud with John Henry present:

> I know where I'm going. It's like I've known all my life. Tomorrow I
> will tell everybody. . . . After the wedding I'm going with them to
> Winter Hill. I'm going off with them after the wedding. . . . Just now
> I realized something. The trouble with me is that for a long time I
> have been just an "I" person. All other people can say "we." When
> Berenice says "we," she means her lodge and church and colored peo-
> ple. Soldiers can say "we" and mean the army. All people belong to a
> "we" except me. Not to belong to a "we" makes you too lonesome.
> Until this afternoon I didn't have a "we," but now after seeing Janice
> and Jarvis I suddenly realized something. . . . I know that the bride
> and my brother are the "we" of me. So I'm going with them, and
> joining with the wedding. This coming Sunday when my brother
> and the bride leave this town, I'm going with the two of them to
> Winter Hill. And after that to whatever place that they will ever go.
> I love the two of them so much and we belong to be together. I love
> the two of them so much because they are the *we* of me.

[Unfortunately, the Anhalts' screenplay has never been published commercially, but since the dialogue is virtually identical to that of the play, I
have quoted the stage version, pp. 51–52.]

The next time we see Frankie, Zinnemann seems to release much of
the dramatic tension that has been built up during the previous episodes,
for this is the first time that we see her outside the environs of her home.
But the release is mostly illusionary: Frankie only seems to be free. In a
medium shot we see her riding her bike to announce to anyone who will
listen that she'll soon be leaving town. Rather than using lyrical pans or
any expansive techniques, Zinnemann subtly imprisons Frankie within

shots in which she moves primarily in and out of the depth of tightly framed images. In the opening bike-riding scene, for example, the camera moves with her as she rides "towards" us. But since she and the camera are moving at the same pace, the image in effect remains stationary: We see no significant change or motion within the frame.

Throughout the movie, Berenice acts as a surrogate mother to Frankie, comforting her when she needs reassurance, scolding her when she's cruel to John Henry, advising her with a steady voice of experience and common sense. A romantic woman herself, Berenice often warns Frankie of the dangers of her excessive romanticism. Sometimes these warnings take a comic form, as when Frankie phones the police to report her missing cat "Charles." With fanciful embellishment, Frankie describes the cat as "almost pure Persian." Shaking her head in amusement, Berenice chuckles and mutters contemptuously, "About as Persian as I is."

When Frankie's romanticism takes a dangerous turn, Berenice's anxieties become more grave, for she's the only person who fully understands the depth of the child's feelings. Berenice repeatedly warns the girl of her folly in believing that she'll be allowed to go with the wedding couple. One of the motifs of the story deals with the idea of the cycles of nature: birth, maturity, death. Associated with this thematic motif is the idea of repetitive cycles of human behavior. John Henry is constantly aping Frankie and Berenice, and in this case the motif is exploited as a comic device. But in Frankie's case it is different. Berenice fears that the girl will condemn herself to repeating the same romantic mistakes that Berenice committed when she was a young woman—the pursuit of an impossible dream. In this respect, the two females resemble a number of Zinnemann's heroines, including Ellie in *The Men*, Alma in *From Here to Eternity*, and Gabrielle (Sister Luke) in *The Nun's Story*.

After her brief happy marriage to Ludie, Berenice condemned herself to a succession of three disastrous marriages, each time hoping that she could recapture a "piece" of Ludie. One of the most moving scenes in the film is that in which she ritualistically recounts the details of Ludie's death to the two awed youngsters:

It was a Thursday towards six o'clock. About this time of day. Only November. I remember I went to the passage and opened the front door. Dark was coming on; the old hound was howling far away. And I go back in the room and lay down on Ludie's bed. I lay myself down over Ludie with my arms spread out and my face on his face. And I pray that the Lord would contage [*sic*] my strength to him. And I ask the Lord to let it be anybody, but not let it be Ludie. And I lay there and pray for a long time. Until night. . . . That night he died. I tell you he died. Ludie! Ludie Freeman! Ludie Maxwell Freeman died! (75)

The scene is powerfully conveyed. Temporarily abandoning his realistic visual style, Zinnemann shoots the scene from a low angle, gradually moving into a tight close-up of Berenice's tear-streaked face. She is totally oblivious of her surroundings, conscious only of the anguish and solitude of her life since Ludie's death. The lights are stylized expressionistically, plunging the three vulnerable creatures into an ethereal twilight.

Frankie refuses to acknowledge any parallel between herself and Berenice, though the child is clearly unnerved by the older woman's penetration. Like a restless animal trapped in a cage, Frankie circles the kitchen table with increasing intensity, talking of how her life will be gloriously transformed when she goes off with Janice and Jarvis. She works herself into a state of near hysteria as she shouts out all the glamorous activities they will share. Finally, she collapses in a state of exhaustion into the comforting arms of Berenice. The lights almost totally extinguished, the three huddle together, Frankie crying softly on Berenice's lap, while John Henry quietly begins to sing the Negro Spiritual that Berenice was humming earlier:

> I sing because I'm happy.
> I sing because I'm free.
> For His eye is on the sparrow.
> And I know He watches me.

Ritualistically, Berenice then sings the second part of the song:

> Why should I feel discouraged?
> Why should the shadows come?
> Why should my heart be lonely,
> Away from heaven and home?
> For Jesus is my portion,
> My constant friend is He.
> For His eye is on the sparrow.
> And I know he watches me.
> So, I sing because I'm happy.

All three join in the final refrain as Zinnemann's camera moves in closer to capture this privileged moment of poignancy. The director later observed that it was "one of the most moving scenes I have witnessed," adding, "I say 'witnessed', not 'directed'" (*Life* 115).

The wedding scene and its aftermath are presented briefly and rather impressionistically in the novel:

> The rest was like some nightmare show in which a wild girl in the audience breaks onto the stage to take upon herself an unplanned part that was never written or meant to be. You are the we of me, her heart was saying, but she could only say aloud: "Take me!" And they pleaded and begged with her, but she was already in the car. At the last she clung to the steering wheel until her father and some-body else had hauled and dragged her from the car, and even then she could only cry in the dust of the empty road: "Take me! Take me!" But there was only the wedding company to hear, for the bride and her brother had driven away (138).

In the stage play, the wedding scene is not presented directly, but is observed by Berenice from the kitchen. The movie version is by far the most powerful presentation. Zinnemann photographs it in such a man-ner that Frankie makes a compositional "third" in the ceremony. By means of a deep focus shot, she is positioned between the bride and groom as the minister recites the words of the marriage. Zinnemann also cuts to close-ups of Frankie's face as the minister's words form the conti-nuity of the scene. As soon as the wedding is concluded, Frankie takes her suitcase to the honeymoon car and waits in the back seat.

The ensuing scene is photographed mostly through the windows of the car, preserving Zinnemann's characteristic motif of enclosures within enclosures. (As in *High Noon*, there are a great many shots of doors and windows in this film, all of them suggesting confinement.) Janice and Jarvis, a pleasant but totally commonplace couple, try to reason with Frankie to get out. But she refuses, insisting that she "belongs" with them. In exasperation, her father pulls her out, and she falls down in the dusty road, screaming, "Take me! Take me!" Alex North's music rises to a cli-mactic crescendo as the high-angled camera cranes down to a tightly framed shot of the collapsed youngster. In the background we can see the lower bodies of the bewildered wedding guests surrounding her. Suddenly two strong arms reach down and pick her up: Berenice supports the hys-

116

FIGURE 8.2. THE MEMBER OF THE WEDDING (Columbia Pictures, 1952). Harry Bolden and James Edwards look on as Brandon de Wilde tells Ethel Waters that he feels sick.

terical child back into the house. This shot, so reminiscent of Griffith's final shot in the homecoming sequence of *The Birth of a Nation*, is at once both powerful and tactfully understated. We don't need to know whose arms reach into the frame: it could only be Berenice, the only person who can understand the girl's anguish. That evening Frankie runs away from home. But her experiment in freedom is terrifying. Zinnemann shoots much of this sequence in a highly stylized—almost surrealistic—manner, reminiscent of film noir. The dark, eerie alleys in which the frightened girl finds herself look like sinister tunnels streaked with harsh shadows. Honky-tonk music and disembodied voices echo as in a nightmare. After a fearful encounter with a drunken soldier who makes a pass at her, the youngster runs home, to the sanctuary-prison of her house, a broken creature. When she arrives, she discovers that John Henry is seriously ill.

Berenice's world comes crashing about her at the same time. In addition to her worrying about the runaway Frankie and the suffering John Henry, she's wracked with anxiety that her stepbrother Honey (James Edwards) will be caught by the police, who are pursuing him for a hit-and-run accident in which the victim was a white man. A major subplot of all three versions of the story concerns the black characters and their imprisonment within a white society. This subplot is most fully developed in the novel. Berenice's friend, T.T. (Harry Bolden), responds to this entrapment by playing the obsequious Uncle Tom. But Honey refuses to demean himself. He plays the role of the razor-wielding, insolent "bad nigger" to the hilt, and has served a prison sentence for his arrogant independence.

Berenice disapproves of Honey's contempt for white people, his "reefer" smoking, and even his trumpet playing, which brings him no income. But she loves him, and prays to God to preserve "the only family I got left." A gifted musician, Honey plays the trumpet whenever he feels he's being hemmed in by a hostile white world. "I got to bust loose or die," he explains to his sister when she upbraids him for not settling down. His nickname is "Lightfoot," a name that Frankie finds infinitely appealing because of its romantic suggestion of freedom and worldly experience. But eventually Honey is caught by the police and sent to prison for ten years. (In the novel and play he commits suicide by hanging himself in his jail cell.)

In the stage version, and even more in the movie, the focus tends to shift from Frankie to Berenice. The concluding sequence of the film opens with a shot of Frankie—"Frances" would be more appropriate—

looking up at John Henry's bedroom window. She's dressed in a teenager's jumper and wears a charmingly feminine beret on her head. It is moving day, and inside the denuded Addams kitchen, Berenice sits thoughtfully on a trunk, contemplating the tragic turn of events that have occurred in the past few months. Frankie is filled with joyful enthusiasm for her two new friends, Mary Littlejohn and Barney Mackean—the very same Mary and Barney that she expressed such contempt for in the early portions of the movie. Frankie guiltily admits that she can barely remember John Henry's appearance. When she promises she'll visit Berenice often in the future, the wiser woman smiles knowingly and replies, "No you won't, baby. You'll have other things to do. Your road is already strange to me." With thoughtless but unintentional cruelty, Frankie departs with Barney, leaving Berenice alone in the kitchen.

In a low-angle shot emphasizing her heroic endurance, Zinnemann moves in for a close-up of this indestructible woman. Almost imperceptibly, in an effort to choke back the tears, she hums a few bars of "His Eye Is on the Sparrow." Like many of Zinnemann's protagonists, she faces the future utterly alone.

WORKS CITED

Hitchcock, Alfred. "*Rear Window.*" In *Focus on Hitchcock*, ed. Albert J. LaValley. Englewood Cliffs, N.J.: Prentice-Hall, 1972. 40–46.

McCullers, Carson. *The Member of the Wedding*, the novel. New York: Bantam Books, 1958.

———. *The Member of the Wedding*, the play. New York: New Directions, 1951.

Zinnemann, Fred. *A Life in the Movies: An Autobiography*. New York: Scribner's, 1992.

CHAPTER NINE

Spirituality and Style in
The Nun's Story (1959)

ARTHUR NOLLETTI JR.

In the closing scene of Fred Zinnemann's *The Nun's Story* (1959), Gabrielle Van der Mal (Audrey Hepburn), known as Sister Luke, leaves the convent after having struggled for seventeen years to attain spiritual perfection, a struggle that begins in the late 1920s and concludes shortly after the outbreak of World War II. Based on Kathryn C. Hulme's best-selling novel, the film was an enormous critical and commercial success. Besides receiving eight Academy Award nominations (including Best Picture), it won the New York Film Critics Awards for Best Actress and Best Director and the National Board of Review honors for Best Picture, Best Director, and Best Supporting Actress (Dame Edith Evans). In the opinion of many, it represents not only Zinnemann's finest achievement and the best American film ever made on religious life, but it contains Audrey Hepburn's greatest performance in the most demanding role of her career.[1]

Since its release, however, *The Nun's Story* has not received the kind of critical attention it deserves, especially from film scholars, who have found such 1959 films as *Some Like It Hot, North by Northwest, Rio Bravo,* and *Imitation of Life* to be of much greater interest. Perhaps this is because of the film's religious subject matter and the fact that cinema studies as a rule is more preoccupied with the claims of society and politics than with spiritual values, which transcend those claims. Perhaps this is also because film studies tends to concentrate on broad, popular genres (comedy, Westerns, melodrama, horror, etc.)—and *The Nun's Story* most decidedly does not fit in here. Whatever the case, the film's relative neglect is part of the overall neglect that Zinnemann's work has suffered since the heyday of auteurist criticism when he was dismissed as an impersonal filmmaker.[2]

In *The Nun's Story* Zinnemann is "impersonal" in that he refuses to impose his personality or point of view on the material. But, far from being a flaw, this is one of the film's greatest strengths, for it allows viewers to decide for themselves whether Sister Luke's renunciation of her vows constitutes a personal victory for having prevailed over a repressive institution or a personal defeat for having failed in her vocation. For this reason alone, the final scene, in which she walks away from the convent forever, is all the more rich and moving. It is also distinguished by the fact that it is played out in virtual silence. As is well known, Zinnemann had to fight over the protests of Jack Warner and composer Franz Waxman, who wanted a full orchestral score at this point. But he prevailed, and in doing so, created what has been rightly called "the most perfectly poised of all endings" (Fitzpatrick 384). In fact, this ending makes possible a third way to interpret Sister Luke's story: as *both* a personal victory and a personal defeat.

Zinnemann's refusal to insist on any single interpretation of his material makes *The Nun's Story* a "profoundly ambiguous film" (Fitzpatrick 382). Yet the few scholars and critics who have studied the film have tended to view it in too narrow a context. Take, for example, Brandon French's often insightful analysis in *On the Verge of Revolt*. For her, *The Nun's Story* is "an unwitting allegory of the demise of conventional secular marriage and the age-old female conflict between service to the self and surrender of the self to the male order" (125). This argument has much to commend it. Indeed, what is surprising is not that *The Nun's Story* lends itself to feminist criticism but that there has been so little attention paid to the film using this extremely vital approach. Unfortunately, French's interest is strictly limited to the secular implications of Sister Luke's story, which leads her to overlook, even at times to distort, the film's all-important spiritual dimension and style. Thus, she dismisses the convent as a tool of patriarchal society, claiming that it "teaches women that they are 'nothing' and encourages them to perceive the annihilation of the self as the ultimate spiritual achievement, a state of grace"

(135). Actually she is right and wrong at the same time—right because what she says is literally correct, but wrong because she fails to recognize that religious life can have validity, even though it is rooted in patriarchal society. In failing to see this, she ends up leaving her readers with the distinct impression that Zinnemann's film shares the same overriding theme and concern as such films as Jacques Rivette's *The Nun* (*La Religieuse*, 1965) and Jerzy Kawalerowicz's *Mother Joan of the Angels* (*Matka Joanna od aniołow*, 1961), in which the convent serves as the metaphor for a repressive environment bent on crushing individualism.

There is no question that the right of the individual is a central theme in Zinnemann's work, one that has its origins in his own life.[3] As a contract director at MGM, he went on suspension rather than accept a compulsory assignment. "I was not meant to be a company man," he has tersely said (*Life* 44). And during the McCarthy era, he was one of the members of the Directors' Guild who refused to be intimidated by the board's efforts to enforce a "loyalty" oath (97). One can see Zinnemann himself in many of his characters: in Julia's humanist ardor; Marshal Will Kane's refusal to compromise; Prewitt's insistence on going "his own way"; Thomas More's unwillingness and inability to sanction his monarch's divorce and remarriage; and, of course, Sister Luke's problem of conscience. Yet we should not automatically assume that Zinnemann's championing of the individual means condemnation of the institution. In *From Here to Eternity* and *A Man for All Seasons*, to cite just two examples, it is not the U.S. Army or the British monarchy that is indicted. After all, Prewitt and Thomas More remain steadfastly loyal to their professions and never utter so much as a single word against them. What is indicted are those individuals who abuse their authority.

In *The Nun's Story* there is no such abuse. Rather, the determining difference is that "the demands of the convent are absolute" (Fitzpatrick 382). One can view these demands (and the convent experience as a whole) as beautiful and ennobling or horrifying and repressive, depending on one's own values and beliefs. In either case Zinnemann undoubtedly realized that *The Nun's Story* could not succeed without a knowledge of the inner workings of the convent, and without a deep respect for religious life and care and sensitivity in depicting that life. He therefore is careful to impart the genuine sense of religious dedication that characterizes those women who are able to adapt themselves to the rigors of their chosen order (Gow 58–59). As he has said, "When you do a film like this you must have, at least, an external appreciation of what religious life is about" (*Life* 158). Elaborating on this point, he has added: "although it is a story of a woman who loses the way to her vocation, the strongest memory I retain is the total faith of so many nuns we met and the marvelous serenity with which they went about their duties and devotions" (*Life* 171). Indeed, without this background of "total faith," Sister Luke's "exhausting inner struggle" and her progress toward spirituality and away from religiosity (Kauffmann 50) would be robbed of meaning.

⊞

The Nun's Story belongs to a genre that is rare in American cinema: the spiritual film.[4] In this chapter I wish to examine Zinnemann's film as an example of this genre, noting the nature of its spirituality and detailing the stylistic means by which Zinnemann creates this spirituality. In the process, I will also trace the evolution of Sister Luke's own individual form of spirituality, comparing and contrasting it with that of the convent. In order to better understand the spirituality that Sister Luke ultimately finds for herself, it is first necessary to articulate the communal spirituality that serves as the foundation of religious life.

At the heart of all Christian spirituality, including the rules and regulations that govern the convent, is the notion of being born again in Christ. These rules by necessity take external forms, such as the actual training that the nun undergoes, and with that training the various exercises, penances, and discipline of the Holy Rule.[5] As Zinnemann's film clearly illustrates, this is the ascetic side of religious life. There is also another side, one that is much harder to achieve and ultimately more important: the mystic. Here one accedes to God's power and love. However, this can only be done after the rules and regulations have been internalized, after one has overcome the ego and self-centeredness by the "emptying" of self, kenosis (Mitchell 127).

This emptying of self cannot be achieved by will. It requires "humility and strength, perseverance and detachment, abandonment of everything and resignation of God's will in all things" (Mitchell 129). As Mother Emmanuel tells Sister Luke, "Remember that you are an instrument. In yourself you are nothing until you are raised up." Consequently, the nun, like all Christians, is enjoined to imitate Christ himself, who humbled himself by becoming man and by dying on the cross, the supreme act of selfless love. As the symbol of the paradox of "dying," of emptying oneself to be born anew, the cross is the single most important icon of Christianity, and is focused on frequently throughout the film. In most of these instances Sister Luke is praying at the foot of the cross intently, fully aware that it signifies what she wishes to be. Yet her religious progress is stymied because intellectual pride prevents her from tolerating imperfections in herself, and because she is obsessed with mastering the state of spiritual perfection. It is a never-ending dilemma for her, for as she laments at one point, "Pride is not burned out in me. When I succeed in obeying the Holy Rule, I fail at the same time because I take pride in having succeeded."

It is probably true that Sister Luke's real calling is not the religious life but nursing. (Her greatest desire is to go to the Congo and work in a bush station.) But to put too much emphasis on this matter is not only to deny her genuine religious devotion but also to miss the point of her story. For her story is not about appropriateness of vocation, or even success or failure in that vocation. Rather it is about the search for self, one of the most universal and heroic of all struggles. And for Sister Luke, this struggle means—first, last, and always—finding her way to God.

The spiritual film by definition is interested in reflecting and expressing interior states of consciousness and experience. It is preoccupied with that which is beyond normal sense experience and the finite. Its provenance is the Holy, the One, the Ideal, or God. It need not be specifically religious in theme or subject matter, but one of its most pressing concerns has to do with the individual's relationship with God. This is the concern that *The Nun's Story* shares with such films as Dreyer's *Passion of Joan of Arc* (*La Passion de Jeanne d'Arc*, 1928), Delannoy's *God Needs Men* (*Dieu a besoin des hommes*, 1950), Bergman's *Winter Light* (*Nattvardsgästerna*, 1962), Pialat's *Under the Sun of Satan* (*Sous le soleil de Satan*, 1987), Cavalier's *Thérèse* (1986), and Bresson's *Diary of a Country Priest* (*Le Journal d'un curé de campagne*, 1950).

The genre of the spiritual film is defined not only by its content but by its visual style, an aesthetic of austerity in which everything but the essential is eliminated in order to concentrate on the experience of the soul as it contends with God. Somewhat paradoxically, the only way in which the ineffable or Holy or God can be expressed is through concrete forms, objects—what Paul Schrader calls "surface aesthetics." These objects absorb, bespeak, or point to the spiritual, going beyond their denotative meanings to suggest another dimension or plane of experience, what might be called the potential or ideal. In film, the spiritual style is characterized by an attenuated, deliberate rhythm; a predominant mood of solemnity; subtlety of emotional expression; restrained camera style; an often painterly evocation of backgrounds and setting; intense stylization of human figure and face; and what Dudley Andrew calls "a rigorous delimitation of means [that] permits only certain forms and objects to be put into play" (31). The keynote of this "delimitation of means" is concentration, intensification, and repetition—a mode of viewing that leads the viewer to a sense of meditation and harmony.

All of these characteristics—this austerity of means and "rigor of visual design" (Fitzpatrick 383)—are to be found in *The Nun's Story*. In fact, they are the aesthetic key to the film.[6] To be sure, as a director trained in the classical Hollywood style, Zinnemann avoids the extreme formalism of such spiritual filmmakers as Dreyer, Bresson, and Ozu. Yet, interestingly enough, this most self-effacing of directors, who favors straight set-ups and eschews gratuitous camera movement, wanted to film the convent scenes in black and white to heighten the contrast with the scenes in the Congo. But Jack Warner vetoed the idea as "too tricky" (*Life* 166), so Zinnemann and cinematographer Franz Planer got the effect of black and white by focusing on the nuns' habits and in general working within a strictly limited palette of pastels (blues, grays, and beiges). Thus, while Zinnemann was denied the extreme formalism he sought in this instance, he managed something no less important: to find another way to create the "delimitation of means" essential to his film.

In *The Nun's Story* this process of concentration, intensification, and repetition is most evident in Zinnemann's use of (1) dialogue; (2) religious rituals, iconography, and settings; and (3) close-ups of the human face. The first forty minutes establish the particular role of dialogue. After Gabrielle bids farewell to her father (Dean Jagger), who explains that she is too "strong willed" to be a nun, and as she and the new entrants undergo their training, dialogue is basically limited to instruction in the Holy Rule, prayer, individual and group recitation, and voice-overs. All of this is in keeping with the law that governs convent life, the Grand Silence. This law, which is observed from after chapel in the evening to after chapel in the morning, is itself motivated by the belief that a nun should strive to be in constant communion with God. Even during those hours when the Grand Silence is not observed, casual conversation in the film (as in the convent) is kept to a minimum. Hence, when Sister Luke and another young novice, Sister Christine (Patricia Bosworth), form a friendship to stave off loneliness and voice their various doubts and feelings, we recognize the seriousness of their lapse immediately, while also understanding the need for this lapse. Not until Sister Luke leaves the mother house does conversation in any real sense of the word re-enter the film, and even then it is never really casual. As we shall see, the most important of these conversations—certainly the most psychologically subtle and incisive ones—take place between Sister Luke and the atheistic surgeon Dr. Fortunati (Peter Finch), who serves as a catalyst in her eventual decision to renounce her vows.

As might be expected, the staging of religious rituals, the presence of Christian iconography (in particular, the cross), and even the various quarters of the convent itself (the chapel, the corridors, the cells where the nuns are housed, and refectory where they eat) also figure prominently. Obviously, they denote meanings and values particular to the Roman Catholic faith. But more importantly, they not only point to a spiritual reality, an elusive, intangible state of being to which each young woman, including Gabrielle, aspires, but they induce in themselves a feeling of spirituality. As such, they are signifiers of all that is to be interiorized.

In this respect the film's first forty minutes again prove crucial. Focusing on the process of the making of a nun, they are highlighted by the formal ceremonies that mark the specific stages in this process, from postulancy through novitiate to the taking of final vows. Of these ceremonies, that of vesture, which runs six-and-a half minutes, is the longest, most elaborate, and detailed. Here the postulants enter the chapel dressed like brides, the white of their garments standing out against the background of soft blue and gold hues. As part of the ritual, their hair is shorn. In one particular shot, one that is lovely and disturbing at the same time, we see a large tress of Gabrielle's hair fall into a gold platter that reflects her image. Her physical beauty is never more evident perhaps than at this moment when she is rejecting the vanity of the world. Praised for documentarylike realism, these ceremonies are Zinnemann's own additions to the screenplay and are there because he rightly felt that they needed to be ("Conversation with Zinnemann"). In one sense, of course, they are not essential to the telling of Sister Luke's story. That is, while the information they relate is needed, this information could have been provided by the narrative in a number of ways. The very fact that Zinnemann chose to devote more than one fourth of his film to these ceremonies and scenes of convent life—an unusually high proportion of the narrative—attests to the importance that he put on evoking the feeling and integrity of religious life as a profoundly spiritual experience.[7]

FIGURE 9.1. THE NUN'S STORY (Warners Bros., 1959). Zinnemann deep in thought on the set. (Courtesy Academy of Motion Picture Arts and Sciences)

This evocation of spirituality begins the moment Gabrielle gets her first glimpse of the inner sanctum of the convent. After parting with her father, she leaves the public waiting room. The door is closed behind her. Shortly thereafter, another door is opened before her.[8] As it opens, she sees a long, starkly beautiful corridor bathed in gold-beige light, at the end of which hangs a crucifix from ceiling to floor, symmetrically centered under arches.

An even more wondrous sight immediately follows, one that holds a complex of meanings. Sister Margharita, Mistress of Postulants (Mildred Dunnock) escorts Gabrielle and the other entrants into chapel for evening prayers. From her position in the choir loft, Gabrielle steals a glance at the sight below: the chapel proper filled with the entire community. In a composition that is perfectly symmetrical and devoid of movement, we see what she sees. At the far end of the chapel (and upper part of the frame) there is an altar. Directly behind it are three stained glass windows (themselves icons of the Holy Trinity) and a crucifix suspended before the middle panel. Spanning the frame from top to bottom are parallel rows of kneeling nuns separated by a broad central aisle that is empty except for a lectern. The rows nearest the aisle are dominated by white wimples, while those further back are dominated by black.

Suddenly this static picture comes to life. One of the nuns on the right rises, moves down the central aisle, and prostrates herself before a figure seated at the near end of the chapel. This figure we later learn is Reverend Mother Emmanuel, the head of the Congregation (Edith Evans). A few moments pass. Then the nun stands, bows, and takes her place in a row of white-wimpled nuns on the left side of the aisle. Like Gabrielle, we have only the vaguest idea of the meaning of the ritual we are witnessing and what the arrangement of rows, the various colored habits, and the act of prostration mean. Like her, we can only observe with fascination the beauty before us: the purity of the gestures, the collective silence, the geometric design, the architecture and splendor of the physical setting—in short, the "surface aesthetics" that take the form of mise en scène.[9] It is a "spectacle" that demands veneration and elevates the soul even before it is "explained" in the scenes to come as an image of love and humility. Indeed, in its unique and mysterious physicality lies a vision and an invitation to penetrate the inner meaning of the physical sign, to perceive that—like Blake's "world in a grain of sand"—it is all that is made because it is made by God. This vision transcends any particular religious sect or ritual. But at this point in the narrative, Gabrielle has no sense of this. For her, religion and spirituality are one and the same. Nor does she realize that she is different from the others, a fact that Zinnemann makes sure we never forget. As he has said, there is a "subconscious quality of independence present in all her actions," and the film is made up of "dozens" of such moments (*Life* 163). Thus, here and throughout the film, he singles her out and conveys her point of view in shot/reaction shot, which, along with the close-up, is one of the film's most important stylistic paradigms.

Zinnemann's use of the close-up of the human face, as has been noted, "can be traced back to the silent cinema" (Garbicz and Klinowski 441). In fact, we are reminded of Dreyer, a director for whom Zinnemann has expressed admiration (*Life* 8), in the way that the face is made the site of the film's interior drama. Primarily it is Audrey Hepburn's face that is privileged, since this is Sister Luke's story, but the faces of other nuns are also scrutinized as studies in contrast. Emblematic in this regard is the scene in which the new postulants are brought before Mother Emmanuel to be formally admitted into the congregation. As part of this ceremony, they are instructed to lie prone on the floor, their faces buried in their arms. Gabrielle, however, in close-up, steals a glance at Mother Emmanuel, who, in close-up, sees her doing so.

What is especially noteworthy about Zinnemann's close-ups is their painterly quality, their indebtedness to portrait painting of masters like Holbein, who favored simple, frontal poses and who, through a reduction of means, sought a more abstract beauty of form (Langdon 11). Here both women are viewed from a frontal position, their faces virtually expressionless, their features alone projecting pure personality. Audrey Hepburn's radiantly youthful face is dominated by her large eyes, which can suggest a wide range of feelings and emotions, not the least of which are resolve and intelligence. In her face one feels a latent vitality that is always about to blossom into overt expression. By contrast Edith Evans's face is that of the ascetic. Lined and somewhat pallid, it is characterized by an almost total stillness of expression that cannot be compromised by even the slight upward turn of the lips or the eyes that briefly acknowledge Gabrielle's presence. Hers is a stillness of spirit, and in her presence we feel her serenity, largesse, and grandeur. She is the perfect nun, "a living rule."

In this scene Mother Emmanuel instructs the postulants that "it is not easy to be a nun," that "it is a never-ending struggle for self-perfection," in which "some of you will have more trouble than others." As she says this, Zinnemann cuts to Gabrielle, indicating that these words are particularly applicable to her. Yet, as I have already said, it is not simply Mother Emmanuel and Gabrielle who are individualized through close-ups. When Mother Emmanuel cautions that "Poverty, chastity, and obedience are extremely difficult. Each of us here can assure you of that," Zinnemann gives us a close-up of two anonymous nuns seated side by side against a bare, gray wall. The one on the left is the older, perhaps in her forties; the one on the right cannot be much beyond her twenties. Nevertheless, we are struck by their similarity, which is overdetermined by the symmetry of Zinnemann's composition, their stance, and the look on their faces: an absence of expression and slightly lowered eyes. It is a "still life" that provides eloquent testimony for Mother Emmanuel's words. In this and other portraits of often anonymous nuns that appear throughout the film, we get a sense of what it means to be a nun, of the cost of the sacrifices that each woman must make, and of the humility that makes possible the ultimate goal and reward of religious life: closer union with Jesus Christ. We also never forget, of course, the way in which Sister Luke's face is different.

So far I have discussed Zinnemann's style as if it were entirely one of austerity. Yet his desire to contrast the convent scenes with those in the Congo, scenes that "burst out into all the hot, vivid, stirring colors of Central Africa" (*Life* 166), indicates that he sees the need for another style as well, a complementary one. Here Paul Schrader's appropriation of Jacques Maritain's "abundant means" and "sparse means" is relevant. For Schrader, these two means are essential to spiritual art. The former is concerned with "practicality, physical goods, and sensual feelings"—life in the outside world; the latter is the "proper means of the spirit" (154)—what I have been referring to as "austerity." Both must work together, but in a careful ratio and in a movement that "disposes of its inherent abundant means and substitutes sparse means" (159) until what is finally reached is "stasis": the image stops. When this happens, "the viewer keeps going, moving deeper and deeper, one might say into the image" (161).

In *The Nun's Story* Zinnemann achieves a subtle interplay of abundance and sparseness of means. We have already discussed the visual forms that the latter takes, particularly in the early convent scenes. Abundance, simply put, takes the form of visual sumptuousness (dynamic camera movement; sweeping panoramic views; highly saturated colors; compositions filled with motion and activity, etc.). Now we need to examine how these two forms interact, and how abundance gradually gives way to sparseness as part of Sister Luke's spiritual progress.

Abundance of means is evident in early scenes, such as the credits sequence in which Gabrielle takes a walk along the cobblestone street outside her Bruges home and in the scenes that follow with her father.[10] But once she enters the convent, this element is contained and subdued. There is the single shot of the exterior of the School of Tropical Medicine in Antwerp where Sister Luke prepares for her work in the Congo. Dominated by bright colors, this shot anticipates the Congo, and is a respite from the austerity of the convent. It also marks the first time that she has stepped foot outside the convent. But it is only an isolated shot, and as it turns out, Sister Luke is assigned to a staff position at a mental sanitarium in Brussels.

Finally, she is sent to the Congo. Here the screen comes alive in a veritable abundance of means, the most dynamic use of color, camera, and cinema in the film. Three shots introduce us to the Congo, including an aerial view of the mighty river itself and the lush, green landscape it cuts through. Then, in a long tracking shot taken from inside a train and representing Sister Luke's point of view, we see large stretches of open space, a small village, natives waving to the train as it passes by, and finally the station itself, her point of destination. On the platform, an army band plays a rather cacaphonous-sounding march while a rush of people—whites and natives alike—scurry about to greet the arriving passengers. Beyond the platform lies the Congo, its muddy waters dotted with boats, its banks busy with trade. Native song fills the air, and from the distance comes the hum of native drums.

Teeming with human activity, and vibrant in its colors of red, gold, and green, the Congo is a fecund place where the purpose of life seems simple and clear: life is to be lived here and now. In every way a contrast to the restraint of convent life and its muted colors, the Congo exults in its physical and sensuous reality. In fact, when one thinks of the Congo, one never thinks of interiors, only of exteriors and the openness and freedom that they signify.

Sister Luke sees the Congo as a place where she can take "flight" from her ongoing spiritual struggle. To some extent she is right. Thanks to her work supervising nurses and assisting Dr. Fortunati and to the generous and sympathetic support of her superior general, Mother Mathilde (Dame Peggy Ashcroft), she enjoys the only real happiness she has known since entering the convent, even though she is initially disappointed by being assigned to work in the European hospital instead of the black one. But as she soon learns, there is no such thing as flight from self. Her per-

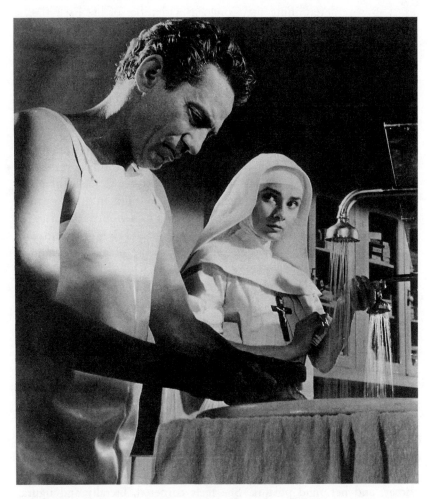

FIGURE 9.2. THE NUN'S STORY (Warner Bros., 1959). Sister Luke (Audrey Hepburn) and Dr. Fortunati (Peter Finch). (Courtesy Collectors Book Store, Hollywood, Calif.)

sonal struggle intensifies, and so does her longing for God's presence. Thus the Congo becomes, in part, a place of confinement.

How does Zinnemann express these dual meanings of the Congo? By creating a tension between abundance and sparseness, or to be more exact, by overdetermining the Congo as a signifier of life itself (i.e., a world of nature), then by limiting Sister Luke's contact with this world by placing her, increasingly, in interiors. Her hospital work, of course, is work she loves more than any other, and so initially at least she seems to suffer no hardship. Yet these particular interiors—small hospital rooms cast in monochromatic shades of tans or blues—and the sparse means (austerity) they bring back into the film—serve to exteriorize her suppressed and deepening conflict.

In a series of quite subtle and moving psychological confrontations, Dr. Fortunati, who clearly is in love with Sister Luke, but never speaks that love out of respect for her vows, tries to get her to realize that her independent nature makes her unsuited to religious life. In the most trenchant of these confrontations he speaks openly to her on this subject for the first time. A short scene—it runs one minute and twenty seconds and consists of eleven shots—it is exemplary in its use of mise en scène to achieve sparseness of means.

Set in extremely cramped quarters at one end of a hospital room, it finds Fortunati and Sister Luke examining an x-ray. Fortunati is seated on a bed against the right wall; Sister Luke stands against the left wall, which is barely an arm's length from him. As the scene opens, a curious thing occurs: a native assistant leaves the room, walking directly forward in the composition and momentarily blocking the two principals from view. This serves not only to emphasize in yet another way the closeness of these quarters but to establish the mood of the scene and the discomfort Sister Luke is to experience at the hands of Fortunati. In fact, as Fortunati needles her, forcing her to defend what he correctly identifies as her tension (and not, as she contends, discipline), we see the pained expression on her face, the dark circles under her eyes, her nervous clutching of her throat, and her rigid posture. She feels cornered, literally and figuratively—as indeed, she is. Thus the net that is draped over Fortunati's bed and which frames him also frames her in reverse shots, thereby compressing space in still another way. So, too, do the tight, alternating close-ups, which make this intimate scene all the more visually austere and emotionally unrelenting, as it builds to its climactic moment. Here Fortunati strikes a real nerve. "As a surgeon, it's not my business to probe the mind," he tells her, "but I'd say that tension is the sign of an exhausting inner struggle." She breaks down: "Do you realize that every time you talk to me like this I should go down on my knees before my sisters and proclaim my fault?" Grieved by the pain he has caused her, he apologizes and hurries from the room. However, he has begun the process of "distilling the conflicting essences within her" (Kauffmann 50) and of helping her find the way to her own spirituality. As such, in these confrontation scenes he is fighting on her behalf for her very soul.

It is important to reiterate that overall the Congo scenes are characterized by both abundance and sparseness—sometimes in juxtaposition, sometimes in a blend of both means—and that a number of scenes, for example, Sister Luke's accompanying of Mother Mathilde on her daily rounds, are almost exclusively in the abundant style. It is also important to keep in mind, as I have already stated, that sparseness of means becomes more prominent as Sister Luke's struggle intensifies. Be that as it may, when she is forced to leave the Congo to return to the mother house in Belgium, the abundant style makes one final, magnificent return. Ushered to her compartment on the train, she finds it decorated from one end to the other with brilliantly colored flowers. As the train pulls away from the station, gradually picking up speed, Zinnemann gives us a tracking shot from Sister Luke's point of view, the companion shot of her arrival. Appropriately, her last image of the Congo is Dr. Fortunati. Waving his good-by, he turns and walks away. An unforgettable direct cut brings us back to the exterior of the mother house in Belgium. All the colors have been drained away, and it is raining. The remainder of the film will be dominated by sparseness of means as Sister Luke, now virtually alone, resolves her struggle.

Instructed by Mother Emmanuel to renew her spiritual life for a "few quiet months" in the mother house, Sister Luke simply cannot get the Congo out of her blood, no matter how hard she tries. Aware of Sister Luke's struggle, Mother Emmanuel assigns her hospital work near the Holland border. But this cannot forestall the inevitable. When the Nazis invade Belgium, she cannot remain neutral, as nuns are expected to be. Lending her support to the Belgian underground, she declares, as she falls to her knees, "What I do from now on is between You and me." She no longer can obey, and being unable to obey, she knows that she is no longer a nun. When her beloved father is killed by the Nazis, she takes the final, decisive step and asks to be released from her vows.

At this point, apropos of the spiritual style, *The Nun's Story* is so bare, so sparse, that it is ready for "stasis," in which the image simply stops and the viewer is left to move deeper and deeper into contemplation. This "stasis" comes in the closing scene; indeed, it is the raison d'être of this "most perfectly poised of all endings" (Fitzpatrick 384).

Made up of nine shots and running four minutes, this scene finds Sister Luke alone in an anteroom where she is to change her nun's habit for street clothes before departing the convent forever. As she removes the first item of clothing, her wimple, and places it on a nearby rack, the camera tilts upward to an image of a cross on the windowed arch of a doorway. The soundtrack becomes silent, and when we return to her, she is now dressed in a gray suit and almost entirely transformed to her former self, Gabrielle Van der Mal. We see her carefully remove the ring from her finger that symbolizes her marriage to Christ. Then she places a hat in her suitcase, closes the suitcase, and presses a button to signal to the porteress in another room that she is ready to leave. After a few seconds, a door unlocks with a loud click that shatters the silence. In the final shot, the longest in the scene, Gabrielle opens the door to its full width and makes her way down the narrow cobblestone street. The camera remains positioned inside the room, framing her in the doorway. At first she walks tentatively, then more confidently, before turning and stopping briefly, the muffled sounds of traffic now audible in the background. Then she takes a few steps and disappears from view. Punctuating her leave-taking is the sound of the Angelus bell striking three times and calling those in the convent to prayer.

Throughout *The Nun's Story*, Sister Luke moves progressively away from the communal spirituality of religious life toward an individual spirituality. But what exactly is the nature of this spirituality that she finally arrives at? We are left to ponder this question while contemplating the open doorway and the world that lies outside it.

Earlier Sister Luke had declared, "What I do from now on is between You and me." In doing so, she not only announced her break with the Holy Rule, she affirmed her own being by coming to the implicit realization that spirituality is not a "thing" or a "state" or a "condition" but a "freedom." In the words of comparative philosopher Donald W. Mitchell, spirituality is in fact "a horizon of absolute freedom and love in which we are all what we truly are while reflecting that freedom and love in unique and particular ways" (13). Interestingly, this "horizon" is given visual expression in the last shot of the film, in the image of the street that leads away from the convent and in Gabrielle's long walk down this street.

It is true, of course, that she takes no joy in leaving the convent, for she regards her inability to obey and her renunciation of vows as indisputable evidence of personal failure. Indeed, she never loses her belief in the value of communal spirituality for those who are suited to it—hence her expression of happiness when she learns that Lisa, a young nurse (Diana Lambert) with whom she has worked closely, is preparing to enter the convent even as she leaves it. Yet she also realizes that given her character—her independence of mind, her inability to make the Holy Rule the priority in her life—she has no other choice but to leave. What she does not see is that there is no fault to be found, no blame to be placed, in leaving.

As she walks away, she leaves behind the turbulence of seventeen years. But still she remains framed in the doorway, and this fact has undeniable significance. She has left the convent, but the convent will always be a part of her. Even the spirituality that she arrives at owes much to the convent, for it is grounded in faith and is animated by compassion and love for others and by the doing of good works. These are the impulses and beliefs that have always been the center of Gabrielle's being. Where she departs from the communal spirituality of the convent is in her recognition that God is just as present in the secular realm as in the religious. Thus she can say of Dr. Fortunati, in direct contrast to Mother Mathilde, who sees him as a genius, a devil, and an unbeliever, "I think always he's very close to God in those unearthly hours when he operates." This utterance, in fact, very nearly states outright the cornerstone of her own belief: "that being with others as a layperson in the world becomes through the practice of love a way to union with God" (Mitchell 172). On the face of it, this belief is not in any way radical or earth-shattering, except for Gabrielle, who has had to journey seventeen years into her self to discover it. In short, Gabrielle Van der Mal, once known as Sister Luke, resolves to continue her good works in the outside world. In all probability she will serve as a nurse in the underground, at least as long as she is needed. Her progress, however, has not really ended; it has simply found a new path. Now she not only acts out God's intention that each human being be free, but in that freedom and its attendant love and grace, she finds her true selfhood and union with God. It is this knowledge that gives the film its resonance, its transcendence, long after the final image has faded from the screen.

NOTES

1. Unfortunately, Hepburn's role and performance in *The Nun's Story* are rarely discussed today, no doubt because they are at odds with the image of the Givenchy-dressed gamine for which she is most fondly remembered.

This neglect is even more curious since her role as Sister Luke clearly pre-
saged her work as a goodwill ambassador for UNICEF in the last years of
her life.

2. There is no need here to rehearse Zinnemann's treatment at the hands of
auteurist critics. But it is interesting to note that Andrew Sarris seems to
have partially recanted his original opinion of Zinnemann and a number of
other directors he lumped together in the now-notorious category, "Less
Than Meets the Eye." He states that these directors "seem to fit into an *objet
d'art* category," then goes on to comment: "These are directors who are
more concerned with cultivating the unique qualities of each individual
work rather than projecting their own personalities. . . . The Politique des
Auteurs has traditionally underestimated the *objet d'art* directors because of
the auteurist emphasis on the stylistic unconscious" (quoted in Studlar and
Desser 274).

   For Zinnemann's opinion of auteurism, see "Conversation with Fred
Zinnemann" in this volume.

3. See, e.g., Gene D. Phillips, *The Movie Makers: Artists in an Industry* (Chicago:
Nelson-Hall, 1973), pp. 103–12, and John Fitzgerald, pp. 378–86.

4. For a stimulating discussion of the treatment of religious themes in film,
consult André Bazin's "Cinema and Theology," which focuses on a handful
of films, especially Delannoy's *La Symphonie Pastorale* and *God Needs Man*.
Although Bazin identifies three categories of religious movie, his principal
interest is in what I have called "the spiritual film." His essay was first published in French in *Esprit* (February 1951), and has been translated into
English by Alain Piette and Bert Cardullo (see *South Atlantic Quarterly* 91
[Summer 1992]: 393–407).

5. In his autobiography Zinnemann states, quite correctly, that *The Nun's Story*
was a period piece about the convent even when it was made in 1958 and
that some of the way things were done had changed considerably since the
film's setting of the late 1920s through the early 1940s. Of course, things
were to change even more in the mid-sixties with the Second Vatican Coun-
cil. Nuns were freed from some of the most antiquated customs and regulations; e.g., the habit was modified, as was the stricture regarding silence, and
in cloistered orders, the rules of enclosure were relaxed. However, as Julia
Lieblich points out in *Sisters: Lives of Devotion and Defiance*, since the early
1980s, the new conservative hierarchy in the Church has tried to undo these
and other reforms of Vatican II (188–89). Even so, none of the above
changes or the efforts to reverse them invalidate the convent experience that
is depicted in Zinnemann's film.

6. As Garbicz and Klinowski say, "The aesthetic key to the film is the classical purity of construction, composition of the frame, color, acting—all used with strict consistency" (441). It is this "strict consistency," in fact, that enables Zinnemann to create a genuine spiritual style *within* the Hollywood classical style. This fact has been insufficiently appreciated.

7. In terms of narrative structure, *The Nun's Story* conforms on the whole to the Hollywood classical style. But in its inclusion of these scenes, which "interrupt" the story, Zinnemann's film demonstrates yet another characteristic that it has in commmon with European film.

8. The opening of this door to reveal what is not meant for the outside world to see appeals to the popular (and powerful) notion of the convent as a fascinating and exotic place. No doubt this was one of the principal reasons that Kathryn Hulme's novel became a bestseller. Even today, this notion of the convent retains power—hence the byline for the Warner Bros. home video of the film: "The award-winning story of the world behind convent walls."

9. This view is also held by Henry Hart. Praising the way that Zinnemann's direction, Franz Planer's photography, Alexander Trauner's art direction, and Maurice Barnathan's set decoration work in concert, he writes: "Some of the interior sets for the mother house induce a sense of spirituality merely by their design and decor. And some of the stagings of the convent rituals make us aware, by symmetries of mass and contrasts of color, of the lesser but eye-delighting fruits of cloistered life" (354).

10. It is worth pointing out, however, that the last section of the credits sequence is clearly an example of austerity (sparseness of means). Here we see the stark black-and-white image of a church or perhaps a convent reflected in the waters of a canal. A voice-over informs us that the religious life is one of sacrifice. The austere, inverted visual imagery tells us even more: that for Gabrielle, the religious life will be an unending struggle. She will be a divided self.

WORKS CITED

Andrew, Dudley. "Desperation and Meditation: Bresson's *Diary of a Country Priest.*" In *Modern European Filmmakers and the Art of Adaptation.* Ed. Andrew S. Horton and Joan Magretta. New York: Frederick Ungar, 1981. 20–37.

Bazin, André. "Cinema and Theology." Trans. Alain Piette and Bert Cardullo. *South Atlantic Quarterly* 91 (Summer 1992): 393–407.

Fitzpatrick, John. "Fred Zinnemann." *American Directors: Volume II.* Ed. Jean-Pierre Coursodon with Pierre Sauvage. New York: McGraw-Hill, 1983. 378–86.

French, Brandon. *On the Verge of Revolt: Women in American Films of the Fifties.* New York: Frederick Ungar, 1978.

Garbicz, Adam, and Jacek Klinowski. *Cinema: The Magic Vehicle—A Guide to Its Achievement. Volume Two. The Cinema in the Fifties.* New York: Schoken Books, 1983.

Gow, Gordon. *Hollywood in the Fifties.* New York: A. S. Barnes, 1971.

Hart, Henry. "*The Nun's Story.*" *Films in Review* 10 (June–July 1959): 351–54.

Kauffmann, Stanley. "*The Nun's Story.*" *A World on Film: Criticism and Comment.* New York: Harper and Row, 1966. 49–51.

Langdon, Helen. *Holbein.* Oxford: Phaidon Press and New York: E. P. Dutton, 1975.

Lieblich, Julia. *Sisters: Lives of Devotion and Defiance.* New York: Ballantine Books, 1992.

Mitchell, Donald W. *Spirituality and Emptiness: The Dynamics of Spiritual Life in Buddhism and Christianity.* New York and Mahwah, N.J.: Paulist Press, 1991.

Sarris, Andrew. "Johnny, We Finally Knew Ye." *Reflections in the Male Eye: John Huston and the American Experience.* Ed. Gaylyn Studlar and David Desser. Washington and London: Smithsonian Institution Press, 1993. 273–76.

Schrader, Paul. *Transcendental Style in Film: Ozu, Bresson, Dreyer.* New York: Da Capo Paperback, 1972.

Zinnemann, Fred. "Conversation with Fred Zinnemann." Interview. By Arthur Nolletti Jr. March 17–18, 1993.

———. *A Life in the Movies: An Autobiography.* New York: Scribner's, 1992.

CHAPTER TEN

⊞

Behold a Pale Horse *(1964):* *Zinnemann and the Spanish Civil War*

LINDA C. EHRLICH

In an essay entitled "Modernism and the Photographic Representation of War and Destruction," Bernd Hüppauf writes: "Representations of modern warfare in film and photography are faced with a structural dilemma: their moral commitment more often than not is linked to a visual code that clashes with aesthetic requirements of visualizing a reality that has become highly abstract" (96). This abstractness from the immediacy of history and its moral concerns marks Fred Zinnemann's dilemma in presenting a cinematic version of the aftermath of the Spanish Civil War in his 1964 film *Behold a Pale Horse.* One recourse he finds to overcome this abstractness is through a secondary character, Father Francisco, who—like many secondary characters in Zinnemann's films—serves as the inspiration for and, in some ways, the stronger partner of the protagonist.

The Spanish Civil War was a monstrous event, setting brother against brother, and destroying in its wake the soul of a nation. On one level, Franco's victory in 1939 ended the conflict, but it also imposed a false unity on the fierce ideological divisions that tore the country apart. To portray the spirit of opposition to Francoist forces, Zinnemann cast the gentle-mannered Gregory Peck against type as an aging, disillusioned resistance fighter (modeled after the fierce fighter Zapater, or "Artiguez" in the novel on which the film is based, *Killing A Mouse on Sunday* by

139

Emeric Pressburger). Zinnemann was unable to fully reproduce either the monumental proportions of the man, or of the landscape in which the story takes place, although he does present a compelling vision of the struggle of an individual to regain his moral center.

Behold a Pale Horse retains a fleeting sense of the struggle between forces of good and evil that distinguishes other Zinnemann films like *High Noon* (1952), *A Man for All Seasons* (1966), and *Julia* (1977). The title is taken from a passage in *Revelation* in the Bible, and is cited at the beginning of the film. (This is the same passage from which the title of Ingmar Bergman's film *The Seventh Seal* originated: When the fourth seal of the angel's book is broken, one can see "a pale horse, and his name was Death, and Hell followed with him.") This chapter will examine Zinnemann's film through two windows: (1) the treatment of the relationship between the protagonist and the two secondary characters who inspire him; and (2) the presentation of the effects of the Spanish Civil War as compared with other cinematic representations of this historical event.

SYNOPSIS

As Peter Monteath has noted, there is a tendency toward mixing documentary and fiction in the literature and films of the Spanish Civil War.[1] Zinnemann's use of documentary footage at the beginning of *Behold a Pale Horse* helps prepare the viewer for the Spanish and French milieu that follows. After the documentary sequences (into which the actors are inserted near the end), an intertitle announces that it is now twenty years later. Paco (Marietto Angeletti), the young son of a murdered resistance fighter, is crossing the border into France, intent on convincing the former resistance fighter Manuel Artiguez (Peck) to return to Spain to kill the Guardia Civíl commander Viñolas (Anthony Quinn), who had tortured and murdered Paco's father.

In a bare apartment in the French town of Pau, Paco finds a deeply demoralized Artiguez living on #17 Spanish Street. There are no clues into how Artiguez has been making his living in France during those years, although we know that during his first years in exile, he had made four or five raids back into Spain each year to taunt the ruling Francoist forces and to steal money for the resistance cause.

In recent years, however, Artiguez seems to have lost his nerve. It will take a series of secondary characters, most importantly Paco and

Father Francisco (Omar Sharif), and an unusual sequence of events, to motivate his final return to Spain. Artiguez's mother Pilar (Mildred Dunnock) lies dying in a hospital in Madrid after having been taken there (against her will) by Viñolas's men. Paco informs Artiguez in detail of the layout of the hospital (which the boy had infiltrated many times to be with his incarcerated father).

Viñolas and his men are intent on observing all who come and go from the ward where Artiguez's mother lies dying. She explicitly asks for Father Francisco when she hears that the young priest will be part of a pilgrimage to Lourdes, thus passing by the town in France where her son lives in exile. Swallowing her basic mistrust of priests, she implores him to honor the wish of a dying woman, to tell her son not to come to Spain to be with her in her last hours. Later, Viñolas tries to extract from the priest Pilar's final words, but the priest refuses to go against his promise to a dying woman.

Father Francisco then witnesses a shocking interchange in Viñolas's room that illustrates how the Guardia Civíl attempts to manipulate events and information to its own advantage. Learning that Pilar has died, Viñolas plots to keep the news from Artiguez. We begin to sense that the moral dilemma facing the young priest might echo, or surpass, that of Artiguez in his decision whether or not to cross over the Pyrenees to Spain one more time.

In his subsequent decision to return to Spain to enter the trap Viñolas has set for him around the hospital, and in full knowledge of his mother's death, Artiguez rediscovers a sense of virility and purpose. There is something poignant, however, about the way he must don glasses to focus on his target across the street, and how at the last moment he loses his one chance to kill his real enemy, Viñolas, when he chooses instead the lesser target of Carlos (Raymond Pellegrin), the smuggler-spy (and supposed friend) who had betrayed him.

HEROIC STATURE

In films like *A Man for All Seasons* and *Julia*, Zinnemann is rightly praised for his characters who assume larger-than-life proportions while never losing their basic humanity. The director stated that what he found important in these films was the struggle of the "individual against machinery. . . . A man [who] is afraid and overcomes his fear shows true courage, whereas a hero without fear, who doesn't know what fear is, basically comes from a fairy tale" (Gow 15–16). Before filming *Behold a Pale Horse*, director and crew made contact with political refugees living on the French side of the border to observe how they maintained their life in exile. They found that many still kept their fiercely anti-Church attitude because of the Church's complicity with Franco's forces. Many dreamed of a return to Spain.

Throughout much of the film, Manuel Artiguez appears to be motivated primarily by impulses of revenge, nostalgia, and machismo. It is difficult to recognize in him the (dormant) passion of a former resistance fighter. Paradoxically, it falls to a figure of the duplicitous Church, and a man of a particularly timid appearance, to inspire this protagonist. Although Father Francisco feels inner conflicts in leaving the security of his group to seek out Artiguez, he recognizes what he perceives to be a higher duty—a request made to a priest on a deathbed. He also recognizes a second duty, one implied in Pilar's question, "Whose laws must you priests follow—God's laws or Viñolas's?" In his performance, Omar Sharif leaves open the possibility that Father Francisco might also grow to feel an awakening of sympathy for the Resistance cause.

In one telling conversation between Artiguez and Father Francisco, the rugged profile of the former Resistance fighter appears stronger in the low-key lighting of dawn. Artiguez rather glibly assures the young priest that it could not have been the Republican side who killed his father in the village of Lorca both men knew so well. For a moment, we catch a glimpse of the committed fighter of twenty years earlier. The priest has the final response, however: "What does it matter which side killed him?" This secondary character becomes not only the wiser one but also the one more in touch with underlying realities.

An examination of several other Zinnemann films reveals this same pattern of a seemingly weaker character inspiring the more headstrong protagonist. In *The Men* (1950), for example, Ellie (Teresa Wright) insists on staying with Bud (Marlon Brando), her fiancé, despite the injury which has left him a paraplegic. Only through her faith and persistence, and the no-nonsense care of Dr. Brock (Everett Sloane), does the fiery protagonist begin to regain a sense of proportion in his life.

In *The Member of the Wedding* (1952) the focus is on the struggles of the twelve-year-old tomboy, Frankie (Julie Harris), but it is Berenice (Ethel Waters), the black housemaid of the family, who offers guidance to the troubled child. In an odd trilogy, with little John Henry (Brandon de

Wilde), these three occupy a space in which caring, anger, and growth are inextricably intertwined. Without Berenice's intervention in a host of situations, Frankie would be lost. This motherless child relies on the generosity of the surrogate mother's spirit even as she rebels against it. In an uncharacteristically pessimistic Zinnemann ending, the film concludes with Frankie flippantly leaving the distraught Berenice and running off with a new-found friend.

Another example of this pattern of a secondary character assisting the protagonist can be found in the Lillian Hellman character in *Julia*, played by Jane Fonda. Lillian decides to conquer her timidity and assume the dangerous task of carrying funds to her friend Julia (Vanessa Redgrave) to assist her in her Resistance efforts during the early 1930s. Wearing an oddly shaped hat full of the hidden funds, Lillian endures nerveracking hours on a train, unsure of whether the people around her are friend or foe. The meeting between Lillian and a crippled Julia in a Berlin cafe, in which Julia sternly informs her friend not to succumb to sentimentality, is one of the most remarkable meetings between a Zinnemann protagonist and secondary character. While the iron-willed Julia might seem beyond the need of assistance from others, her actual situation is more vulnerable than that of the tremulous Lillian herself.

In *Behold a Pale Horse*, the young boy Paco, like Father Francisco, is another secondary character who plays a crucial role in revitalizing the weary resistance fighter. At first he goads Artiguez to return to Spain, but when he suspects a trap, he puts aside his own desire for revenge and wisely urges the resistance fighter not to go. This pattern of a member of the younger generation goading someone older to do his or her duty is not a new theme in the Zinnemann ouevre. One of the roles of Margaret (Susannah York), Sir Thomas More's daughter in *A Man for All Seasons*, is to help her father stay on the narrow path. In *High Noon* it is ultimately the marshal's young Quaker bride (Grace Kelly) who saves not only his life but his sense of purpose. This relationship between the moral lessons of a younger person and the response of the older protagonist is not, however, a one-way relationship. The younger characters need the older ones as the more powerful manifestations of their own passions. As Manuel Artiguez is gunned down in the hospital by the Guardia Civíl, he has a vision of Paco catching the soccer ball he had earlier given the boy, thus effectively merging child and man.

In actuality, the list of secondary characters in Zinnemann films who offer essential guidance to aid the protagonist is even longer. In *High*

Noon, the marshal's ex-mistress (Katy Jurado) overcomes the vestiges of jealousy and regret to instruct his new wife in how to be a caring partner for such a man. In *A Man for All Seasons*, More's seemingly befuddled wife (Wendy Hiller) comes around as the increasingly troubled protagonist's inner support. In the same way, the irascible Dr. Fortunati (Peter Finch) in *The Nun's Story* (1959) appears to be an obstacle but actually serves as the necessary impetus to push the awakening consciousness of Sister Luke (Audrey Hepburn) toward a greater sense of autonomy. As in the case of Father Francisco, an unlikely ally, even a teacher, can be found for the hero or heroine in these more minor roles.

SETTING AND HEROIC STATURE

At the time *Behold a Pale Horse* was being shot, Franco refused to allow Zinnemann to film in Spain. Production designer Alexander Trauner constructed an elaborate set in the Studio St. Maurice in Vincennes to replicate the Madrid street on which the hospital would be located. Most of the exterior shots were taken around Pau, Lourdes, and Gotein, on the French side of the Basque region. In the scene of the visit of the Spanish priests to Lourdes, the director inserted footage of actual worshipers (taken before the making of the feature film).

In general, however, the sets in *Behold a Pale Horse* add little to our understanding of the characters or of the action. The hospital could be anywhere; Artiguez's poor, cramped room in Pau could be in any small European town. This lack of geographical specificity is echoed in the cast, who hailed from the United States, Italy, France, Egypt, and England. As William Johnson notes in his *Film Quarterly* review: "In Pau, Zinnemann avoids the pitfall of easy picturesqueness, showing us neither stunning views nor decorative dilapidation" (47).

Only the mountains over which Paco descends, and later Artiguez ascends, hint at the force of that particular topography. As the messengers, informers, and resistance fighters cross over the Pyrenees into Spain, the breathtaking peaks dwarf the men. These mountains, covered with snow throughout the year, remind us of the height of hope and defeat in this civil war in which the first bombings of civilians were felt around the world.

While growing up in Austria, Zinnemann developed a love of mountains, and he recalled how legend relates that the Breche de Roland

FIGURE 10.1. BEHOLD A PALE HORSE (Columbia Pictures, 1964). Crossing the Pyrenees. (Courtesy Museum of Modern Art/Film Stills Archive)

in the Pyrenees (which Artiguez crosses) is the area where the medieval hero Roland was said to have cleft the rock in two with his sword. Mountains also become a major character in the last Zinnemann film, *Five Days One Summer* (1982), set in the Swiss Alps. The series of ascents and descents punctuating the stark mise en scène of *Behold a Pale Horse* alternates with a sense of claustrophobia and stagnation, as in the close-framing of the Pau apartment. The 8,000–foot-high Pyrenees, in contrast, offer a sense of possibility, exaltation, and challenge.

In his autobiography, Zinnemann writes: "In some pictures, as in *The Men*, the exteriors are, by design, only a background. In others, such as *The Search* or *Teresa*, the location is an actor, a dramatically active ingredient in itself" (90). Other settings in Zinnemann films that achieve center stage include the towering ceilings of the convent of La Byloke in Ghent, Belgium where the novices in *The Nun's Story* are trained, the Hawaiian beach near Diamond Head in *From Here to Eternity* (1953) where the famous love-making scene takes place, the courtroom for Sir Thomas More's final trial in *A Man for All Seasons*, and the steamy, timeless kitchen of Frankie's home in *The Member of the Wedding*. As in the alternation of sweeping vistas and confined interiors seen in *Behold a Pale Horse*, the towering ceiling of the cathedral in *The Nun's Story*, and the multileveled courtroom in *A Man for All Seasons*, place the protagonists both as the powerful center of the composition and as the trapped victim.

THE SPANISH CIVIL WAR: HOLLYWOOD AND EUROPEAN CINEMA

In the opening documentary montage sequence of *Behold a Pale Horse*, the narrator proclaims: "The whole world found itself involved in this struggle. The whole world looked toward Spain." Although this has an attractive dramatic ring to it, it is not entirely true. By glossing over the political complexities of the Spanish Civil War, Zinnemann fails to fully establish the kind of background setting that would make his characters more comprehensible. Although it would be impossible here to discuss all films with a Spanish Civil War theme, a look at some of the most representative cinematic treatments by American and European films helps us gain perspective on Zinnemann's efforts in *Behold a Pale Horse*. In terms of the cinema, the Spanish Civil War was particularly notable as the first European war that occurred in the sound-film era, and at a time when the movie camera was becoming increasingly portable.

In his hopes to draw in a large audience for *Behold a Pale Horse*, Zinnemann had counted on the fact that the Spanish Civil War had been "a dress rehearsal" for World War II. Unfortunately, earlier films, like the Paramount production of *For Whom the Bell Tolls*, directed by Sam Wood and released in 1943, had already "defined" that historical period for the majority of the filmviewing audience. Three years of prerelease publicity for Wood's three-hour film had its effect—even the Franco government had tried to influence the outcome of the film! In addition, the novel by Ernest Hemingway, published in 1940, was already extremely popular by the time the film was released.

Wood's film focuses on the life of a group of rebels in the La Granja mountains of the Spain of 1937, with the interweaving of a love story between an American instructor of Spanish, Robert Jordan (Gary Cooper) and a young Spanish woman, María (Ingrid Bergman). Jordan, a volunteer to aid the Republican side, encounters the rebels, including Pilar (played by the Greek actress Katina Paxinou), Pablo (Akim Tamiroff), the lazy and unreliable husband of Pilar, and El Sordo (Joseph Calleia), the guerilla chieftain. In contrast to the sense of languor that initially marks the aging Artiguez in *Behold a Pale Horse*, a sense of immediacy fills the relatively sparse dialogue of Dudley Nichols's scenario for *For Whom the Bell Tolls*. Time is short, supplies are short, the enemy is gaining power. The production design by William Cameron Menzies offers a contrast of splendid mountain peaks with tighter shots within the rebels' cave. The love scenes, which take place in the open, have a timeless sense about them.

Two earlier films on the Spanish Civil War were the 1937 Paramount production *The Last Train from Madrid* and the Walter Wanger production *Blockade* (1938), starring Henry Fonda and Madeleine Carroll. The release of the latter film was met by protests from political interest groups from both the right (the Knights of Columbus, Catholic organizations) and the left, despite the fact that the producer called the film "nonpartisan" and disavowed anything but its entertainment value. As in *Behold a Pale Horse*, this apparent reluctance of the filmmakers to speak directly to an American audience about the full horrors of the civil war weakens the overall effect of the film. With contributions by composer Kurt Weill and other émigré artists, *Blockade* was set in an unnamed country, easily recognizable as Spain. By the end of the film, Marcos (Fonda) addresses the audience directly in a thinly veiled appeal to end the quasi blockade of the Republican efforts.

In European cinema, a prominent interpretation of the Spanish Civil War was that of French novelist and Spanish Civil War veteran André Malraux, who helped make a film based on the last section of his novel *L'Espoir* (*Man's Hope*, published in 1937).[2] Novel and film deal with both a successful raid by pilots in a Republican air squadron and the death of an Italian pilot in the group during one of the raids. Made under difficult conditions between mid-1938 and the beginning of 1939, the film of *L'Espoir* was completed just one day before Franco's troops entered Barcelona. The start of World War II delayed the first public screening until 1945.

Joris Ivens's documentary *The Spanish Earth* (1937), with a screenplay by John Dos Passos and Ernest Hemingway, and music by Marc Blitzstein and Virgil Thomson, was commissioned by writers like Archibald MacLeish, Lillian Hellman, and Dorothy Parker to raise funds for ambulances for the Spanish resistance forces. The film ends on a note of invitation to life, work, and hope, as the international brigades struggle to keep open the routes of supplies to the capital. The sense of immediacy of films like *The Spanish Earth* and *L'Espoir* contrasts with the distanced contemplation of the event in *Behold a Pale Horse*—a distance brought on not only by the temporal and geographical distance but also by the sense of abstractness in which the later film was conceived.

As in *Behold A Pale Horse*, a depiction of postwar malaise enters into *La Guerre Est Finie* (*The War is Over*, 1966) by French director Alain Resnais (with a screenplay by Spanish writer Jorge Semprun). In the film, an aging Spanish resistance fighter exiled in Paris, Diego Mora (Yves Montand), dejectedly recalls the effects of twenty-five years of fighting against Franco. In an earlier short documentary film entitled *Guernica* (1950), Resnais presents a skillful montage of the painting by Picasso with a reading of the poetical text by Paul Eluard (narrated by Maria Casarès) to evoke what he called "a hymn to innocence and peace."[3]

In the documentary genre, *The Good Fight* (1983), directed by Noel Buchner, Mary Dore, and Sam Sills and narrated by Studs Terkel, presents an in-depth reconstruction of the history of one of the international brigades who fought in the Spanish Civil War, the Abraham Lincoln Brigade. This film offers a tribute to the people who risked loss of citizenship and life to join a fight in a foreign land for a cause that most of them felt transcended national boundaries. The Brigade's fifty-year reunion was the impetus for another documentary, *Forever Activists! Abra-*

ham Lincoln Brigade Veterans by Judy Montell (USA, 1991).

More recently, in Ken Loach's *Land and Freedom* (1995), a Communist from Liverpool, David (Ian Hart), joins the Republican forces and experiences first hand the exhilaration and political treachery of the war. Structured through a flashback format, the film ends on a note of disillusionment as David realizes how the Stalinists have betrayed the antifascist forces.

When *Behold a Pale Horse* is viewed along with these other cinematic representations from Hollywood and European cinema, its relative strengths, individual style of expression, and sense of ambiguity become clearer. Even more telling as contrasts, however, is the representation of the war in the Spanish cinema itself.

SPANISH CINEMA'S INTERPRETATION

In the Viñolas character, Zinnemann, following Pressburger's lead, indulges in stereotypic images of Spain—castanets on the soundtrack, an amateur bullfight, the strong male figure on a white horse. Anthony Quinn plays him with an appropriate amount of egoism, "machismo," deceit, and faint flickers of self-doubt. His character reinforces the smug way the Francoist forces attempted (and in many cases succeeded) in manipulating the Church to their own purposes.

Zinnemann's approach to this post–Civil War tale can thus be seen as a mixture of the clearly drawn, the stereotypic, the noble, and the ambiguous. By examining the attempts by Spanish directors to present a "moral center" to the war and its aftermath, the relative merits of *Behold a Pale Horse* become more evident.

Until Franco's death in 1975, there were few references to the Spanish Civil War in the Spanish cinema. Propaganda during Franco's regime tended to show the enemy as unwelcome aliens, representing foreign intervention in an internal Spanish matter.[4] After Franco's death, Communists regained full civil rights, and film censorship was officially abolished in December 1977. From the seventies, a reexamination of Spanish society through the lens of its cinema began to take place, at first through the veil of highly obscure narratives.

An emblematic image of this reexamination occurs in Saura's *La prima Angélica* (*Cousin Angelica*, 1973), with its image of a Falangist with a broken arm in a cast, locked in a fascist-style salute. Saura's earlier film,

El Jardín de las delicías (*Garden of Delights*, 1970), the first to explicitly mention the Spanish Civil War, offers a cryptic view of a man, Antonio Cano, who is left with brain damage after an automobile accident, like a nation whose memory has been eradicated by the war. Antonio's attempts to recover his memory must begin with reenactments of the Spanish Civil War (complete with newsreels and mock attacks) and continue up to (often surrealistic) confrontations with problems of contemporary Spain. Antonio's loss of memory leaves him in a childlike state, seemingly unable to make, or recover, the transition to adulthood. In the same way, his family is locked in memories of what might have been, and is unable to face dramatically altered present realities. As Katherine S. Kovács writes:

> Implicit in the structure and themes of *The Garden of Delights* is the notion of the family's illness as representative of the malady afflicting Spain after 30 years of Franco. They will not recuperate until, like Antonio, they begin to reconstruct an authentic past, not on the basis of what they are told or shown, not on the basis of newsreel footage, public ceremonies, or photographs, but by means of the workings of the inner psyche . . . thereby releasing them from the hold of ideology, discourse, and representation. (51)

Haunting images from Victor Erice's *El Espiritú de la Colmena* (*Spirit of the Beehive*, 1973), set in the Castille of the 1940s, present a picture of Spanish adults, alienated from the Franco regime, who live in an inward-looking world without communication with each other or with the society at large. A small child, Ana, serves as a link between the oppressive silence of the adult world, the hope of a friend embodied in a wounded resistance fighter, and the fantasies of a new generation. Ana's father, ensconced in his white beekeeper's garb like an alien from another universe, bears a spiritual resemblance to Artiguez in *Behold a Pale Horse*, in that both men have become shadows of their true selves under the shadow of a harsh political regime.

The documentary mode has proved particularly powerful for the Spanish presentation of this theme. *Canciones para después de una Guerra* (literally, "Songs for after a War," 1971) by Basilio Martín Patino contrasts the images presented in official postwar documents with the songs that were popular during that period. Completed between 1968 and 1971, the film was not shown publically until 1976 because of the condemnation of Spanish censors. Catalán director Jaime Camino's *La Vieja*

Memoria (*Old Memory*, 1977), a three-hour documentary on the individual and collective memory of the Spanish people concerning the war, mixes fictional devices with face-to-face interviews in a way that involves the audience in a search for truth about the Civil War. In defense of this docu-drama approach, Camino stated: "Memory is not history but is subjective recall" (quoted in Kinder 37).

A more recent Spanish feature film, *Libertarias* (*Libertarians*, 1995), directed by Vicente Aranda, takes as its subject matter a brigade from the Mujeres Libres (Free Women) movement in 1936, in the front in Aragón. It is one of the few films about the crucial role women played during this historical period. Focusing on six women in the brigade (including trained soldiers, a nun, and prostitutes), it presents a group of women who declare that they would rather "die on their feet like men than live on their knees as servants."

As the above description implies, *Libertarias* partakes of ideological shades of black and white with few greys. The Republicans are depicted as models of courage and idealism; the enemies are shown as the basest types. Nevertheless, this focus on women who declare they are "equivalent, not equal" ("las mujeres somos equivalents, no iguales") offers a view of the Spanish Civil War that adds one more dimension to the recreations, and acts of recovery, of this historical period.

As Leger Grindon notes in his *Shadows on the Past: Studies in the Historical Fiction Film*, films about the past are often ways of trying to deal with the present. He specifically mentions *High Noon*, as an example of this principle, with its theme of an individual deserted by his friends in the face of adversity. (*High Noon* appeared at the time of the McCarthy hearings.)[5] In addition, Grindon notes that historical films can serve as an escape into nostalgia, an appeal to authority and truth, or as a search for origins. On one level, the history of the cinema is the history of the twentieth century itself, and so this close marriage between history and its cinematic presentation is a natural, if often troubled, one.

CONCLUSION

At the close of *Behold a Pale Horse*, a wounded and dazed Viñolas limps out to the street by the Madrid hospital, as members of the Guardia Civíl rush up to congratulate him on the killing of Artiguez. Perplexed, he asks under his breath to one of his officers: "Why did Manuel Artiguez come

FIGURE 10.2. BEHOLD A PALE HORSE (Columbia Pictures, 1964). Artiguez (Gregory Peck) taunts Father Francisco (Omar Sharif). (Courtesy Larry Edmunds Bookshop, Inc.)

back?" As if in response, the director presents a shot of the body of the former resistance fighter lined up next to that of his deceased mother. The film ends with a high-angle shot of everyday Spanish citizens (not extras, but a real crowd on a Spanish street), moving around a car in which the body of Artiguez is being carried away. The survivor, Father Francisco, gazes from the window, quietly mouthing what seems to be a prayer. As in the opening of the film, documentary impeccably merges with fiction.

Viñolas's confusion over Artiguez's motives can be seen as an echo of Artiguez's own confusion in an earlier scene about the nature of Father Francisco's motives in risking his religious career, and even his life, to help the worn-out fighter. He doubts the priest; he taunts him (at one point dangling a woman's nylon stocking in his face); he even hits him. Unlike Viñolas, however, Artiguez is able to recognize that there are moral challenges that the good man cannot avoid. In this sense, the tender-hearted priest assumes the moral center of the film, even as he is overshadowed by the more vociferous hero.

The Spanish title of the film, *Llega el día de la vergüenza*, could be translated as "the day of shame arrives." This is the shame of the resistance fighter, of the commander of the Guardia Civil, of the priest, of the Spanish people themselves. Through *Behold a Pale Horse* and the other films discussed above, we can begin to visualize more clearly the reality of the Spanish Civil War and the subsequent memories of that catastrophic event. However, like any tumultuous historical period, it can ultimately be represented only in part.

In *Cinematic Uses of the Past* Marcia Landy writes of historical representations as "a pastiche of conceptions about the world" rather than as a presentation of dominant cultural ideas and values, as they might seem" (1). It is in this sense of a pastiche that *Behold a Pale Horse* can be viewed as not only a contribution to the growing list of films that help us to understand the Spanish Civil War and its aftermath but also as an interesting variant in the Zinnemann oeuvre.

NOTES

1. See *The Spanish Civil War in Literature, Film, and Art: An International Bibliography of Secondary Literature* (Westport, Conn.: Greenwood Press, 1994).

2. The film, with score by Darius Milhaud, is also known as *Sierra de Teruel.*

3. Cited in notes for "For Whom the Bell Tolls: Reverberations from the Spanish Civil War" film exhibition, Film Society of Lincoln Center (April 25–May 3, 1996), p. 15.

4. In terms of pro-Nationalist works in Spanish cinema, most attention has been paid to *Raza* (Race, 1941), the only film scripted by Franco himself under the pen name "Jaime de Andrade." This semiautobiographical film was directed by José Luis Saénz de Heredía, a cousin of the founder of the Falange. In *Raza*, the handsome and courageous heroes are contrasted with the villains who are represented as a mixture of communists, politicians, and criminals.

5. Other films discussed by Grindon in this context include: Eisenstein's *Alexander Nevsky* (1938), made at the time of Hitler, in which Nevsky battles Teutonic Knights; Laurence Olivier's *Henry V* (1945), whose presentation of the victory at Agincourt mirrors the time of the Normandy landing; and Spike Lee's *Malcolm X* (1992), which links a depiction of post–World War II race relations with an examination of the current racial situation in this country.

WORKS CITED

"For Whom the Bell Tolls: Reverberations from the Spanish Civil War" film exhibition, Film Society of Lincoln Center (April 25–May 3, 1996): 11–15.

Gow, Gordon. "Individualism Against Machinery: Fred Zinnemann in an Interview with Gordon Gow." *Films and Filming* 24.5 (February 1978): 12–17.

Grindon, Leger. *Shadows on the Past: Studies in the Historical Fiction Film.* Philadelphia: Temple University Press, 1994.

Hüppauf, Bernd. "Modernism and the Photographic Representation of War and Destruction." *Fields of Vision: Essays in Film Studies, Visual Anthropology, and Photography.* Ed. Leslie Devereaux and Roger Hillman. Berkeley: University of California Press, 1995: 94–124.

Johnson, William. "*Behold a Pale Horse.*" *Film Quarterly* 18.2 (Winter 1964): 46–50.

Kinder, Marsha. *Spanish Cinema: The Politics of Family and Gender.* Los Angeles: The Spanish Ministry of Culture and USC School of Cinema-Televison, 1989. A catalogue for a film series that was organized by Katherine S. Kovács and Marsha Kinder.

Kovács, Katherine S. "Loss and Recuperation in *The Garden of Delights.*" *Cine-Tracts* 4.2–3 (Summer–Fall 1981): 45–54.

Landy, Marcia. *Cinematic Uses of the Past.* Minneapolis: University of Minnesota Press, 1996.

Monteath, Peter. *The Spanish Civil War in Literature, Film, and Art: An International Bibliography of Secondary Literature.* Westport, Conn.: Greenwood Press, 1994.

Zinnemann, Fred. *A Life in the Movies: An Autobiography.* New York: Scribner's, 1992.

CHAPTER ELEVEN

◫

Fred Zinnemann, A Man for All Seasons *(1966),* and Documentary Fiction

JOEL N. SUPER

While *A Man for All Seasons* (1966) was, from the start, a studio film, in significant ways it was produced as an independent film. Financed by Columbia Pictures, the film was made in England, far from Columbia's corporate headquarters. Because the decision makers at Columbia apparently found it hard to believe that they could sell restraint, craftsmanship, and serious historical subject matter to film audiences in 1966 (especially with no American stars), the budget was very limited.[1] From Zinnemann's perspective, their ignorance and the resulting low budget were positive factors because they kept the front office out of the way during production, allowing him the freedom he preferred. Before they wrote off the possibility of a successful film, however, "the boys in the front office" might have considered why the stage version of *A Man for All Seasons* had been so popular and remembered that Zinnemann had a history of choosing successful projects. Like many of Zinnemann's films, *A Man for All Seasons* filled a void in the film market and drew on his documentary fiction technique. Moreover, it demonstrates his recurring interest in filming stories generated by political upheaval and reflects in interesting ways the documentary aesthetic he developed early in his career in films like

The Wave (1934), *The Search* (1948), *The Men* (1950), and *Teresa* (1951).

Various writers practicing a reductive sort of auteurist analysis have tried to define Zinnemann's major concern and recurring theme as the solitary individual of integrity against the corrupt and cowardly world. Zinnemann himself has supported this focus by agreeing that this theme does, in fact, attract him. *A Man for All Seasons, High Noon*, and *From Here to Eternity* are often cited as paradigms of this recurring theme, and other, less well-known films like *The Nun's Story* and *Behold A Pale Horse* can be used to illustrate it as well. Certainly, a film where the central character is a martyr lends itself to the interpretation that Zinnemann's preferred theme is one of individual conscience. But this view doesn't illuminate the critical and popular success of *Man for All Seasons* as well as it might.

Winner of the New York Critics Circle Award, the Screen Directors' Guild Award, and Academy Awards for best actor, director, picture, screenplay, cinematography, and costumes, *A Man for All Seasons* possesses the broad audience appeal and critical approbation Zinnemann had successfully achieved numerous times before. His previous films must have demonstrated to him the excellent results possible when he chose distinctive and serious subjects that interested him. Zinnemann never explicitly stated that he aimed for one particular market when he began a film, probably because he did not. Certainly, one wouldn't think of *From Here to Eternity* and *The Nun's Story* as part of an oeuvre aimed at the same market segment. And yet, in a sense they were: they were (consciously or unconsciously) aimed at the *whole* market. That is to say, Zinnemann sought an audience that spanned generations and market niches; the success of many of his films demonstrates that his respect for the audience and interest in the subject brought in a wide audience. We see this respect throughout his career in his refusal to indulge in gimmicks or pander to the audience, his avoidance of genre films, and in his consistent choice of projects that demonstrate a profound respect for the dignity of persons. Even when he worked from studio-mandated scripts, his films never indulged in formulas, cheap eroticism, or easy stereotypes. For him, this working method was a personally congenial and demonstrably successful one. He followed it again in choosing to direct *A Man For All Seasons*.

Zinnemann's source for *A Man for All Seasons* was, like many of his films, an adaptation. (He nearly always worked from adaptations, whether drawn from novels or plays.) While similar to *The Member of the Wedding, A Hatful of Rain*, and *Oklahoma!* because of its theatrical origins, *A Man for All Seasons* differs markedly from lesser-known films like *The Wave*, which had "a script of sorts" (Zinnemann 31), and *Teresa*, *The Search*, and *The Men*, which were produced from original scripts. Those films, which I call his documentary fictions, are explorations in fictional narrative heavily influenced by the documentary impulse. Often, the documentary fictions like *The Search* incorporated or drew on actual events and experiences the director and crew encountered during preproduction. This involvement with developing the source material was important to Zinnemann's artistic development and has its influences in *A Man for All Seasons*, which he also produced—hence he oversaw all major artistic facets of the production.[2] In this chapter we will examine the relationship between *A Man for All Seasons* and these documentary fictions, focusing on the impact that political actions or events have on the protagonists, the archetypal ordinariness of the protagonists, the role of location shooting, the formal patterning and dispassionate style, and the use of nonactors and "unknown" actors.

By the time he made *A Man for All Seasons*, Zinnemann had long since concentrated on adaptations, perhaps because they were more commercially successful than the documentary fictions. Bearing in mind the terrible quality of most film adaptations, Zinnemann's are remarkable in their sensitivity, quality, and success. *A Man for All Seasons* was no exception.

The success of Robert Bolt's play in London and on Broadway had demonstrated that contemporary critics and audiences were receptive to both the subject—the dramatization of Thomas More's life—and its intimate treatment.[3] Robert Bolt himself seemed to be a bit mystified at the appeal of the subject when, in a letter, he noted that "the play has been commercially successful in a bewildering variety of countries" (*Sight and Sound* Dossier 20). The film version proved equally successful with an even wider audience and with film critics; it was generally highly praised, several writers even asserting that the film was better than the play.[4] At first, this popularity might seem strange, given the subject matter, but several explanations offer themselves. For one thing, many viewers seem to have felt a sense of relief at the chance to take a break from the relentless innovation for the sake of innovation that they perceived in contemporary films. *Saturday Review*'s Hollis Alpert wrote, "It must be said that the film bows not at all to current cinematic fashions: no Godardian nonsense, no Fellini-like flashes of brilliance; but a film of modest refinement" (58). *Time* commented that "Seldom in these days of coast-to-coast screens and retina-wrecking color is a play so tastefully transformed into a film" (119). Judith Crist also suggested her pleasure in a film that resisted "panoply and spectacle," relying instead on discipline, precision, and concision (205). And in an "impoverished" cinematic season, John Simon considered the film "a godsend," largely for the pleasure of watching Paul Scofield's performance in close-up (262). If one's aesthetic predilections run to "bad boy" originality, an improvisational approach, or a preference for the epic, these observations could be read as damning with faint praise. But we could also read them as a justifiable audience preference for character exploration and an engagement with issues over the vaunted pleasures of vapid "spectacle." At any rate, budget constraints would not have permitted Zinnemann to make a spectacle out of the film even if he had wanted to, and in adroitly translating the play's intimate tone to the screen he was working in his usual disciplined manner. The scale of *Oklahoma!* and *The Nun's Story* demonstrate that he could successfully paint on a giant canvas; the intimate scale of scenes like the king's wedding reception and More's glimpse of dancing courtiers as he passes a door in Hampton Court palace demonstrate that the director was an accomplished miniaturist as well.

The second reason for the film's great success may be gauged from the *Saturday Review*'s comment that "the film . . . rings with words of more intellectual and psychological excitement than are normally common in movies" (Alpert 58) and *The Film Daily*'s observation that "Naturally cultivated patrons can get more out of it than the patron of lesser taste" (Herbstman 4). Ignoring the condescension of the latter remark, these comments reflect the general assessment that the acting and direction were the most significant achievements of a vehicle that many feared was too dialogue-heavy to be successful as a film. *Time* magazine concluded that "the actors are borne lightly on the lucid stream of language that flows throughout the film" (119). The dramatist/screenwriter's treatment of the subject matter made all the difference. Like Shaw in *Saint Joan*, Bolt managed in *A Man for All Seasons* to treat a saint in a secular way. He focused on the power issues raised by a nonconformist, and did not indulge in dramatic hagiography or religious biography. Like *Saint Joan*, *A Man for All Seasons*, in both its dramatic and cinematic versions, does not set out to explore or critique the protagonist's religious convictions. Instead, the film accepts these convictions as the necessary starting point of the conflict in a society with a state church, dramatizing the personal consequences of the resulting political machinations. Box office results proved that, despite what the businessmen may have thought, the dramatization and exploration of this conflict interested a large audience.

A Man for All Seasons shares with Zinnemann's documentary fictions the desire to explore how the protagonists are affected by political actions or events beyond their control. In each of these films, the feature film's extreme time limitations obliged the writer and the director to investigate the political and the ideological by localizing the conflict around an individual. *The Wave*, for instance, concentrates on Miro, a poor Mexican fisherman whose experience with exploitative middlemen radicalizes him into a labor organizer. Zinnemann's comment that Paul Strand, producer of *The Wave* was "the most doctrinaire Marxist I had ever met," suggests that Zinnemann himself had little sympathy for Marxism, but this film does not make *his* politics the issue (Weaver 199). As in most of his films, Zinnemann concentrates instead on character and an artful interpretation of the material. He focuses on the consequences of Mexico's brutal social and economic organization for the Mexican fishermen and their families: powerlessness and poverty, leading to death. The film's opening scenes dramatize this general situation. Since the poor fisherman, Miro, cannot get a salary advance from his employer to pay a doctor to treat his son, the child dies. The carefully filmed funeral underlines the point, with dignity and restraint.

This focus on how the political affects the personal is just as clear in *The Search*, *The Men*, and *Teresa*. In *The Search* the Nazi takeover of Czechoslovakia has separated a little boy, Karel, from his family, and he becomes one of many displaced children wandering about Europe after the war. In *The Men* Bud Wilochek suffers through the trauma of paraplegia incurred by a war injury. In *Teresa* Philip Cass tries to extricate himself from a debilitating dependency on his mother while he and his war bride Teresa struggle to make their marriage work. The suffocating atmosphere of his family's apartment intensifies the struggle.

In varying degrees, these three postwar films explore the intersection of the political becoming personal, just as *Behold a Pale Horse* and *Julia* do much later. They do not openly deal with the actual mechanics of the political in the way that *The Wave* and *A Man for All Seasons* do, but the wrenching political dislocations and uncertainties of World War II are the primary source of the protagonists' problems in all three films. Without his war injury, Bud's life and desires would be unremarkable. It is the war that gets the indecisive and dependent Phil away from his mother long enough for him to meet and marry Teresa. After this, the rampant unem-

162

FIGURE 11.1. THE WAVE (Dept. of Fine Arts, Federal Government of Mexico, 1935). The fishermen of Alvarado. (Courtesy Museum of Modern Art/Film Stills Archive)

ployment that demobilization helps produce thwarts his chances of break-
ing from his dependence and thus serves the narrative's essential causal
function. Zinnemann underlines the fact by opening the film in the
Unemployment Office. In the most extreme case, Karel and the other
children in *The Search* are victims of hideous political persecution and
lose everything they have ever had: family, home, nation. These early
films indicate a recurring interest in Zinnemann's work, for throughout
his career Zinnemann returned to films where political events have caused
a problem and then form a backdrop to the action. The overtness of the
political discussion or dramatization of the machinery shifts and changes,
but it is there in at least nine of his films, most clearly in the documentary fictions and *A Man for All Seasons*. Zinnemann is not generally
thought of as a director interested in politics. And he is not interested in
politics per se. But more than other social realists like Huston, Kazan,
Wyler, or Kramer, he seems to gravitate to films with plots generated by
political upheavals and events.

In this context, Zinnemann's willingness to produce a version of
Bolt's "politico-theological" play for the screen seems more than just the
opportunity to work on an interesting project. Like Brecht, who focused
the conflict around Galileo in order to dramatize the power struggle
resulting when new scientific knowledge was seen to challenge traditional
Christian understandings of the universe, Bolt isolates a crucial moment
in European politics—Henry VIII's split with the Roman Catholic
Church. The drama comes from More's response to this political situation, a narrative strategy Zinnemann had previously found highly effective. This is a film about the man who wrote *Utopia*, knew Erasmus and
Holbein, and had had a long and interesting career as a scholar, lawyer,
and private man before he became Henry VIII's Lord Chancellor, but
Bolt focuses on the political by concentrating on More's rise and fall in
politics rather than more broadly on his life. In doing so, he dramatizes
one of *the* political questions of the age. As Richard Marius, a More specialist, makes clear, the critical problem of the Reformation for most
Europeans was the political question, "What is the relationship of the
national state to the universal Christian community?" (936). More's
refusal to aid the king in obtaining a divorce and his subsequent martyrdom dramatize one man's answer to that question. Both the play and the
film also dramatize a more local issue: freedom of speech. As Paul Turner
points out in his introduction to More's *Utopia*, today we may easily forget that More's silence in refusing to swear to the Oath of Succession was

a political crime in Tudor England, where no freedom of speech—even freedom of thought—existed. More's refusal to acknowledge publicly the king's new marriage was dangerous precisely because it was a matter of state as much as a matter of private conscience. Because of More's eminence, even after his resignation as chancellor, his "private" views, even when unexpressed, were unavoidably (and dangerously) political because they threatened Henry's attempt to recast the relationship between church and secular power in England.

The politics, however, are more complicated than they may at first look and are necessarily treated at greater length than in Zinnemann's other films. Bolt, Marius claims, skews More's portrayal by grounding his refusal to acquiesce to Henry's plans in a dogmatic assertion of papal authority. Marius argues, instead, that it was not so much More's allegiance to the pope, but his profound fear of anarchy and his lifelong belief in hedging the power of any office with constitutional checks and balances that drove his political thought and this expression of it.[5] Perhaps Marius is thinking here of the scene between the Duke of Norfolk and More where More explains to the Duke that Henry's actions are not benign—they are a declaration of war on the Church. But other scenes focus as much on the law and the presentation of anarchy as on papal authority. More defends the law, for example, when his wife, daughter, and Will Roper demand that he have Richard Rich arrested. Although Rich has done nothing illegal, they say he is dangerous to More and thus More, as Chancellor, should arrest him. A script change from the play and subtle camera work still focus the issues on the law in the scene quoted below. In the film adaptation Bolt has eliminated references to God from the dialogue and thus emphasized More's belief in the law as his only refuge against the despotic powers of the monarchy:

> **Alice:** While you talk, he's gone!
>
> **More:** And go he should, if he was the Devil himself, until he broke the law!
>
> **Roper:** So now you'd give the Devil benefit of law!
>
> **More:** Yes. What would you do? Cut a great road through the law to get after the Devil?
>
> **Roper:** Yes! I'd cut down every law in England to do that!
>
> **More:** Oh? And when the last law was down, and the Devil turned round on you—where would you hide, Roper, the laws all being

flat? This country's planted thick with laws from coast to coast—man's laws, not God's—and if you cut them down—and you're just the man to do it—d'you really think you could stand upright in the winds that would blow then? Yes, I'd give the Devil benefit of law, for my own safety's sake.

Zinnemann underscores the centrality of this belief through a slow, deliberate tracking shot toward More as he delivers it, ending with a medium close-up. A dissolve then justifies More's view that the law remains the only refuge (however imperfect) against intrigue and power: it reveals the perfidious Richard Rich arriving at Thomas Cromwell's inn in the dark to begin informing on More.

Bolt clearly indicates in his preface to the play that he interprets the conflict between the king and More in a political light. It is the clash between Henry, "the monstrous baby whom none dared gainsay . . . an archetype, one of the champions of our baser nature" and "the whole edifice of medieval religion" (vii). This focus remains in the film. Bolt also notes the important fact that Henry's motives for a divorce "are presumably as confused, inaccessible and helpless in a King as any other man" (viii), but that the political imperative to produce a male heir was certainly a major motive in his desire to divorce Catherine of Aragon.[6] Bolt saw Henry's argument that the pope had no real right to appoint bishops as a root of the conflict, the play's "politico-theological background." His primary interest (in both the film and the play) lay in dramatizing the way the participants lived the collisions between abstractions like "theology" and "politics." Even in the parliamentary English monarchy, a substantial element of the personal influenced politics, in the form of the king. The film, drawn so heavily from the play, maintains this dramatization of the political through the personal. Bolt's focus on the concrete in the face of abstraction is bound to have appealed to Zinnemann, whose social realist aesthetic so often led him to concentrate on just such concrete subjects in his films. In his experience the catharsis produced through the dramatization of abstractions had always appealed to the filmgoing public.

Although *A Man for All Seasons* and the documentary fictions share a common interest in political upheavals and their effects, they differ completely in the social status of their protagonists.[7] As many others have noted, Zinnemann's dramas typically deal with ordinary individuals. This is true from characters like George Heisler, Spencer Tracy's character in *The Seventh Cross* (1944) to the sheepherders of *The Sundowners* (1960).

166

FIGURE 11.2. A MAN FOR ALL SEASONS (Columbia Pictures, 1966). Sir Thomas More (Paul Scofield) defends the law to his family (Corin Redgrave, Susannah York, and Wendy Hiller). (Courtesy Collectors Book Store, Hollywood, Calif.)

In particular, all the documentary fictions deal with world events or systems and their impact on characters almost archetypal in their averageness. In *The Men*, for instance, the central characters are an ex-soldier and his fiancée. Bud Wilochek, the paraplegic soldier, played football in college. Ellie, the fiancée, is played by Teresa Wright, an actress whose roles in *Shadow of a Doubt*, *Mrs. Miniver*, and *The Best Years of Our Lives* defined Hollywood's average young woman. He is an orphan; she is the daughter of well-to-do parents. A variety of wounded enlisted men (many of them actual wounded veterans) with their medical, personal, and family problems shade the definition of the "average" experience and weave Bud and Ellie's "averageness" into a fairly complex tapestry of that characteristic. In *The Wave* the central characters are poor fishermen, individualized but typical. In *The Search* the central characters are similarly individualized but typical American soldiers, United Nations Relief and Rehabilitation Administration (UNRRA) workers, and a displaced child; in *Teresa* "average" rests in a veteran, his war bride, and his blue-collar family. Insofar as the documentary fiction films share a concern, they all seem to explore examples of average, everyday people coping with personal disaster or misfortune brought on by impersonal systems or events—Mexico's exploitative economic system or World War II. Each narrative thus creates fictional but representative characters, often using nonactors.

In *A Man for All Seasons*, however, Zinnemann's focus shifts to consider the effects of political events on society's upper strata. In this film he deals with a luminary, a famous and powerful man of his age. Here Zinnemann works with a real person refined into fiction, rather than the fictional but representative characters common to the other films. And unlike the three postwar documentary fictions, where the Veteran's Administration or UNRRA steps in to ameliorate the consequences of political dislocation, no benevolent government bureaucracy mitigates personal suffering here. Instead, the bureaucracy actively conspires to produce the suffering, maneuvering to rid itself of More, an impediment to its goals. This permutation is really typical of Zinnemann and is part of why it can be hard to write about him—he does not pigeonhole easily. Indeed, while Thomas More was not an average person in the way Miro, Bud, Phil, or Karel represent average people, for a rich and powerful man, he was by all accounts simple in his tastes and as humble as such a person can be. And he, too, was left adrift, practically without friends. In these respects, the protagonists of the documentary fictions and the protagonist of *A Man for All Seasons* are flip sides of the same coin.

In a similar way, the use of location shooting in *A Man for All Seasons* is both typical and atypical, when considered beside the earlier documentary fictions. It is atypical in that it is much more bucolic. Scenes on the river or in the empty countryside, in the garden, and along the garden wall all create the sense of an underpopulated world that is moving at a much slower pace than the societies of later films. This is especially true of the long, lingeringly beautiful shots on the river as the credits run and the several scenes where characters travel by boat. To prevent us from forgetting that this beauty was the real setting of a real conflict, Zinnemann includes a carefully composed montage of churches and cathedral towers that both underlines this pastoralism and checks it. By using composition, framing, and juxtaposition, the shots of Salisbury and Wells cathedrals, together with the lonely tower at Glastonbury Tor and a fortified church by the sea, remind us that a power struggle was occurring in this place. Its last shot—close-ups on gargoyles, cutting to a close-up of Anne Boleyn at the window with her new husband—drives the point home. There are, however, no equivalents for the crowded tenement streets, antiseptic and anonymous bureaucratic rooms filled with people, or ruined train stations packed with travelers that characterize the postwar films. Of course, there is a pragmatic explanation for avoiding crowds and cities, as re-creating period settings and costuming hundreds of extras runs up a budget. The outdoor settings did, however, offer Zinnemann some compensation by allowing for the typical accidents of location shooting which help produce the spontaneous feeling and realistic texture he liked to capture. In his autobiography Zinnemann details a few of these accidents, such as the way the wind arose, as if on cue, to punctuate the king's anger during his garden scene with More, an effect similar to the wind whipping Teresa's veil around during the wedding scene in *Teresa*. Zinnemann also notes the hunting-up of essential locations, such as a pristine tidal river to stand in for the sixteenth-century Thames and a suitable period house for More's residence. Given his previous experience choosing locations from what was available and using them to their best advantage (such as the ruins, train station, and river scenes in *The Search*), he found that the low budget for *A Man for All Seasons* merely obliged him to work in a way he had successfully worked before.

A Man for All Seasons also shares with the documentary fictions a tendency to use outdoor settings to emphasize crucial scenes. In the documentary films this preference takes various forms: a Mexican beach,

Nuremberg's ruins, the grounds of the Birmingham Veteran's hospital, or Central Park, among others. In *A Man for All Seasons* and *Teresa* this preference also produces a consistent inside/outside alternation, resulting in a distinct formal patterning. The opening sequence of *A Man for All Seasons*, for instance, begins with shots of the fantastic statuary outside Hampton Court Palace, cuts to inside, where the Cardinal finishes a letter and a messenger runs down a corridor with it and out into a waiting boat. The credits come up over the shots of the river, and when the messenger arrives in Chelsea at Thomas More's manor house, the scene moves back indoors, then out once again as More leaves to make the journey back to Hampton Court. This regular, calculated inside/outside movement creates both visual variety and a sense of immediacy and spontaneity.

The critical scenes with Richard Rich also take place outdoors during and after the sequence described above, where Zinnemann's almost casual staging belies the import of More's dealings with Rich. In the first of the two scenes, More rebuffs Rich's effort to discuss a post, and in the second, when Rich returns, refuses (kindly) to recommend him for a court appointment. Instead, he offers him a teaching post and then gives him a silver cup which a petitioner has tried to use as a bribe. In retrospect, after Rich has perjured himself and thus condemned More to death, we realize that the beautiful shots of the tranquil river that precede the second scene, and the peaceful garden setting in which it happens, provide an ironic contrast to the consequences of More's refusal. This conscious, but subtle use of setting to comment on the action is typical of Zinnemann's documentary fiction work. In *The Search*, for example, our first view of Karel and the other DP children comes as they arrive in a bombed train station.

In *A Man for All Seasons* Zinnemann makes notable use of locations in other scenes as well. When More's daughter Margaret meets him to relay the news that a new act of Parliament about the king's marriage will require an oath, this scene occurs outdoors, in a fierce wind. The film includes a brief new scene of Secretary Cromwell addressing Parliament, highlighting the movement from indoor to outdoor by a dissolve from Cromwell's speech to More walking in the wind. The significant speech of the scene—"If He [God] suffers us to fall to such a case that there is no escaping, then we may stand to our tackle as best we can. . . . Our natural business lies in escaping . . ."—is shot in close-up, with very little depth to the frame. Here Zinnemann drops the ironic contrast of setting and action, and allows the mise en scène to emphasize straightforwardly the terrible gravity of this development. The scene then dissolves again, this time to a barred window, filmed from inside the cell, indicating that More has found no way of taking the oath. These uses of location and their contrasts to comment on or underline the action are quite typical of Zinnemann's documentary fictions, especially *Teresa*, where all of Phil and Teresa's significant encounters occur outdoors, from their first meeting to the scene where she leaves him. Like the documentary fictions, in *A Man for All Seasons* Zinnemann carefully explores the character's life and circumstances; natural or "found" settings play an integral role in furthering that exploration. Zinnemann's documentary fictions do not look the same, but the visual style is always restrained and dispassionate, enabling one to identify each as the work of the same director.

A Man for All Seasons adopts a similarly dispassionate style, creating what movement it can within and between frames, working under a limited budget and with a script that had changed little from a relatively static stage play. One of the changes allows for a brief interval of silence to punctuate the many dialogue scenes and demonstrates Zinnemann's facility at creating subtle frame dynamism through staging. For the film, Bolt eliminated several characters, including Signor Chapuys, the Spanish Ambassador. He replaced the scene where Chapuys and More obliquely discuss the issues around Henry's proposed divorce with one where the bishops assemble to hear the king's demand that they follow Parliament and acknowledge him Supreme Head of the Church in England. Zinnemann stages the brief scene starting with a procession framed straight on in medium close-up; gradually, the procession moves screen right as the camera tracks back. As the camera continues to move, it reveals the enormous convocation space and the procession moving screen right in the foreground and screen left (on an upper level) in the background, at the top of the frame. A cut reframes so that part of the group moves toward the camera, soon filling the foreground with a sea of brown and black cassocks as the end of the procession continues to move screen left in the background. This brief, snaking procession in the huge space produces not only a dynamic frame appropriate to the film's pace, but also an effective graphic contrast to the close, dark scene between Rich and Cromwell that precedes it. Scenes like these manifest Zinnemann's distinct formal interests based on each film's goals, and it is this interest, and the precision with which it is deployed, that defines the Zinnemann aesthetic both in the early documentary fictions and *A Man for All Seasons*.

Unlike the documentary fictions, which take the stories of many real individuals and combine them into representative fictional characters, *A Man for All Seasons,* as we have seen, fictionalizes actual historical characters.[8] Yet in fictionalizing these people, Zinnemann turns to a method he solidified in making his documentary fictions; he casts the film largely with actors essentially unknown to most Americans, the major segment of the target audience. This time, however, Zinnemann casts no nonactors; thus he gives up the verisimilitude and freshness they brought to those films for the polished professionalism of English acting. Like *The Search* and *The Men,* though, the major role does go to an "unknown" of sorts: Paul Scofield had only made three British films prior to this one. He was well known to English theatergoers, and reasonably well known to Broadway audiences for the New York production of the play, but his status with movie audiences was equivalent to Montgomery Clift's in *The Search* or Marlon Brando's in *The Men* when they first worked with Zinnemann, giving the director an actor with the freshness of an "unknown," together with the capacity to deliver challenging dialogue. Supporting characters brought the same qualities to the film. Older audience members may have recognized Wendy Hiller for her work in *Pygmalion* (1938), *Major Barbara* (1941), or *Separate Tables* (1958), and Susannah York might have been familiar to some for her roles in *Freud* (1962) and *Tom Jones* (1963), but they were not stars in any blockbuster sense. This is also true of Robert Shaw, whom audiences might feel "looked familiar" (*From Russia with Love,* 1962) or Leo McKern, who had done many films prior to this one. John Hurt and Corin Redgrave, it's safe to say, were unknown in the States, and little known in the United Kingdom. Orson Welles and Vanessa Redgrave, who had been nominated for an Oscar for *Morgan!* (1966), rounded out the cast and provide the exceptions to the rule. Their parts were important, but their screen time was quite short, so their greater celebrity could add authority to the film without overpowering it.

Aside from the impossibility of hiring stars on his low budget, Zinnemann characteristically preferred talented "unknowns" to stars because he believed stars often distracted the audience and got in the way of the story. Minimizing the distractions caused by star personas or casting slightly against type—as he did by casting Deborah Kerr as the Captain's frosty, promiscuous wife in *From Here to Eternity*—maximized the possibility for actor and director to explore the fictionalized character. In a film like *A Man for All Seasons,* which relies heavily on dialogue and interiority (typical of his work), it is essential to work with fine actors. As Zinne-

172

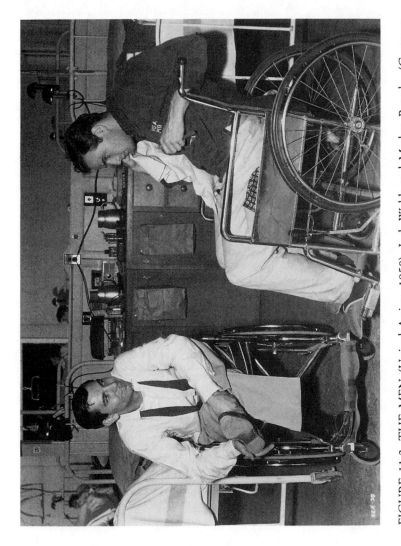

FIGURE 11.3. THE MEN (United Artists, 1950). Jack Webb and Marlon Brando. (Courtesy Museum of Modern Art/Film Stills Archive)

mann has pointed out, Vanessa Redgrave, in a scene lasting forty-five seconds, had to "convince the audience that she [Anne Boleyn] was capable of changing the course of an empire" (206). Redgrave's success in this challenge is one example of how witnessing the performances and listening to Bolt's prose constitute one of the film's great pleasures. It also demonstrates the efficacy of Zinnemann's working method.

Unlike the earlier documentary fictions, *A Man for All Seasons* also presents the challenge of maintaining viewer interest when many audience members already know the plot's outcome. The acting needs to be uniformly strong to carry this off, and it is. Zinnemann's sensitive casting and the cast's ensemble acting, which creates excellent unity and balance, successfully complete the characters' fictionalization. Creating some sense of unity was the challenge of the documentary fictions: to blend or synthesize the highly different acting styles of actors like Jack Webb and Everett Sloane with the Method acting of Marlon Brando and the amateur acting of actual paraplegics like Arthur Jurado. *The Search* and *The Men* manage to carry off the synthesis in part because of the superior talent of Clift and Brando combined with the fact that they were essentially unknown as film actors.[9] On the other hand, *Teresa's* synthesis is not as successful. It is difficult to pinpoint why—is it flawed by John Ericson's relative inexperience and weak ensemble acting, or have the actors done the best they could with a weak script? Zinnemann has ascribed the problem to a "script split in its purpose," incomplete before shooting started, and with too much emphasis on the mother's dominance (90). Granting this, it still seems that although Ericson was unknown to film audiences, his freshness could not compensate for a performance lacking the interiority Brando and Clift brought to their parts or the maturity and finesse Scofield brought to his. In *Teresa*, only Pier Angeli seems to possess both the freshness and the skill needed for her part. The other documentary fictions had managed the challenge of synthesizing actors differing as much in background, experience, and philosophy as those here—Rod Steiger, Ralph Meeker, Peggy Ann Garner, Patricia Collinge, and the amateur Bill Mauldin—but they do not coalesce here. *Teresa*, like the other documentary fictions and *A Man for All Seasons*, has very little "action" of the typical sort to engage a viewer. Without enough compelling performances, the film cannot achieve the emotional intensity the earlier films produce. It nonetheless requires mention here because, like the others, it takes its characters and their weaknesses seriously and treats them with dignity. Since, in their documentary capacity, these fictionalized charac-

174

FIGURE 11.4. TERESA (MGM, 1951). John Ericson and Pier Angeli (Courtesy Collectors Book Store, Hollywood, Calif.)

ters represent actual people and real social problems, the dignity of their treatment extends beyond the filmic world and implies the same attitude toward actual persons.

This always-present sense that the filmmaker has drawn from actual people and circumstances to create an imaginative portrait of the characters' lives and circumstances permeates *The Wave* and the other documentary fictions. Zinnemann's characteristic compassion and respect are based always in the specific, not in the abstract: the fishermen of Alvarado, Mexico, in 1934, the DP children of UNRRA camps in Germany during the winter of 1946–1947, the paralyzed veterans of Birmingham Hospital in 1949. *A Man for All Seasons* cannot, of course, achieve the same sense of the present tense, given its historical subject. But in addition to its treatment and interests, it reveals its kinship to the earlier films through the same strong sense of compassion and respect for the characters, grounded in the specific and individual. These films demonstrate that Zinnemann, far from seeing politics as eliminating the possibility of an individual narrative, sees it as providing both the impetus and the context for such a narrative. In these films, most especially *The Wave* and *A Man for All Seasons*, the personal response is not only possible within a political environment, it is essential.

This continuity across films seems especially appropriate, considering the latter film's major character and what we can glean of his world view from his best-known work. In Book Two of Thomas More's *Utopia*, the author learns about the Utopian's customs and philosophy from the traveler Raphael Nonsenso. Having just returned to Europe from Utopia, this fictive narrator asserts that the Utopians are "blind to the existence of that notorious Universal, M A N . . . a pretty conspicuous figure, bigger than any giant you ever heard of—but though we pointed him out quite clearly, none of them could see him" (90). Richard Marius interprets this Utopian inability to comprehend abstraction as part of the overall adherence to a language that only spoke of persons in their individual concreteness, and further notes that More himself had "a certain repugnance for the abstract," believing that "men learned best . . . by exposure to the specific" (935). Two facts of Utopian life clearly support the notion that More found these issues central. First, the Utopians excel at inventing useful, everyday things. Second, they exempt only a select few promising men and women from work to study full time, expecting the rest of the people to work with their hands and study in their leisure time. The scholarly More's ideal world, where the concrete results of individuals' collective work would take precedence over the intangible results of study and abstraction, suggests a good deal about More's values. This social arrangement does not express contempt for intellectual work, but suggests that without action, such work loses value. More importantly, it suggests that where intellect is valued above all other human qualities, an unjust society will result. Montgomery Clift's character in *The Search* seems to express this same belief in the need for individual action when he suggests that, however difficult and impractical it might be, in adopting Karel he would do more good by "rebuilding a kid's life" than by engineering another bridge. Although *A Man for All Seasons* looks so different from the documentary fiction films, in spirit and approach we see both Zinnemann's diversity and consistency as a film artist. We can hear insistent echoes of the documentary fictions in his focus on the individual, not the universal. More, with his preference for the active, the concrete, and the specific, seems to have been an earlier resident in the intellectual neighborhood Zinnemann still inhabits.

NOTES

1. A letter from Robert Bolt to Bob O'Brien at MGM dated March 1, 1965, speculates that Columbia is lukewarm about the film because it needs a big hit and does not believe *A Man for All Seasons* has hit potential.

2. A letter from Patrick Carey to Zinnemann dated April 25, 1966, supports this view. Carey, the second unit director, responds in great detail to Zinnemann's request that the opening river sequence set the film's tone by discussing the desirability of including birdcalls characteristic of rural sixteenth-century England, trying to avoid shots of "modern forest," which did not exist at the time, and setting out ideas for the way shots should look.

3. Reviews of the play were almost universally positive, even effusive. See Walter Kerr, "A Man for All Seasons," *New York Herald Tribune*, Nov. 23, 1961: 166; John McClain, "New Hit Paced by British Star," *New York Journal American*, Nov. 24, 1961: 164; Norman Nadel, "Bolt's 'Man for Seasons'," *New York World-Telegram and The Sun*, Nov. 24, 1961: 167; and Howard Taubman, "The Theatre: 'A Man for All Seasons,'" *The New York Times*, Nov. 23, 1961: 165. All are reprinted in *New York Theatre Critics Reviews* 22 (1964).

4. Pauline Kael is a notable exception here, finding the film "tasteful and moderately enjoyable" but ultimately too subtle and irrelevant to contemporary life. See "Heads that Roll," *The New Republic* Feb. 25, 1967: 35–36.

5. Marius notes that More's biography of Richard III (later, the chief source of Shakespeare's play), demonstrates his abhorrence of arbitrary, unchecked action for private good. In addition, he notes that long before the great Peasant's Rebellion of 1525 More had postulated that some would interpret Luther's attack on the pope as just cause for an attack on civil magistrates. This, More believed, would only produce chaos.

6. The politics that had preceded Tudor ascendancy had been bloody, and many thoughtful people wanted to avoid another round of internecine wars. Bolt asserts in his introduction to the play that all competent statesmen of the period agreed that a queen on the throne of England was unthinkable if civil war were to be avoided. In the film Cardinal Wolsey's warning to More carries a similar import: "Let the dynasty die with Henry the VIII and we'll have dynastic wars again . . . blood-witted barons ramping the country from end to end! Is that what you want?"

7. In this respect, the film seems to be part of a shift toward famous or important protagonists. The protagonist of *Behold a Pale Horse* (1964), for instance, was based on the anti-Franco hero Zapater. Later, *Julia's* protagonist is Lillian Hellman; Zinnemann's last film, *Five Days One Summer* (1982), invents a prominent Scottish doctor as protagonist.

8. The method for creating scripts for *The Search* and *The Men* had been for some combination of writer, director, and producer to spend time with the real subjects of the film—displaced children in Switzerland and paraplegic veterans at Birmingham Veteran's Hospital in California—and incorporate details of their stories into the fictional characters. These films also included actual displaced children and wounded veterans, and *Teresa* included Italian villagers as extras.

9. Zinnemann asserts in his autobiography, perhaps apocryphally, that after its American premiere someone asked him, "Where did you find a *soldier* who could act so well?" (69).

WORKS CITED

Alpert, Hollis. "A Film for All Seasons" *Saturday Review* December 17, 1966: 58.

Bolt, Robert. Letter reproduced in "Fred Zinnemann, *Sight and Sound* Dossier," Supplement [January 1996].

———. *A Man for All Seasons: A Play in Two Acts*. New York: Random House, 1962.

Carey, Patrick. Letter reproduced in "Fred Zinnemann, *Sight and Sound* Dossier."

Crist, Judith. "A Film for All Time" *The Private Eye, The Cowboy, and the Very Naked Girl: Movies from Cleopatra to Clyde.* New York: Holt, Rinehart and Winston, 1967. 203–205.

"Fred Zinnemann: *Sight and Sound* Dossier," *Sight and Sound* Supplement [January 1996].

Herbstman, Mandel. "*A Man for All Seasons.*" *The Film Daily* December 22, 1966: 4.

Marius, Richard C. "Thomas More: Church, State and Ecumenicity." *The Christian Century* July 19, 1967: 934–36.

More, Thomas. *Utopia.* Trans. Paul Turner. Harmondsworth, England: Penguin, 1971.

Simon, John. "Art Taint and Art Attained." *Private Screenings.* New York: Macmillan, 1967. 260–64.

"To Serve Wittily." [Review of *A Man for All Seasons*] *Time* December 16, 1966: 119.

Weaver, Mike. "Dynamic Realist." *Paul Strand: Essays on His Life and Work.* Ed. Maren Stange. New York: Aperture Foundation, 1990.

Zinnemann, Fred. *A Life in the Movies: An Autobiography.* New York: Scribner's, 1992.

CHAPTER TWELVE

◨

Shooting a Melon:
The Target Practice Sequence in
The Day of the Jackal *(1973)*

LLOYD MICHAELS

Movies are difficult to talk about, Christian Metz has suggested, because they are easy to understand. This aphorism may help to explain the rather truncated, if respectful reviews that followed the release of Fred Zinnemann's *The Day of the Jackal* in the spring of 1973 and the nearly total lack of critical attention the film has received during the past two decades. Most reviewers complimented the director's technical proficiency, especially the editing of the complicated, multinational plot about an attempt to assassinate French President Charles de Gaulle, so as to maintain suspense despite the audience's knowledge that the general died of natural causes. Several, like *Time's* Richard Schickel, reversed the usual judgment and called the movie an improvement on Frederick Forsyth's best-selling novel. But the picture also seemed distinctly minor when compared with Zinnemann's earlier work, a genre piece lacking the resonance and ambition of *The Nun's Story* (1959) and *A Man for All Seasons* (1966) or even the allegorical implications of *High Noon* (1952). Film scholars have virtually ignored it: historians and auteurists relegating it to brief discussions, theorists of all stripes finding little or nothing to interest them. If television listings and video store inventories can be taken as anecdotal evidence, the film has been kept alive by ordinary viewers who find in it an entertaining, well-acted yarn that moves steadily towards a satisfying climax while requiring only minimal attention.

At least one sequence deserves closer scrutiny, however, if only because, like the silent scene in Antonioni's *Blow Up* in which the photographer studies a succession of his enlargements, it serves as the pivot on which the entire film turns, as well as the moment that often remains most vivid in the viewer's memory. Appearing near the middle of both films, these privileged parts seem to lift the story to another, more philosophical level by reflecting on the shadowy, evanescent nature of human character and, by extension, the imaginary realm of cinema itself. In *The Day of the Jackal*, this transcendent sequence occurs when the would-be assassin, known as the Jackal (Edward Fox), takes his specially designed rifle to a bucolic meadow and fine-tunes the scope by firing at a melon he has hung from a distant tree. It is this deceptively easy part of the movie— a paradigm, perhaps, of "pure cinema"—that I want to talk about here.

The scene, based on four pages in Forsyth's novel and consisting of seventeen shots in two minutes and fifteen seconds, serves most obviously to anticipate the intended result of the conspirators' plot—the sniper's attack against de Gaulle—and to define the cold-hearted precision of the professional assassin.[1] In terms of the film's narrative trajectory, it both culminates the Jackal's various preparations and initiates the execution of his plans; moreover, as a rehearsal of the film's aborted climax, it satisfies the audience's desire to see, at least in symbolic form, the ultimate act of violence denied in this case by history. In addition to these diegetic functions, the target practice sequence also works in intratextual and self-reflexive ways, fixing our attention on a lost object destroyed before our eyes.

The framing long shots that begin and end the sequence mark the dimensions of the Jackal's disruption of the natural order. Shot #1 establishes the picturesque landscape, the tree centered at the vanishing point of the perfectly balanced composition. Shot #17 is a reverse long shot, the melon hanging in front of the camera in the upper part of the frame, then exploding in a burst of red as the test bullet finds its target. The shocking effect stems in part from this violation of the scene's harmonious visual design, which had been reinforced by the peaceful chirping of birds, and also from the reverse angle, which directs the Jackal's assault not simply against the melon, but against us, who have been carefully positioned in the line of fire. The aesthetic distance established in the opening shot as well as the scientific perspective we have been invited to adopt during the intervening shots in which the assassin adjusts his sights—always aiming outside the frame and away from the spectator—has been shattered as easily as the fruit of this lost paradise.

The second shot, a close-up of the Jackal painting a crude face on the melon, identifies the symbolic identity of the target as an effigy of the intended victim, Charles de Gaulle. In effect, the melon becomes a mask, one seen again through the crosshairs of the rifle scope in four successive masking shots (#s 9, 11, 13, and 15). As so often seems the case, even in similar thrillers like *The Taking of Pelham, One, Two, Three* (1974) and *Escape from Alcatraz* (1979) made in the same period as *The Day of the Jackal*, the mask exerts a disproportionately disturbing effect precisely because it has replaced the face that had concealed the character hidden behind it—or, in this case, has transformed the melon that served as a stand-in for the familiar face of Charles de Gaulle.

Compounding this process of replacement (and, thus, withdrawal) in all films is the fact that the face being masked is, of course, an *actor's* face, himself a stand-in for the fictional (or historical) character he is impersonating. Add the point made by Metz in "The Imaginary Signifier," Leo Braudy in *The World in a Frame*, and John Ellis in *Visible Fictions* about the inherent paradox involved in the cinema's mode of signification—the simultaneous presentation and withdrawal of the perceived object—and we can begin to account for the strange epiphany often experienced while witnessing masks on the screen. "The cinema image is marked by a particular half-magic feat," Ellis has remarked, "in that it makes present something that is absent. The movement shown on the screen is passed and gone when it is called back into being as illusion" (58). Thus, it might be argued that film has always had a natural predilection for such character types as the double, the vampire, the confidence man, the spy, and, in the case of *The Day of the Jackal*, the cipher. To return to the defaced melon, its cartooned surface signifies a de Gaulle who is absent from the scene, absent from the film (subsequently impersonated from long range by a virtually anonymous actor),[2] and absent from reality (deceased two years before the film's production).

The last three masking shots of the sequence (#s 11, 13, and 15) depict the mask, shot. The stylized, generic form of this particular presentation of the image—a target carefully aligned through a rifle's telescopic sight—subtly suggests the unseen presence of a third elusive char-

FIGURE 12.1. THE DAY OF THE JACKAL (Universal Pictures, 1973). Zinnemann in the crosshairs. (Courtesy Academy of Motion Picture Arts and Sciences)

acter beyond the frame, not the Jackal (who has adopted the name of a long-deceased child, Paul Oliver Duggan, and travels on twenty-three different passports, one of which belongs to Charles Harold Calthrop, the man being pursued by the French police) and not Charles de Gaulle, but rather the director, Fred Zinnemann. The analogy between the sniper's activity and the filmmaker is inscribed in the scene both by the Jackal's meticulous adjustments of his instrument after each "take," seen in tight closeups in shots #10, 12, and 14, and by the camera's fidgety zooms in shot #5, when he hangs the melon on a branch, and at the end of shot #6, when he first sights the target. Zinnemann's awareness of the connection has been memorialized in a special photograph he chose to include in his recent photographic memoir, showing his head posed in profile in front of the melon and between the crosshairs of the scope. Zinnemann's caption reads: "I wonder if someone would have liked to pull the trigger" (219).

What is the point of the analogy? Because *The Day of the Jackal* is primarily a genre piece and not a self-consciously reflexive film on the order of *8½* or *Persona*, one can only speculate. The photograph, and its caption, suggests Zinnemann's sense of the latent aggressiveness in the filmmaker's art as well as the artist's own vulnerability, the mutual antipathy between the performer and the audience that remains imperfectly repressed in their need to exhibit and witness deceptive images of reality. The parallel may also speak to the issue of George Orwell's famous essay on "Shooting an Elephant," the recognition that we all wear a mask, and our face grows to fit it (299). Or perhaps the link between the two forms of shooting lies in Susan Sontag's observation about photography, that the act of recording a moment of violence is simultaneously an act of nonintervention (11). No less the cool professional than his fictional assailant, Zinnemann withholds his psychoanalytical insights and moral judgments of the Jackal, just as he effaces any political opinions about the famous French leader.

The final shot in the sequence—the melon exploding in front of the camera, the now empty air it had occupied suspended by Zinnemann for an extra second—compounds our sense of its status as a "lost object," Metz's term for the imaginary scopic regime presented by the cinema (59). By withdrawing this object, leaving only a tracing (a presence of absence), Metz has argued, the filmic signifier replenishes the spectator's desire. In the case of the hanging fruit, shot #17 presents an unusually complex matrix of presence/absence:

1. the melon itself, like all images on film, not really present at the time of projection just as the spectator is not really present at the time of shooting;
2. the Jackal, present in the extreme distance, literally beyond the vanishing point, but not seen in the long shot that records the final effect of his assault;
3. de Gaulle, as noted earlier, absent from the scene, absent from life (like so many other actors in older movies), but represented in effigy by the painted melon;
4. the painted face on the melon, not really a caricature of de Gaulle or any other human face but an abstraction, now turned away from the camera, concealed from the spectator's vision by the reverse angle, for the only time in the sequence;
5. the emptiness—spatial and aural (the muffled impact of the bullet, the silence of the birds)—that follows the destruction of the melon, leaving behind only a vestigial fragment of fruit dangling from the vacant mesh bag.

While the sequence as a whole draws upon the generic conventions of the thriller for much of its immediate impact, this final shot evokes another profoundly disturbing moment of violence recorded on film, Abraham Zapruder's home movie of the Kennedy assassination.[3] The viewer may be reminded, albeit on a subconscious level, of that earlier, terrifying vision of a world leader destroyed by a distant, anonymous sharpshooter. For a moment, despite our knowledge of de Gaulle's actual fate, the exploding "brain" of the melon makes his assassination seem possible. Indeed, no account of the resonance of this particular sequence seems complete without noting how the Zapruder footage has become part of the American movie audience's collective unconscious.

In a broader sense, Zinnemann's film speaks to the basic mystery of human character that the cinema, with its projection of phantoms long departed from the scene, may be especially well suited to portray. Thus reviewers like the one from *Newsweek* who complained that the assassin's "Motives and outlook are never explored, his background and personality do not exist" (101) have missed the point made so clearly through the metaphor of the exploding melon. Ultimately, *The Day of the Jackal* reminds viewers of the evanescence as well as the fragility of human character when, in the epilogue, the true identity of the man called "the Jackal," himself assassinated, remains a mystery he takes to the grave.

NOTES

1. Forsyth's original version of the scene lacks both the intensity and formal virtuosity of Zinnemann's film. In the novel, the Jackal changes his clothes, paints the top and bottom of the melon brown and the center pink before adding the cartoon face, then fires nine practice shots and walks back to check the target three times before loading the explosive bullet.

2. Adrien Cayla-Legrand, a French actor who specialized in impersonating de Gaulle.

3. Writing about a different shot, Frank McConnell also has noted a connection between the Zapruder movie and *The Day of the Jackal* (166).

WORKS CITED

Ellis, John. *Visible Fictions: Cinema, Television, Video.* Boston: Routledge and Kegan Paul, 1982.

McConnell, Frank D. *The Spoken Seen.* Baltimore: Johns Hopkins University Press, 1975.

Metz, Christian. *The Imaginary Signifier: Psychoanalysis and the Cinema* Bloomington: Indiana University Press, 1982.

Orwell, George. "Shooting an Elephant." *Classic Essays in English.* Ed. Josephine Miles. Boston: Little, Brown, 1961.

P.D.Z. "*The Day of the Jackal.*" *Newsweek* 28 May 1973: 101.

Schickel, Richard. "*The Day of the Jackal.*" *Time* 28 May 1973: 91

Sontag, Susan. *On Photography* New York: Dell, 1977.

Zinnemann, Fred. *A Life in the Movies: An Autobiography.* New York: Scribner's, 1992.

CHAPTER THIRTEEN

"Do You Understand?" History and Memory in Julia (1977)

STEPHEN PRINCE

Julia (1977), Fred Zinnemann's second to last film, demonstrates the continuing importance of Zinnemann's ethic and aesthetic of social realism. Due in part to his early documentary training and to his first-hand observations of the rise of fascism in his native Austria, Zinnemann was, throughout his career, always keenly drawn to a filmmaking style and subject matter that enabled him to dramatize the connections between people and their historical moment, particularly in the crises of conscience that history may set up for the individual. In 1948 Zinnemann wrote that his goal as a film.naker was "to dramatize contemporary history for a large American audience and to make them understand in emotional terms what the world outside looks like today" ("Perspective" 113). Since then, over the years, he reiterated his interest in dramatizing the challenges that historical periods might set for the individuals living through them. "I have always been concerned with the problem of the individual who struggles to preserve personal integrity and self-respect" (Buckley 38). Zinnemann said that the theme that preoccupied him above all others "has been expressed as follows by Hillel two thousand years ago: 'If I am not myself, who will be for me? And if I am only for myself, what am I? And if not now, when?' This seems to me to be a universal theme" (Phillips 26–27). Zinnemann felt strongly that this theme emphasizing the individual's need to act in response to historical crisis entailed a corresponding responsibility for the filmmaker. Despair or cynicism, as an aesthetic or an existential stance, was too easy and was an evasion of the social issues that the filmmaker confronted through the drama. "One of the crucial things today is trying to preserve our civilization," said Zinnemann, and film could provide a record of this effort (*American Film* 12). Zinnemann urged the need for a positive portrayal of human potential: "I just like to do films that are positive in the sense that they deal with the dignity of human beings and have something to say about oppression, not necessarily in a political way but in a human way" (*American Film* 13).

Zinnemann was drawn to the *Julia* project because he found the story of the friendship between Lillian Hellman and Julia so compelling and because of the issue of conscience at the heart of the story—"the fact that a woman who is leading a comfortable life is suddenly faced with the question of life or death and decides to go ahead and risk taking the money into Germany" (*American Film* 13, 62). The film is based on a short account that appeared in Hellman's collection *Pentimento* of her childhood friend, Julia, who dropped out of medical school to become active in Austrian socialism and subsequently, during the Nazi period, in the antifascist struggle. While Julia is living in Vienna, Hellman achieves national success as a playwright with *The Children's Hour*. While in Paris, en route to a Moscow Theatre Festival, Hellman receives a mysterious request from Julia. She is to journey to Moscow by way of Berlin (now under the Nazi regime) and ferry $50,000 to Julia, which will be used to help free political prisoners. Hellman agrees and meets Julia briefly and for the last time in Berlin. She delivers the money and learns that Julia has a daughter. As her life in the resistance is very dangerous, Julia wants Lillian to look after this child. She intends to bring her child to the United States where Lillian will meet her, but Julia is killed by the Nazis before this can happen. Learning of Julia's death, Lillian returns to Austria searching for the child, but does not find her. Hellman's account ends here, with the daughter's fate a mystery and with the memory of Julia poignantly enduring.

Zinnemann presents this narrative with his customary respect for the materials of history. The careful reconstruction of the different time periods in the narrative is exacting, intelligent, and precise, and the visual design that brings the narrative to life offers a poetic reaffirmation of the enduring significance of history and of the individual's place within it. We should first discuss Zinnemann's historical reconstruction of the prefascist and fascist eras and then how the film's poetic visual design conjoins the inner subjectivity of memory with the outer, objective brutalities of history in a way that affirms Zinnemann's ethic of social realism. Alvin Sargent's screenplay presents the narrative in a very elliptical way. It fragments the story by shifting continuously between different time frames: Lillian's journey to Berlin with the money in 1937; episodes from her childhood friendship with Julia in the early 1920s; her brief meeting with Julia at Oxford in 1925 and then, again, in a Vienna hospital where Julia lay critically wounded following the 1934 Florisdorf riots; Lillian's relationship with Dashiell Hammett (Jason Robards) and her developing career as a writer from 1934–1937; and, finally, Lillian's reflections as an older woman upon all of these episodes from her earlier years. This elliptical structure required Zinnemann and his crew not merely to recreate earlier time periods in a visually convincing way but to coordinate the characters' constantly changing physical appearances with changes in costuming, props, and sets in a way that would preserve the integrity of each time period.

Zinnemann has said that for his own career and working methods the influence of documentary filmmaker Robert Flaherty is of paramount importance. "Professionally, he was my godfather" (*Life* 26). Zinnemann noted that his memories of Flaherty's documentary approach were especially vivid when he was working on *Julia* (25–26), and he brought a documentarian's emphasis to the production design. Cinematographer Douglas Slocombe said that Zinnemann was especially intent that the film have a realistic style even though all of the narrative events are filtered through Hellman's memories (Samuelson 250). Zinnemann's respect for history is evident in these choices about style that were intended to impress upon viewers the realism of the events they were watching. Zinnemann, for example, was adamant about doing a careful reconstruction of Sardi's restaurant in New York City as it appeared in the 1930s for a scene in which Hellman is enthusiastically greeted by the restaurant patrons following the premiere of *The Children's Hour*. Zinnemann required that every piece of artwork originally on the walls of Sardi's be reproduced for the film. Each was photocopied, then rephotographed or repainted and mounted on the walls of the set. Zinnemann also required that the set be filmed with only American extras (filming of the scene occurred in England at the E.M.I. studio).

Not enough American extras could be found in England so Zinnemann ordered that the remainder be flown in from the United States. Cinematographer Slocombe was impressed with the authenticity that Zinnemann thereby achieved:

> In actual fact, [Zinnemann] was quite right, because, although one's first reaction was that these people were only in the background, there is a certain way that Americans dress, the way they sit . . . just every aspect of their clothing and their behavior is very, very different [from the English], and Zinnemann insisted on having all that authentic. It seemed like a rather expensive way to prove his point, but it paid off. (Samuelson 286)

As an additional means of ensuring the authenticity of the film's historical reconstruction, Zinnemann retained a technical advisor for the film's sequences involving Julia's and Lillian's travels to Europe aboard a transatlantic oceanliner. These ships no longer exist, and Zinnemann sought the advice of a retired liner pilot. The liner sets were built and filmed in England, where a variety of locations were doubling for America. The American sets filmed in England were designed by Gene Callahan, an American production designer. The film, in fact, had three production designers because of Zinnemann's insistence that the sets corresponding to the principal locales of the story—the United States, England, France, and Germany—be designed, as far as possible, by production personnel corresponding to those nationalities. This, too, was a function of Zinnemann's search for authenticity. Slocombe remarked that, "It was in line with Zinnemann's thinking . . . that the technicians of a particular country somehow know more about the idiosyncrasies of their own country than a foreigner would" (286).

Zinnemann's elaborate measures to achieve an authentic historical reconstruction of the narrative's various locations and periods also included relying on his own experience and knowledge. The episodes dealing with the fascist takeover in Vienna, Julia's wounding during the Florisdorf riots, and Lilly's visit to her in the hospital must have resonated with Zinnemann's vivid memories of the Austria of his youth and, particularly, the ominous atmosphere of encroaching fascism. In his autobiography, he writes of the cultural bewilderment that beset Austria in the later 1920s and the discrimination against Jews that permeated the society. This was the soil in which fascism would take root.

An Austrian brand of Fascism had now begun to flourish; the Nazis were but a cloud on the horizon but people no longer laughed at Hitler. His book, *Mein Kampf,* became obsessive reading, a gospel for millions. Boys came to school with swastikas in their lapels. "Aren't you ashamed?" I asked one. "I'm proud of it," he said. (11)

Zinnemann also writes with repugnance of Hitler's march into Austria in 1938 where he was welcomed by jubilant crowds. The Florisdorf fighting dramatized in the film, in which the Austrian army attacked a socialist workers' district, was a significant symptom of the fascist wave that would sweep Austria and in which Zinnemann's parents would perish, "two out of six million," he wrote (55). The film illustrates the rise of the Nazis in Europe, significantly, with photographs, rather than dramatic recreations, that serve as authentic historical documents, and these photographs are very similar to those that Zinnemann placed in his autobiography to illustrate the same phenomenon. In the autobiography, he writes about the indifference of people in Europe and America to the gathering storm, and, in the film, Julia writes angrily to Lillian of the approaching Holocaust and of people who refused to see what was coming.

Zinnemann, then, could authenticate the Vienna scenes of the film by locating them in relation to his own history and to that of his Viennese family and could find in Julia a character whose views of the European crisis closely resembled his own. Furthermore, the authenticity of the production design that Zinnemann sought to achieve is connected with, and is validated by, the film's stance in regard to the outer realm of history and the inner one of personal memory through which the narrative is organized. These two arenas, through which Hellman's crisis of conscience (whether to ferry the money to Julia) is disclosed, are brought into alignment by the film's visual design and in a way that honors the ethic of social realism that underlay Zinnemann's search for authenticity. We turn now to an examination of this visual design.

As previously noted, the narrative is fragmented into a collection of episodes that recount the story of Lillian's friendship with Julia. The viewer sees them in varying episodes of childhood, youth, and adulthood, and these glimpses are presented out of proper chronological sequence. Furthermore, all of these episodes are framed as an act of recollection by the elderly Hellman so that the entire film becomes a journey into Hellman's memory of the past. The first image is a longshot of the elderly

Hellman fishing from a small boat in misty, soft light. Overtop this image, she begins the spoken recitative of her recollections about Julia by explaining the concept of "pentimento."

> Oil paint on canvas, as it ages, sometimes becomes transparent. When that happens it is possible, in some pictures, to see the original lines: a tree will show through a woman's dress, a child makes way for a dog, a large boat is no longer on an open sea. That is called pentimento because the painter "repented," changed his mind.

While this recitative derives from the prefatory note in Hellman's book, it has been reinflected in a significant way by the film. After Lillian explains "pentimento," the editing by Walter Murch presents a series of images linked by dissolves. The longshot of the figure in the rowboat dissolves to a close-up of gentle waves bathed in golden light, then a dissolve to a shot of the steam locomotive leaving Paris and that is carrying Lilly to Berlin with Julia's money, then a dissolve to the waves, and then a dissolve to an extreme close-up of Lilly's eyes. The narration that accompanies this latter shot changes the tense, as Hellman wrote it in her book, from past to present: "I'm old now and I want to remember what was there for me once and what is there for me now." This shot then dissolves to a longshot of Lilly and Dash's beach house in 1934 where she is struggling with her writing and the first narrative episode takes place.

This tense change from the book's preface to the film's spoken recitative signals the vital and engaged stance with history that will be manifest in the film's presentation of Lillian's memories. This tense change stresses the ongoing nature of memory and reflection and, therefore, of the history which continues to live through these memories. The film is edited so that the dissolve functions as the primary visual device of narrative structure, creating as the film progresses an accumulating series of overlapping images. Shifts in time and space between scenes are signaled with dissolves, not cuts or fades which would have the effect of separating images. The dissolve does not merely connect the shifting time frames of the narrative and the differing spaces of its scenes, but it does so in a way that superimposes the images over top of one another, much as Hellman has explained in the context of the painted image that becomes a pentimento. As the tense change in the spoken recitative had done, the dissolve suggests the continuing presence and reality of the past, its endurance into and within the present.

But the film's elaboration of a pentimento structure goes well beyond this use of the dissolve as the primary visual unit for organizing narrative. Throughout the film, the different temporal frames interpenetrate one another in an evocation of the fluidity of consciousness (the events in the film being contained as the contents of Lillian's memories), its mercurial ability to shift space and time according to the logic of emotional free association. Thus, the audio-visual design layers voices from differing time periods over images of other time periods to create a fluid, moving set of associations that evokes the structure of memory, grasped in the metaphor of pentimento. For example, in the 1934 frame which finds Lilly at the beach house with Dash, she asks him whether she ought to go to Paris to continue working on her play (it's not progressing very well at the house with Dash). She lies down on their bed as dialogue from her past appears in voice-over. Lilly (as a girl): "But what about Paris, what about Rome?" Julia (as a girl): "You aren't listening." Lilly: "I am listening." In the middle of this last line, the scene dissolves from Lilly's adult face to a long point of view shot from inside a car as it drives onto a wooded estate. A subsequent cut to Lilly's face (as a girl) shows that the point-of-view in the previous shot belongs to her as she rides in the car's front seat. Arriving at Julia's grandparents' summer lodge, the girls run from the car. Julia is angry. The grandparents took her to Europe and Egypt where Julia's developing social consciousness was disturbed by the poverty she encountered and her grandparents' wealthy indifference to it. What about Paris, what about Rome? Lilly asks. Julia tells her she's not listening and asserts that it is wrong to be so wealthy and not to use it to help those who are worse off. Julia says, "It's wrong"/ cut to close-up of Lilly/ "it's wrong, Lilly"/ dissolve to misty image of the elderly Lillian fishing from her small boat/ "Do you understand?" As the editing of this dialogue with the corresponding series of images demonstrates, Julia's dialogue with Lillian from 1922 at the summer lodge reverberates through the 1934 time frame as well as the master frame of Hellman's elderly years.

This question—"Do you understand?"—is referenced to the organizing frame of the story (the fishing image and the chain of memories it unlocks) as the significant issue the film poses (not just to Lilly but to its viewers) regarding oppression, historical trauma, and the ethic of commitment that Julia embodies. This ethic and example are so important, as is the history that underlies them, that they transcend the subjective memories by Hellman that enclose them. We will return to this point in a moment as it holds the key to the film's peculiar audio-visual structure.

FIGURE 13.1. JULIA (Twentieth Century Fox, 1977). Lillian (Jane Fonda) and Johann (Maximilian Schell). (Courtesy Larry Edmunds Bookshop, Inc.)

After a beat, while the fishing image remains on screen, Julia's voice is heard but from an altogether different time frame, 1925: "I heard from Oxford, from medical school. I was accepted." Lillian's voice: "When will you go?" Julia's voice: "At the end of the summer"/ cut from the fishing image to the scene of Lilly's farewell to Julia at dockside. (This is one of the few notable instances where a cut is used to shift scenes and time frames.) Lillian and Julia say their farewells, and Lillian leaves Julia with another statement as legacy: "Work hard, take chances, be very bold." A spoken recitative from Hellman's twilight years now overlaps these images at the docks: "I wasn't to see her again for a long time"/ dissolve to Oxford and Julia now radiant with her commitment to socialism/ "until I went to visit her at Oxford."

This pentimento structure, imaginatively realized throughout the film, creates a series of interconnected frames in which voices and images refract one another as the film circles about the elusive figure of Julia and her legacy for Lillian. That legacy is the example of commitment to a just cause and, through it, a testimony as to how the raw material of history (the fascist period against which Julia struggles) may be lived out, and contested by, individuals of conscience such as Julia. Lillian lacks Julia's fortitude, but when asked to place herself in a situation of some danger for the sake of her friend, she agrees. Significantly, Zinnemann and Sargent expand the terms of Lilly's choice, and emphasize the crisis of decision she confronts, through their presentation of Julia's messenger, Johann (Maximilian Schell), who contacts her in Paris and gives instructions on how the money is to be ferried. In the written account of this meeting that Hellman published in *Pentimento*, Johann gently admonishes Lillian not to do what Julia has asked unless Lillian is truly capable of doing it. In the film, by contrast, Johann cautions her on this point several times, prompting Lillian, in anger, to ask him to please stop saying it. By reiterating Johann's warning to Lillian, Zinnemann and Sargent emphasize the crisis of conscience that Julia's request forces upon Lilly, which is precisely the kind of interior, psychological drama that Zinnemann has always been drawn to in cinema.

As Lillian returns to her hotel from the meeting with Johann, trying to decide whether to do as Julia has asked, another set of voices from the past overlaps the time-space of this imagery. It is Julia, as a young girl, saying, "Lilly, you don't have to come this way. Go down under, wade across." A dissolve connects Lilly's anguished walk back to the hotel with a small drama from her youth. A fallen tree lies across the elevated banks of a riverbed. Julia crosses to the other side by walking on the fallen tree. Lilly tries to do this, ignoring Julia's warning, initially heard as voice-over in the other time frame but which is now repeated. Halfway across, suspended over the stream, Lilly freezes and nearly falls from the tree. After Julia rescues her, Lilly apologizes and Julia says that it is all right, she'll do it successfully next time. A dissolve connects Lilly's young, smiling face as she looks affectionately at Julia to a close-up of Hitler's portrait. It hangs on the wall of the German consulate in Paris where the adult Lilly has gone to apply for her visa to Berlin. This is the "next time" for Lilly. Julia has said that Lilly is afraid of being afraid and so will sometimes do what she cannot do. This is the basis for Lillian's inability to answer Johann immediately. She asks to have several hours to think things over. Lillian can remain within, and rest in, her fears. Or she can, and does, confront the questions that Julia knows she will successfully resolve, and which Zinnemann has found to be of abiding significance: If I am not myself, who will be for me? And if I am only for myself, what am I? And if not now, when?

The film's shifting time frames, its overlapping voices and images, are structural embodiments of these issues. They make the past a living presence in the narrative and suggest that history, as an arena that contains both oppression and principled responses to it, is, properly understood, not a matter of past events but of a continuous and living interconnection among people and the situations in which they act. Thus, the film takes a very positive perspective on the enduring value of history and on the significance of past events and behaviors which continue to shape subsequent lives and minds. This emphasis places *Julia* very close in spirit to *High Noon* (1952), an earlier Zinnemann film that argued eloquently and passionately for the connection between the social and political health of a community and the principled acts of its members (see my chapter on the film elsewhere in this volume). This is an issue of enduring importance for Zinnemann, as the common emphases of these films indicate. In *High Noon*, town Marshal Will Kane understands that the threat of violence posed by Frank Miller and his gang, emanating from the town's past, is also a threat to its future because of the probability that Miller's reappearance will corrupt not just the civic institutions but the fraternal bonds among the people of Hadleyville. Thus, the consequences of Miller's violence spread across the different, implied time frames of *High Noon*'s narrative. In *Julia*, this implication of an interconnected history, of action and reaction moving simultaneously across different frames of time and space, is given a more explicit formal treatment. But in either case, the emphases of these two films show clearly Zinnemann's ongoing, realist engagement with the dynamics of an individual's moral choice in response to social crisis.

Zinnemann's historical realism is affirmed through *Julia's* emphasis upon memory as a living and reliable means of accessing the past. Here, the film is remarkably different from what is today the familiar modernist, and postmodernist, mistrust of language, thought, and memory as vehicles for accessing an outer world of behavior and circumstance. A film like Resnais's *Hiroshima Mon Amour* (1959) is a brilliant meditation on the inability to reconcile the subjectivity of human perception and recollection with the "objective" cataclysms of such events as World War II. Resnais and scriptwriter Marguerite Duras poetically emphasize the necessity of forgetting, on a personal and social scale, and the role this palliative response plays in making possible the next round of atrocities. By contrast, *Julia* affirms an old-fashioned belief in the knowability of history and human behavior because such knowability safeguards the possibility of moral choice and committed action in response to the brutalities that history inflicts.

Early in the film in the 1934 time frame, Lillian and Dash discuss the frustrations she feels as an aspiring writer. Dash goes up to the house and Lillian remains on the beach, alone in the night air. In voice-over, she reflects (from the master frame of the narrative), "I think I have always known about my memory. I know when the truth is distorted by some drama or fantasy. But I trust absolutely what I remember about"/ dissolve to close-up of young Julia/ "Julia." In the close-up, Julia smiles and gazes directly at the camera. Her first shot in the film, and its presentation within Lillian's recitation, confirms her enduring presence in memory and in history as she gazes directly at us from out of the past. Lillian's recitation about the trust she places in her memories affirms the knowability of history and takes the film very far, as we have seen, from modernist and postmodernist accounts of the duplicity of human consciousness in relation to the external world.

Just how far is the film's ethic from the modernist, and postmodernist, outlook is strikingly apparent in what Zinnemann chose not to emphasize. Zinnemann has suggested that the Julia story, as related by Hellman, may be a fabrication and not a factual account of events that she personally experienced. In his autobiography, Zinnemann claims that Hellman told him in the mid-1970s that the real Julia was still living in

New York! Furthermore, Zinnemann writes that research on the Austrian underground indicated that there was only one American woman in the movement. Code named "Mary," she was possibly a Dr. Muriel Gardiner. Hellman, though, had never been friends with, or connected to, Gardiner. Zinnemann writes, "It is believed that a man who knew both ladies might have told Lillian the story. The mystery remains—if it is, indeed, a mystery?" (*Life* 223) Significantly, Zinnemann's acknowledgement that Hellman's Julia story might be a work of fiction did not hinder his ability to apply to it his realist aesthetic and the historical perspective that underlies it. The reason why is not hard to see. The tale might be a fabrication, but the philosophy the film engages and expresses remains true and vitally important. Zinnemann could not back away from this. Whether Hellman's Julia was real or not, Zinnemann chose to honor the character's example and ethic. It made for a better film and one that was faithful to the issues, style, and outlook that shaped his long and distinguished career.

WORKS CITED

Buckley, Michael. "Fred Zinnemann." *Films in Review* 34.1 (January 1983): 25–40.

Phillips, Gene. "Fred Zinnemann Talking to Gene Phillips." *Focus on Film* 14 (Spring 1973): 21–32.

Samuelson, David W. "The Photography of *Julia*." *American Cinematographer* 59.3 (March 1978): 248–86, 320–22.

Zinnemann, Fred. "Different Perspective." *Sight and Sound* 17.67 (1948): 113.

———. "Fred Zinnemann." *American Film* 11.4 (January–February 1986): 12–13, 62, 66–67.

———. *A Life in the Movies: An Autobiography.* New York: Scribner's, 1992.

CHAPTER FOURTEEN

⊞

Real-Life References in
Four Fred Zinnemann Films

CLAUDIA STERNBERG

A number of Fred Zinnemann's feature films show a distinct preference for fictions inspired by historical facts and situations. Borrowing from the study of literature and linguistics, I shall refer to such facts and situations as *etic* references. Etic references also include events, characters, institutions, settings, and historical or regional language which have a real-life existence outside the system of the fictional world in which they appear. Within the fictional system itself, their meaning is generated primarily by their potential for extratextual reference and connotation. Opposed to such references are *emic* elements, which are specific and internal to the fictional system and do not rely on the knowledge of the outside world that the reader brings to the text.[1] Obvious examples of literary eticity include Charles Dickens's allusions to the Poor Law in *Oliver Twist* or Hubert Selby's use of New York topography in *Last Exit to Brooklyn*. Such etic elements often serve as markers of authenticity; they suggest verisimilitude and can help to underscore the social criticism embedded in fiction. For the reader who is removed from the subject matter by time, region, or culture, they may facilitate an understanding of historical, geographical, and cultural conditions beyond the text's fictional and literary qualities. The choice of real-life references has a number of consequences:

their use typically implies an attention to accuracy of detail and a tendency toward an overall realism in language, theme, and character.

The same principles apply to film. However, a number of factors set the medium apart. Literature is essentially governed by the author's verbal choices; etic references are easily collected by way of experience and research. Editorial comment, publishing policy, and certain legal restrictions with regard to personal rights may have a limited influence on the text. Film writers and directors, on the other hand, are subject to diverse and diverting mechanisms in amalgamating fiction with reality. Whether the material stems completely or partly from historical sources or reaches the screen through a preceding fictionalization, each film production has to assess anew the implications of incorporating etic elements. The screenwriter's and director's choices are restricted by budget, producer, censoring agencies, and commercial concerns. Directorial priorities, too, for example regarding location, casting, film stock, and audience expectations, shape the degree and profile of eticity. As etic references can always be replaced by emic ones (or disguised, for that matter, which creates the effect of literature or film *à clef*), these choices do not always become apparent in the final film.

Fred Zinnemann's films *The Search, From Here to Eternity, Behold a Pale Horse*, and *Day of the Jackal*, produced in four decades from 1948 to 1972, show these mechanisms at work. All these films have in common a distinct date and location (postwar Germany; Schofield Barracks before the Pearl Harbor attack; France and Spain in 1959; Paris in 1963); all are based on or refer to facts or faction (United Nations Relief and Rehabilitation Administration reports; novelist James Jones's military service in Hawaii; the life of the Spanish anti-Falangist Francisco Zapater; the assassination attempts on Charles de Gaulle); and all contain many etic references. These dictate and also reflect the director's conception of each film, as the following discussion will show.[2]

THE SEARCH (1948)

At the core of *The Search* is the United Nations Relief and Rehabilitation Administration (UNRRA) and the problem of displaced children in postwar Germany. As an émigré who had lost his family in the Holocaust, Zinnemann was acutely aware of the Nazi atrocities and set out to use "the raw material of contemporary history in order to make a dramatic

FIGURE 14.1. THE SEARCH (MGM, 1948). Ivan Jandl as a displaced child. (Courtesy Museum of Modern Art/Film Stills Archive).

document" (113), as he stated in his article "Different Perspective" in 1948. Thus *The Search* had no literary source; its raw material was the work of the UNRRA, which, in collaboration with the International Tracing Service (ITS) and other organizations, tried to reunite unaccompanied children with their families and repatriate them, since many were completely alienated from their mother countries and languages. These children had been taken from their families and turned over to SS families for "Germanization" or, if not found "racially suitable," had been turned over for "another education," which meant deportation to concentration camps.

The research files of *The Search* contain copies of Nazi documents, interviews with children, biographies, eyewitness accounts, and Zinnemann's notes about the psychological trauma of the children and their subsequent behavior, for instance their silence, eating habits, and symptoms of fear. Richard Schweizer transformed the abundant etic material into a narrative script by adding the mother-son story and the American soldier as its dramatic backbone. The interaction between the shapers and subjects of etic material was inspiring; the relative immediacy of the events was a great advantage. Zinnemann recalls: "We got the stories from displaced persons themselves. . . . An incredible experience." He even speaks of a "creative accident" that led to his *Autobahn* scene (*FZ Retro*). The motorways, built as military routes under Hitler's dictatorship, were now void of traffic and became walking trails for people looking for their lost families. Such a deserted *Autobahn* was used as a setting to show Karel's mother during her desperate search for her son.

The intensity of *The Search* also results from the fact that the UN permitted Zinnemann to work with volunteer children who had been released from concentration camps. How strongly this casting influenced the film is illustrated by the following incident: in one scene, Zinnemann cast ordinary Swiss children, who were not frightened. The camp children, on the other hand, were extremely nervous and needed no direction at all. Thus many of the strong impressions of the movie were derived from real-life sources rather than reenacted scenes, so that their prime impact proved unreproducible in later films of the Holocaust.[3]

Zinnemann's combining of the original location of the ruins in Germany with the exacting preparation of Montgomery Clift, amateur acting, and the insights from the horrifying UNRRA reports approximated Italian neorealist filmmaking conceptually and stylistically.[4] With the American target audience in mind, however, the director felt a certain amount of expositional explanation was required: "At the time . . . no one in America, or very few people, had any idea what had happened. What had happened to children" (*FZ Retro*). An opening voice-over in *The Search*, spoken by a female narrator, introduced the subject matter, and expository narration became a recurring feature in Zinnemann's film-making in or about Europe. *The Search* was designed to utilize the "general acceptance of the film . . . as a method of educating the large American public to a vital modern problem" ("Different Perspective" 113) and an explanatory, "objective" voice reinforces this didactic purpose.

Since the goal was "to dramatize contemporary history for the large American audience and to make them understand in emotional terms what the world outside looks like today" ("Different Perspective" 113), Clift's American soldier, Stevenson, functions as a bridge between the film's material and the spectator. Stevenson refers to Lincoln, baseball, the Statue of Liberty, and Bambi to gain the child's confidence by introducing American symbols for American values. National emblems are included to relate the content of the film to the audience's own society. But at the same time, Stevenson's insecurity and that of his American friends can be decoded as an index for the uncertain position of the American audience, caught between generosity, sympathy, and ignorance concerning the victims of World War II.

Zinnemann was determined not to alienate the American audience, and purposely toned down what was known to him:

> All of us realized, of course, that it would be necessary to soften the truth to a certain extent, because to show things as they really were would have meant—at least in our sincere opinion—that the American audience would have lost any desire to face it, used as they have been through the years to seeing a sentimentalized world. ("Different Perspective" 113)

It was the paradox of a "softened truth" which alienated some non-American spectators. Completing disregarding the filmmakers' targeted audience and perceiving foreign and familiar etic elements in reversed order, they found the European references simplistic and the American ones ostentatious, calling *The Search* American progaganda. Some claimed the film failed to point out the causes of the misery, the Nazi ideology (*FZC*; Audience response survey, England). *The Search* to some degree made the destinies of displaced children more bearable by the happy ending and glorified the U.S. input through the strong feeling of social responsibility in Stevenson, but these modifications were the declared choices of the creative team wanting to reach and instruct a specific audience. Since the war was over and the Nazi domination shattered, the director faced no limitations.

FROM HERE TO ETERNITY (1953)

With *From Here to Eternity*, which was based on a novel fictionalizing the American Army on the eve of the Pearl Harbor attack, restrictions were dictated from the outside. With the shift to an American theme, etic material became a matter of national concern, or to put it less ambiguously, of national censorship. It was not, however, the Pearl Harbor attack (substantiated in the film with original wartime footage as an etic reminder) that was at issue a dozen years after the fact, but the status of the American Army. *From Here to Eternity*, published in 1951, had been a controversial novel; the author, James Jones, had been stationed in Hawaii and laid a certain claim to authenticity. When screenwriter Daniel Taradash and Fred Zinnemann approached the novel, two major censors became actively involved: the Breen Office and the Department of Defense. The conflict was twofold: on one side were the moral issues, prostitution, and adultery; on the other, the harsh criticism of the leadership of the American Army, thin ice for a studio in the McCarthy period.

Zinnemann's course was toward cooperation with the U.S. Army, because it would allow him to use original locations and obtain factual information. But, as Zinnemann has said, even more important than "*external* authenticity" was the need "to capture the *SPIRIT* of the place and the rhythm and precision of the professional pre-War military establishment" ("Letter" 88). Though clearly against the making of the film, the Army agreed to cooperate, but their cooperation was a reluctant one: "They realized that the film would be made regardless. I wasn't going to make it without Army co-operation, but somebody would. . . . They felt that they'd better come to terms" (*FZ Retro*). The agreement was not without conditions, and all stipulations were directed at palliating the problems of the service's internal structures. Eticity was interpreted on an abstract and hypothetical level; any of the film's negative references were seen as potentially damaging to the Army's reputation in real life.

The Departments of Defense and the Army voiced objections to the depiction of violence in the military prison scene and to other parts of the script. They insisted on changes before granting the approval sought by Columbia Pictures boss Harry Cohn and Zinnemann. Their demands, phrased as "recommendations," were discussed with Daniel Taradash and producer Buddy Adler. One of the suggestions was to use a different title for the film in order to avoid an immediate connection with the well-known novel. This feeble attempt at censorship confirmed the status of the novel as no mere fiction, but as a work critical of the American military, whose very title carries with it the etic implications made explicit in Jones's "Special Note," which is prefixed to the novel:

> This book is a work of fiction. . . . However, certain of the Stockade scenes did happen. They did not happen at the Schofield Barracks Post Stockade but at a post within the United States at which the author served, and they are true scenes of which the author had first-hand knowledge. (n.pag.)

The Departments wanted Fatso's brutality to be personal, not representative of the stockade and its use of corporal punishment in general. In the film, the interior of the stockade was not shown, but this omission was compensated for by the death of Maggio, who survives the ill-treatment in the novel. Furthermore, the suggestion was made to have Prewitt killed by bullets from a Japanese plane, but Adler and Taradash rejected this proposal vehemently: "This, we felt, was a typical Hollywood ending and had absolutely no meaning at all." The parties agreed on Prewitt being without uniform when he is shot by American MPs (*FZC*; report on the Army and Department of Defense recommendations, discussed with and partly agreed on by Adler and Taradash, probably written by Adler, February 25, 1952). A further recommendation was related to Captain Holmes, the commanding officer of the unit, who, in the novel, is promoted to the rank of major in another company. The departments wanted Holmes to receive punishment, not reassignment and promotion for his incompetence. This requirement meant turning the whole film around, but here the Army insisted that "he has either the choice to resign or to be court-martialled" (*FZ Retro*). Zinnemann had to give in; in the film Holmes resigns, and the positive image of the American officer is restored.

The film's other and seemingly emic problems—adultery, prostitution, violence, and strong language—were taken care of by the Breen Office. "The important problem remaining in this story, from the Code standpoint," wrote Joseph Breen to Harry Cohn, "is the lack of compensation for the immoral relationship between Warden and Karen" (*FZC*; letter of December 9, 1952). It was therefore demanded that the relationship between Warden and Holmes's wife should not last. Expressions like "Get the hell out of the way," "You dirty sons—" and "Nuts" were to be omitted, and there was a controversy about Warden using a broken bottle as a weapon; the Office suggested that Zinnemann should "find some other bit of business not quite so startlingly effective and easy to imitate" (*FZC*; Breen in a letter to Cohn, August 4, 1952).

When it enforced its own Production Code, the industry's self-censoring agency was also concerned with the etic potential of scenes related to daily life in the Army. It became necessary to eliminate sexual indications in the Prewitt-Lorene relationship; "nothing whatever suggestive of a brothel in the New Congress Club" (*FZC*; Breen's letter of August 4, 1952) was permitted. The Breen Office suggested that Karen put on a robe in the beach scene and Prewitt and Lorene sit up in Mrs. Kipfer's establishment. To meet the provisions of the Code, Lorene was transformed from a prostitute into a hostess in a brothel-turned-club setting. The inference that American soldiers frequented houses of prostitution was left to the imagination of the audience, who, Zinnemann notes, "instantly accepted that the 'club' was in fact a whorehouse" ("Letter" 88).

The implications of the novel had led to the belief that its narrative and characters were a threat to the Army's public image, and alterations to the film were made accordingly. Whether or not "that compromise, which wasn't a happy one, was nevertheless worthwhile" (*FZ Retro*) may be debatable from today's point of view, but at the time the changes in the screenplay enabled Zinnemann to realize some of his own choices, which would otherwise have been impossible to implement. He could film the original Schofield Barracks and use a platoon of military policemen who looked and marched like soldiers, not like extras. Casting and acting were largely left to the director, who, against some early resistance, chose Montgomery Clift as the boxer Prewitt in correspondence with the novel's description of the character. To provide Prewitt with a regional inflection suggested by the literary source, Zinnemann contacted the *Louisville Times*, Berea College, and Liberty Music Shop in New York and asked for audio samples of a Kentuckian Harlan County accent.[5] One major aesthetic decision that went along with the desire to use the original location was the director's choice of film stock:

In retrospect I am surprised to think how many battles I did win during the making of the film. One of them had to do with colour: the sales department ("the boys in New York") made it plain that the film would gross an extra million dollars if it was shot in colour, but I was able to persuade Cohn to agree to shooting it in black and white. This made a great difference to the picture's impact; colour would have made it look trivial. (*"From Here"* 24)

Despite the adjustments, the reactions to the film were mixed in military circles. Colonel B. A. Byrne of the U.S. Army Headquarters in the Pacific, with whom Zinnemann had worked, wrote to the director on October 2, 1953 (*FZC*): "General O'Daniel recently saw the picture while on the Coast. While he shares the feeling—which I am sure is common to the Army—that the picture represents our Service poorly, he was unstinting in his praise of everything stemming from direction." Byrne and O'Daniel deplored both the writing of the novel and the idea of adaptation because both shed a bad light on their institution, but they recognized the quality of the film. Others, however, did not see the film as an autonomous artistic product at all. The *Daily News* of August 29, 1953, reported the banning of *From Here to Eternity* by the Navy (*FZC*):

A high-level conference here in Washington decided not to show *From Here to Eternity* because it was "derogatory of a sister service"—the Army—and was a "discredit to the armed services." The Army, however, has leased *From Here to Eternity* for showing at Army bases, another military source said. This official said the Army cooperated in making the film in hopes of "softening" the effect of James Jones' book by the same name. He said the Army, having cooperated in making the picture, was "stuck" and had to use it. But he said the Army was "so shocked" at the preview that it refused to let its name be used in a "credit" line at the start of the film.

The Army's dissatisfaction reveals the ideological atmosphere of the time and explains why *From Here to Eternity* was received as a critical film despite censorship; "showing conditions in the United States Army as far from ideal, and at times downright brutal, amounted to an antimilitary statement that was daring for its period" (Gow, "Individualism" 14).

BEHOLD A PALE HORSE (1964)

In the early 1960s Fred Zinnemann turned his critical eye back to Europe. When he made *Behold a Pale Horse*, Francisco Franco had been in power for twenty-five years. The film, adapted from Emeric Pressburger's novel *Killing a Mouse on Sunday*, opens with stock footage from the end of the Spanish Civil War and a prologue (*FZC*):

> In 1936 a thousand years of history exploded in Spain. The forces of nationalism joined together against the forces of revolution. Soon the whole world found itself involved in this struggle. The whole world looked toward Spain. Soon it too would be a battleground. (a pause) In 1939 the Spanish Civil War came to an end. (a pause) These were the men who lost—crossing the border to France—and exile.

Aiming at a documentary-style cinematography, Zinnemann again chose black and white film and hired the cameraman Jean Badal, who had filmed the events of the Hungarian Revolution: "I was trying to show the story without intruding, as the camera does when you photograph an event in a newsreel" ("Talks Back" 22). The newsreel style was perfected to ease the transition from fact to fiction when, after the original footage from the Civil War, Gregory Peck as the protagonist Manuel Artiguez appears on screen:

> We found some wonderful newsreel material which we used. And then the job became finding a way to do a scene of Peck who at the end of the war is about to cross the border into France to become a refugee, an exile. We shot this scene in the mountains but then it became a question of making it fit the rest of the film. And we duped it several times over until it became as sparse of detail as newsreel shots do. And now you can't tell the difference. ("Talks Back" 30)[6]

It has been argued that the effect, however perfect technically, is tarnished because of the spectator's familiarity with the appearance of Gregory Peck. Interestingly, casting international stars (Peck, Anthony Quinn, Omar Sharif) was considered a drawback for the story by some film critics (Johnson 47). This cinéaste criticism implies a stronger acceptance of unknown actors and amateurs in films which accentuate etic material and suggests that such films do not necessarily benefit from stars. From a producer's point of view, however, the success of *The Search* (introducing Montgomery Clift)[7] and *The Men* (introducing Marlon Brando) seemed more of a financial risk than a film billed with a top director and well-known film stars.

It is uncertain whether the "intelligence that he [Zinnemann] takes for granted in his audience" (Sussex 198) accounts for the fact that no further specific references are made to the war. The film jumps to the year 1959 when the story about the resistance of Spanish Civil War exiles takes place. As with his other films, Zinnemann accumulated newspaper articles, magazine reports, and photographs, which gave the actors a frame of etic reference and the director material for the desired appearance of the people and their environment.

There were about 100,000 Spanish refugees in France in 1962, modestly supported by the French government. These refugees were mainly radical socialists, but declared anti-Stalinists. Zinnemann interviewed exiles in Toulouse and Perpignan, some of whom were supposed to have worked with the anti-Falangist Francisco Zapater, on whom the Artiguez character was based and who had set up a "school of terrorism" in Toulouse to harass Franco. The exiles informed the team that Franco's amnesty was not for political offenders, and that the Church worked hand in hand with the Falange. During the war, priests had executed wounded enemies, which accounts for the fact that the exiles, often strongly religious, never again set foot in a church. This background is not made explicit in Artiguez's, Pilar's, and Paco's strong anticlerical feelings, although the antagonism between the Church and the population is one of the central conflicts in the film.

The oppressive nature of the Franco regime was felt when location shooting once again proved to be a problematic issue. J. Raymond Bell wrote to M. J. Frankovich of Columbia Pictures on February 27, 1963 (*FZC*): "The Spanish government had been giving us the treatment." *Behold a Pale Horse*, which was to be filmed in Pamplona, Spain, was eventually shot in France, because the Spanish government made it impossible to shoot on Spanish soil. Another agency voiced its concern from France. The Office Catholique Français du Cinéma was worried about the character of the priest Francisco. In a letter the Office suggested that the priest should not be judgmental because "ne pas juger, c'est la phrase principale de l'évangile" ["'Judge not': this is the chief teaching of the Gospel." Editor's translation] (*FZC*, no date). It is likely that this correspondence had become necessary in the first place because the pilgrimage site of Lourdes was used as a location, a choice which required cooperation or at least communication between the production and the Church.

An intrinsic problem of *Behold a Pale Horse* is that the audience encounters a man who, after twenty years of fighting for a seemingly lost cause, goes out one more time for his convictions. It is difficult to filter these convictions through the character's frustration, bitterness, and personal animosities. Zinnemann was not sure whether the American audience would understand the "very Spanish gesture" ("Talks Back" 21) of Artiguez. While he had catered to the audience in *The Search* to ensure understanding, Zinnemann was now determined to sacrifice conventional identification devices, for example the introduction of an American character as witness or participant, or one-dimensional "rooting interest":

> It's a very easy thing to develop. We tell the audience you've got to be for this guy, and you've got to be against this man. If you do it skillfully enough, they'll be happy to do it for you. But, right or wrong, I don't like to do it. ("Talks Back" 21)

Artiguez's hopes for the future of his country are not clearly expressed. His return to Spain could easily be interpreted as an act of self-destruction, but Zinnemann saw it as a statement relating to contemporary politics in general:

> I don't think his decision is a question of resignation. A comparison, which perhaps is a little far fetched, is last year in Saigon . . . nobody in the world knew really what was going on or why a man had to burn himself to death . . . it focused the attention of the world on it, and in some ways led to the downfall of the Diem regime . . . in a sense Manuel's return to Spain and getting killed you might say is also a protest . . . a protest against oppression, against a police state . . . and this happens all the time, this is not fiction in that sense. ("Revelations" 6)

Although Zinnemann wanted to demonstrate that Artiguez "is a sort of Robin Hood character" who has been "helping the Spanish exiles to survive" (*FZC*; Letter to M. J. Frankovich, Columbia Pictures Corporation from Paris, May 30, 1964), the film did not succeed at the box office and with the critics. The confidential report about the trip to Perpignan and Toulouse reveals the impact the personal encounters with the exiles had on the team (*FZC*): "The incredible thing about all these people is their intensity. As soon as they start talking the years seem to drop away. It is as though all of the Civil War happened yesterday." The immediacy and intensity of these interviews may have blurred the fact that the Spanish Civil War and its aftermath was not a hot issue in 1964. Despite available information about liberation attacks, garrotting, prison pleas, and anti-Franco organizations, the Spanish problem had been overshadowed by World War II and had already found its glossy movie representation in *For Whom the Bell Tolls* (1943). While American moviegoers had difficulties in warming to the conflict and characters, European critics again voiced their disappointment at a lack of political stance in *Behold a Pale Horse*. Uwe Nettelbeck, for instance, claims that Zinnemann "did not want to hurt anyone, not the church, and actually not even the fascists" (640). The following letter by Emilio López, Barcelona, to Mr. Rothman (Executive Vice President, Columbia Pictures International, New York) with reference to a screening in Paris on December 2, 1963, reveals how scattered indeed the film's assertions were (*FZC*):

> There will be no critic or spectator that can honestly say that the Spanish political system is attacked or that religious sentiments are offended. If the Captain of the "Guardia Civil" has a small "affair," this is only human and is a sign of "virility." I am confident that the Spanish Authorities, previously influenced by the reading of the novel *Killing a Mouse on Sunday*, will change their unjust and arbitrary attitude. . . . I kindly request that our International Publicity Department be extra careful when making the phrases for advertising the film and avoid any political allusion that may not reflect the humanity contained therein.

The stylistic and narrative policy of "not intruding" had played down the authenticity of the etic material, added to the remoteness of the subject matter, and even allowed an interpretation of the film as politically noncommittal, which helped the producers to sell their product more conveniently.

THE DAY OF THE JACKAL (1973)

Fred Zinnemann is one of the few directors who looked outside the United States for foreign themes and material while at the same time succeeding in obtaining financial support from American backers. This holds true for his adaptation of Frederick Forsyth's novel *The Day of the Jackal*, released as a French-British co-production. Nine European locations, the absence of an American character as a link for the audience, and an all-European cast set *The Day of the Jackal* one step further apart from the other three films.

The film's quintessential etic references are the terrorist activities of the Organisation de l'Armée Secrète (OAS) during the Algerian crisis and its attempted assassinations of Charles de Gaulle in the early 1960s. Journalist-novelist Forsyth mixed actual characters and events of the time with detailed accounts of criminal and police proceedings and added another, fictionalized attack on de Gaulle's life, executed by a hired British assassin, the "Jackal." Zinnemann conducted his own research as usual: technical comments on the organization of the French police were translated into English, railway schedules of 1972 were compared to those of 1963, military gun experts were consulted for the technical details on the rifle and final gunshot scene. In order to get a "real" Charles de Gaulle for the assassination attempt, Zinnemann again wanted to use stock footage. Since the material was black and white, technicians experimented with colorization and filters to avoid a phony look. Despite all efforts, the optical trick did not bring the desired result. So the president's part was taken over by an actor and the scene was staged.

As the assassination attempts had failed almost a decade earlier and de Gaulle died in 1970, it seemed unlikely that *The Day of the Jackal* would face restrictions with regard to its theme and characters. There were slight adjustments to the different audiences, such as the omission of the explanatory prologue in the French version. For the U.S. release a "shadow" was required during the killing of the forger as a moderate censorship measure. However, Zinnemann wrote on January 3, 1972, that it would be advisable to change "authentic names of people involved in the 'Jackal'" in order to protect ourselves against future legal complications" (*FZC*). Thirteen names, ranging from several ministers to de Gaulle's driver, were changed. Zinnemann wanted to keep the original names at least for the prologue sequence: "I hope that it will not be necessary to change the name of Bastien-Thiry, as this would severely damage, at the very outset, the documentary flavour which we are trying to give the film" (*FZC*; letter of January 3, 1972).

The "documentary flavour" of *The Day of the Jackal* was achieved with television newscast-type pictures of statesmen, complemented by film-style high angles of buildings. Narration and a radio news report form a combined voice-over in the expositional scene of the assassination attempt in 1962, and the execution of Bastien-Thiry is reminiscent of the semidocumentary beginning of *Behold a Pale Horse*. The main part of the film focuses on the Jackal's scheme and the authorities' efforts to trace him, interspersed with glimpses of European settings. The scene of the crime is Paris during a parade, and here the film returns to its newscast style. The short and effective gunshot scene is preceded by pictures of the empty square ornamented with fences to hold back the masses, followed by a montage sequence of the police apparatus, guns, uniforms, flags, tanks, and planes orchestrated with marches and anthems.

The professionalism of the assassin, for whom killing is merely a technical problem, rendered in-depth information about de Gaulle or the OAS almost unnecessary; no original footage of the president's telecratic performances was used. *The Day of the Jackal* marked the beginning of a series of assassination and political intrigue films in the 1970s, which reflected the contemporary rise in terrorism and political corruption (e.g., *The Parallax View* [1974], *Black Sunday* [1976], *All the President's Men* [1976]). Presidential assassination was part of the American collective memory, but the release of the film, which also emphasized shortcomings such as illegal procedures within national institutions, additionally coincided with the Watergate scandal in the United States. *Jackal*'s main genre tradition, however, was that of the cunning crime story, which, mostly devoid of political insinuation, had become a variety of the gangster film when the noir potential had been exhausted.

Zinnemann and producer John Woolf held different views on audience considerations. Zinnemann wrote to Woolf on August 31, 1972, that "*The Day of the Jackal* in book form had by far its greatest success in the United States. It seems logical that consideration should be given primarily to the tastes of an American audience" (*FZC*). But Woolf, who saw the film as geared toward international audiences, was anxious not to lose or upset particular markets by affronts to any national feeling or disregard for authorities. He wrote on September 7, 1972 (*FZC*):

It has to be appreciated in our story—which may in fact be true—if de Gaulle had not bent down to kiss the veteran, a British subject would have assassinated him. Shades of Joan of Arc!! The consequences would have been unimaginable. Therefore, although we are not making a political film—I would be ashamed to leave such a possibility in the minds of French and British audiences and it is for this reason that I hold the view that it is essential to demonstrate that the British authorities, stemming from the Prime Minister, did everything in their power to prevent such an overwhelming disaster.

The apple of discord Woolf refers to is the British involvement in the police action taken against the danger of assassination. Woolf suggested increasing the emphasis on the efficiency of the British authorities. Zinnemann felt that the two storylines of the Jackal and Lebel, the French pursuer, were complex—and complicated—enough, but he reluctantly added scenes featuring British activities, risking more confusion in the plot. He wrote to Woolf: "I would like to restate my position, with the understanding that I will shoot the U.K. scenes in question—against my own judgement and conviction—as a personal concession to you" (*FZC*; September 8, 1972). Despite speculations of this kind, *The Day of the Jackal* performed poorly in France, where its main action takes place and whose etic material is at the story's heart.

Fred Zinnemann reached the narrative cinema by way of documentary filmmaking. He was drawn to historical situations in America and abroad which determined his choice of subject matter and shaping of real-life material. Zinnemann's attitude toward eticity is influenced by documentary practices; he shows a strong desire to film original locations and to pay attention to a well-researched accuracy in detail, for instance in costume, mannerism, or language. In the case of Schofield Barracks, location and military authenticity ranked high, even at the cost of having to submit to additional censorship. In casting, Zinnemann frequently employed supporting actors from the respective countries or bilingual actors with inflections rather than heavy accents; regional dialects also matter in his American films, and language barriers are generally portrayed realistically in instances of intercultural communication. To create additional audiovisual support for some real-life approximation, Zinnemann repeatedly used original footage, black and white film stock, and newsreel or TV newscast aesthetics in opening or framing sequences.

While Zinnemann followed his formal preferences throughout, questions of content were subject to interference and shifting emphasis. In 1948 Zinnemann wrote: "The inner truth of the subject matter is of such paramount importance that it must not be sacrificed to ulterior considerations such as star names and conventional treatment" ("Different Perspective" 113). *The Search* fulfills this dictum to a greater extent than the other films of this analysis, yet the film shows more consideration for the audience than *Behold a Pale Horse* which, on the other hand, has a star cast. In order to work within the established industry, it became necessary for Zinnemann to negotiate and at times subordinate his own decisions. Restrictions were imposed on the film by censors within or outside the film industry who wished to sustain a public image or societal fabrication (as in *From Here to Eternity*), and/or by the producers, for example to accommodate international markets (as in *The Day of the Jackal*).

Over the years a shift occurs in the priority Zinnemann assigns to subject matter and in his attitude towards the creation of awareness through political statements. In a letter to producer John Woolf of September 8, 1972, the order is reversed (*FZC*): "The public sees movies for entertainment. They want to be told a story that keeps them continually involved and interested. They are not interested in ulterior political overtones." Not only *The Day of the Jackal* confirms this view, but also *Julia* (1977), in which Zinnemann emphasizes the personal relationship and the American character Lillian, not the political life led by Julia in Europe.[8] In 1983 Zinnemann took on the traditional stance of the industry: "I'm a Hollywood director, who wants to please a mass audience. I don't believe in selling personal beliefs—just in making good movies" ("Fred Zinnemann" 38–39).

In view of his choice and handling of material, the latter statement is not altogether convincing. Zinnemann's films, particularly those with a high degree of (international) eticity, are not standard escapist Hollywood fare. Occasionally, the presence rather than absence of etic references gave rise to criticism. Andrew Sarris accuses Zinnemann of "superficiality of commitment" and labels him "semirealist" (169). Even stronger is Parker Tyler's criticism of *The Men* (1950): "what may seem casually a mere realism of technique is actually a pseudo-realism of content" (11). Some moviegoers, by contrast, reacted with complaints about false uniforms or with compliments on the accuracy of firearms detail (*FZC*).[9] Unaware of the larger scale of directorial choices, modifications, and restrictions, they scrutinized Zinnemann's "well-informed fiction" (Gow, "*Jackal*" 51) for minor inaccuracies in its etic detail.

Etic precision in the cinema is not simply a matter of accuracy and technical possibility. The above variants of perception reveal that the documentarist Zinnemann is caught between his ideal of a "dramatic document" and technicalities of mere "documentary flavour." Moving further toward documentary drama would have required him to give up the narrative advantages of fictional dramatization; on the other hand, abstaining from etic material would have foregone the potential for real-life cross reference and sociopolitical criticism. Though Zinnemann allows "creative accidents" to enter his visuals as a documentary filmmaker would, many strong impressions resulting from the "rawness" of research material or personal encounters do not find their way to the screen, because they would have been transported only by a documentary film. He is a Hollywood director in the sense that he had to balance his own aesthetic choices and commitment to his material as relates to the use of etic elements with the need to satisfy producers, censors, and potential audiences.

NOTES

1. The opposition *etic* and *emic* has been derived from the linguistic opposition *phonetic* and *phonemic* and its further application was developed by Kenneth L. Pike in *Language in Relation to a Unified Theory of the Structure of Human Behavior* (The Hague/Paris: Mouton, 2d revised ed. 1967 [first part of the Preliminary Edition: 1954]). For the purposes of this chapter, the terms *etic* and *real-life* have been simplified and are basically interchangeable.

2. This contribution is based predominantly on correspondence and production files which were made available by Fred Zinnemann and are compiled in the *Fred Zinnemann Collection* (*FZC*) of the Margaret Herrick Library at the Academy of Motion Picture Arts and Sciences, and on public discussions with the director on March 6 and March 20, 1988, during the *Fred Zinnemann Retrospective* (*FZ Retro*), University of Southern California in collaboration with the Max Kade Institute of German-Austrian-Swiss Studies, March 5–26, 1988.

3. The strong effect of original location shooting and nonprofessional acting on the aesthetic appeal of etic material becomes apparent in a comparison with Zinnemann's adaptation of Anna Seghers's concentration camp escape novel *The Seventh Cross*, which was filmed in 1944 as a studio production. Since then, documentary footage has irrevocably shaped the visual impression of the concentration camp and makes the film look stagey and unreal.

4. Zinnemann's programmatic statements in "Different Perspective" resemble Roberto Rossellini's definition of cinema's function, namely "to bring men face to face with things, with realities such as they are, and to make known other men, other problems" (quoted in Armes 205).

5. Zinnemann writes on November 12, 1952 (*FZC*): "Both Mr. Clift and I feel that it would add a very interesting facet to the characterization if in his [Prewitt's] speech there could be an occasional inflection indicating his origin. . . . Also, by ordinary production standards, this entire problem is not regarded as particularly important. However, it happens to be of great interest to Mr. Clift and myself."

6. A similar technique to combine etic footage with emic characters was used in the newsreel sequence in *Citizen Kane* (1941), for the protagonist's backstory in *In the Line of Fire* (1993), and more extensively in *The Unbearable Lightness of Being* (1987). The technique is also the major narrative and stylistic principle in *Zelig* (1982).

7. *The Search* was Clift's second film, but the first to be released.

8. The *FZC* production files for *Julia* contain suggestions by Lillian Hellman that the film should show more of the political climate in Europe in the 1930s and spend more time on Julia. A memorandum by Zinnemann says: "I reminded her [Vanessa Redgrave, who played Julia] of our first discussion in New York when I said that I did *not* want *Julia* to be a political film, to which, I thought, she had agreed" (*FZC*).

9. How readily real-life references and realism are seen as mutual influences is also revealed in Mark Rabinowitz's review of Zinnemann's *A Hatful of Rain*: "I was surprised by some evidences that Fred Zinnemann's direction is getting careless . . . since he was committed to location-shooting, presumably for 'realism,' he should have used locations for minor actions that were geographically related to the location of the main action. It is impossible to get about New York as did the characters in this film" (355).

WORKS CITED

Armes, Roy. *Patterns of Realism*. South Brunswick/New York: A. S. Barnes, 1971.

Gow, Gordon. "*The Day of the Jackal*." *Films and Filming* 8 (1973): 51.

——— . "Individualism against Machinery: Fred Zinnemann in an Interview with Gordon Gow." *Films and Filming* 24.5 (February 1978): 12–17.

Johnson, William. "*Behold a Pale Horse*." *Film Quarterly* 18.2 (1964): 46–50.

Jones, James. *From Here to Eternity*. New York: Scribner's, 1951.

Nettelbeck, Uwe. "*Deine Zeit ist um*." *Filmkritik* 12 (1964): 639–40. Translation mine.

Rabinowitz, Mark. "*A Hatful of Rain.*" *Films in Review* 8.7 (August–September 1957): 355.

Sarris, Andrew. *The American Cinema: Directors and Directions.* New York: Dutton, 1968.

Sussex, Elizabeth. "*Behold a Pale Horse.*" *Sight and Sound* 33.4 (Autumn 1964): 198.

Tyler, Parker. "Violating Reality via the Fact-Fiction Film." *Films in Review* 1.4 (May–June 1950): 9–11, 38.

Zinnemann, Fred. "Different Perspective." *Sight and Sound* 17.67 (Autumn 1948): 113.

———. "Fred Zinnemann." Interview. By Michael Buckley. *Films in Review* 34.1 (January 1983): 25–40.

———. "*From Here to Eternity.*" *Sight and Sound* 57.1 (Winter 1987–1988): 20–25.

———. "Letter from Fred Zinnemann." *Film Criticism* 19.2 (Winter 1994–1995): 86–89.

———. "Revelations." Interview. *Films and Filming* 10.12 (September 1964): 5–6.

———. "Zinnemann Talks Back." Interview. By James R. Silke and Rory Guy. *Cinema* (Beverly Hills) 2.3 (October–November 1964): 20–22, 30.

CHAPTER FIFTEEN

Fred Zinnemann's Actors

STEVE VINEBERG

Fred Zinnemann's movies offer Hollywood big-studio classicism—
meticulous craft put to the service of telling large-scale popular stories
with clarity and feeling—tempered by unusual restraint and touched,
unexpectedly, by the poetic. The restraint and the poetry mark the major
differences between Zinnemann and his closest near-contemporary,
William Wyler, though both were subtle and superlative filmmakers who
lifted craftsmanship to the realm of art, and both were celebrated actor's
directors. But in the years during which Zinnemann came to prominence—the exciting post–World War II era when Hollywood movies
acquired a startling new vibrancy after the cheery fakeness of the mid-for-
ties—Wyler continued to work almost exclusively with established stars,
"personality" actors (many of them extremely talented) who approached
acting in the same way as the performers he'd directed in the thirties
had—Bette Davis, Henry Fonda, Margaret Sullavan. Zinnemann, on the
other hand, was fascinated by the youngsters trained in the Method by
Lee Strasberg and Stella Adler and Elia Kazan—by Montgomery Clift,
whom he directed in *The Search* in 1948 and *From Here to Eternity* in
1953; by Marlon Brando, who made his first picture, *The Men*, with Zinnemann in 1950; with Julie Harris, who repeated her stage portrayal of
Frankie Addams in Carson McCullers's *The Member of the Wedding* for
Zinnemann's 1952 film. In terms of his work with actors, Zinnemann,

219

who collaborated with old-style movie stars as well, stands midway between Wyler and Kazan, the Method actors' icon, who set up shop in New York rather than Hollywood, who directed theater as well as movies, and whose fireball energy and love of flamboyant outpourings of feeling linked him to the young actors who stepped out of his classes at the Actors Studio and right onto the sets for *A Streetcar Named Desire*, *On the Waterfront*, and *East of Eden*.

At their finest, all three men got stunning ensemble work out of their casts. What is amazing about Zinnemann's best movies is the variety of acting styles they show off—the way actors of contrasting background and with contrasting approaches are able to play off each other, like gifted musicians from different generations and milieux thrown together in a pick-up band. In *The Member of the Wedding*, the Method prodigy Julie Harris (twenty-four when she played twelve-year-old Frankie on Broadway, twenty-six in the film) shares the screen with the spooky-funny child actor Brandon de Wilde and the blues singer and musical-comedy star Ethel Waters, whose heyday began in the late twenties and ended in 1943 with the movie adaptation of her biggest stage hit, *Cabin in the Sky*. In *From Here to Eternity* Method-trained Montgomery Clift pals around with pop singer Frank Sinatra (in his first dramatic role) and is romantically paired with Donna Reed, a contract player since the forties whose wholesomeness covered a weird, noir-ish intensity and a capacity for sudden, high-pitched emotion. (Frank Capra had touched on both in *It's a Wonderful Life* seven years earlier.) In the same movie, Burt Lancaster, both a tough-guy actor in the Cagney-Robinson-Bogart mold and a flamboyantly physical performer in the Douglas Fairbanks-Errol Flynn mold, is matched with the Scottish-born Deborah Kerr, a classically trained dancer and stage actress whose air of breeding brought her a Hollywood contract in the late forties. Zinnemann located a neurotic quality in Kerr no one else had seemed interested in. In *The Nun's Story* (1959) he gave Audrey Hepburn, Hollywood's most elegant pixie, her first opportunity for serious work, surrounding her with a distinguished cast of British and American character actors—Peter Finch, Peggy Ashcroft, Edith Evans, Mildred Dunnock, Patricia Collinge (and the soon-to-be distinguished young Colleen Dewhurst). In *The Sundowners* (1960) he cast Kerr again, strikingly against type, as the wife of an Australian sheep drover, a nomad played by Robert Mitchum, who (like Lancaster) came out of the forties film noir.

Though a certain amount has been written about the Method performances in Zinnemann's films, most of the other terrific acting he coached has not been discussed very much. Deborah Kerr is seldom thought about any more, though in the fifties she was generally acknowledged to be a strong and intelligent actress. Her best work—up until *The Innocents*, in 1961—was for Zinnemann. As Karen Holmes in *From Here to Eternity*, the captain's wife who has an affair with an enlisted man (the company's "top kick," Sergeant Milt Warden, played by Lancaster) in the months leading to Pearl Harbor, she shows more sides than in any previous performance. Warden is drawn to her aura of sexual availability, to her wised-up, tough-blonde presence; he begins insinuating the moment they meet, and he has the nerve to drive to her house in the rain when he knows her husband isn't home—ostensibly with papers for him to sign—and push his way into her kitchen to procure himself a drink. She commends him on his ingenuity but admonishes him, "You just got one thing wrong—the lady herself. The lady's not what she seems."

That's the key line for Kerr's performance. Lana Turner specialized in roles like this one seems to be—street-smart, sexually direct women compensating for loneliness or poverty—and Barbara Stanwyck was brilliant in such roles years earlier. But though Karen Holmes carries as much baggage as any of those characters did—a careless, unfaithful husband, a dead child—she has nothing like their knife-edge danger; her style is just a defense, barely covering raw nerves. By the time Warden arrives for their first date, she is a jumble of conflicting impulses like frayed wires; when she unloads on him—three men have tried to pick her up, she feels cheap, she imagines he's decided this is a lousy idea and maybe she should just go home—he has to jump to avoid the loose sparks. Kerr uses the hard R's she has adopted (to blanket over her Scot-tinged English accent) and the cigarettes she pulls on to suggest the tough shell that shatters from the inside every time Warden gets near her. We see what she is really like when they are at a club together listening to music, and she strokes his clenched hand, draws it around her shoulder, kisses his knuckles, nestles into his shoulder. Her lovemaking with Lancaster's Milt Warden, here and in the justly famous beach scene, is urgent and fugitive—a lifeline for Karen.

Kerr's opposite number in *From Here to Eternity* is the dark beauty Donna Reed, who plays Alma/Lorene, the working-class woman from Oregon who landed in Hawaii and took a job as a hostess at the New Congress Club, where her name—picked from a perfume ad because her employer thought it sounded French—suits her slightly exotic, princessy looks and her slightly languid, reticent air. (In James Jones's novel, she's a whore, but the Hays Code was still in effect when the movie came out.) Alma doesn't drink and she's got a vocabulary; she holds her cigarette like a debutante and lives in a fashionable district of town (with a girlfriend); but underneath that high-society affectation—which doesn't seem like one because she believes in it so fervently—is a woman who is desperate for respectability, and at the same time desperately in love with Prewitt (Clift), the career soldier who represents everything she thinks she doesn't want (everything that's low class). He is drawn to her sensitivity, which we see in her silent, touched response to his story about the boxing opponent he beat into blindness—the reason Prewitt swears he will never fight again. That sensitivity can take her all the way into hysteria. In moments of high emotion—like the scene where she tries uselessly to keep him from crawling back to his company after he has gone AWOL and as the Japanese bombs fall—her face begins to melt and her delicate poise crumbles.

From Here to Eternity is a men-at-war saga (even though the war doesn't get going until the last reel)—probably the best to come out of the big-studio era—and the two women are, by convention, on the periphery of the main theme, which is, as I read it, integrity. Karen and Alma's love for their respective men takes them over the edge, but on some essential level they do not understand what those men are about. Karen begs Milt to take officer exams so she can divorce Holmes and marry him, but he hates officers and he just cannot get himself to sign the papers. Alma argues that the army has never done Prewitt anything but damage—she doesn't see why he is so loyal to it. It's only at the end—in each woman's final scene with her lover—that they recognize these men are in love with something from which they can never wrest them away. Appropriately, the last time we see the two women, they are standing side by side on the ship that takes them away from Pearl Harbor forever. This scene (the movie's finale) really belongs to Donna Reed. The women, who have never met before, strike up a conversation, and Alma tells Karen that her fiancé was a bomber pilot who died in the first strike—the son of a fine southern family, Robert E. Lee Prewitt. There is something disturbing about Alma's fiction (Altman's *Thieves Like Us*, made two decades later, ends similarly, with Shelley Duvall inventing a story about her dead outlaw lover), just as there was about her hysteria with Prewitt in the blackout a few moments earlier. Reed's suggestion of instability undercuts what may have been intended as a sentimental ending.

In *The Sundowners*, Kerr plays Ida Carmody, a tough, proud, self-reliant woman who makes the most of her husband's wanderlust because

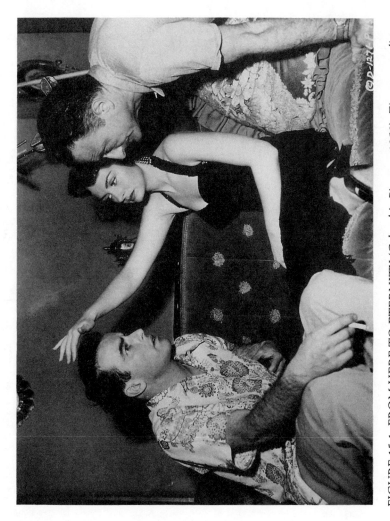

FIGURE 15.1. FROM HERE TO ETERNITY (Columbia Pictures, 1953). Zinnemann directing Montgomery Clift and Donna Reed. (Courtesy Jerry Ohlinger Archives)

FIGURE 15.2. THE SUNDOWNERS (Warner Bros., 1960). Robert Mitchum and Deborah Kerr as sheep drovers. (Courtesy Museum of Modern Art/Film Stills Archive)

she loves him so much. But the careless freedom of her youth has given way to the natural fears of middle age, and now she longs for a home—a longing that consumes her, coming over her like a dry cough, compelling her to pinch pennies and devise strategies to get the whole family working (including their teenage son Sean), so they can earn enough for a down payment on a farm. There is one scene in the movie I doubt anyone who has seen it has forgotten. The Carmodys' horse and cart pauses at a railroad crossing, and for a moment Ida is face to face with a young woman, well-dressed, obviously homebound, applying her make-up. Kerr makes it clear that Ida sees in this stranger everything she's ever wanted and never had—and is afraid she never *will* have. Kerr's eyes narrow and shine, and she seems almost drunk with the unexpected emotion of the encounter—as if it had hauled her out of a deep sleep and brought her into a confrontation with a secret terror.

Even more than *From Here to Eternity*, *The Sundowners* focuses on the emotions of women and men who don't express their feelings easily or (often) directly. When Rupe (Peter Ustinov), Paddy's partner, turns down the jolly, open-hearted hotelkeeper, Gert (Glynis Johns), who has been trying to charm him into marriage, Gert jokes publicly about her rejection; our only hint of how hard she takes it is the way, marching across the yard back to her hotel, she loses her bearings for a second and bumps into a horse's flank. When the Carmodys take their leave of the sheep shearers they have been working with for several months, one of them, a new father, tells Sean (Michael Anderson, Jr.) he hopes the baby grows into a boy just like him, and Sean, unable to handle the baldness of the compliment, shifts away in confusion and sinks his attention in the manual task he's engaged in.

Deborah Kerr's performance is the most eloquent and moving example in the picture of the reluctant emotion of rough and ready outbackers. As in *From Here to Eternity*, she goes right at the neurotic underpinnings of the character, but she offers them to us in the quick, subtle changes of expression that flicker across her face like sunlight. When she broaches the subject of the farm to Paddy, presenting it as Sean's dream more than her own, her eyes grow suddenly sharp and bitter. The actress draws on the distinctive quaver in her voice as her emotional resource for the speech in which Ida conveys to her husband her fear of a homeless old age, and again for the speech to Sean (who has urged her, impulsively, to get a home on her own if Paddy refuses to give up the road). In this passage—the best, I'd say, in Isobel Lennart's screenplay—she warns him that if he ever asks her to choose between Paddy and him, she'll choose Paddy every time. When Ida's finally rounded up enough cash for the down payment, and Paddy gambles it away, half deliberately, she can hardly stand to look at him, but Kerr keeps us aware of the depth of her love and loyalty under her dismay.

Both of Kerr's films for Zinnemann came out in the last decade or so in which the weight of the Production Code could still be felt in Hollywood (though it was being tested with greater regularity), and there is a sexual frankness in the depiction of Karen Holmes's adulterous romance with Milt Warden and in Ida's marriage to Paddy Carmody that is daring for the time and still, I think, unusually articulate and adult. With Karen and Warden, you feel the pull of sexual feelings that battle against reason and certainly against practicality; with the Carmodys, you can see how much these two people like sleeping together—that the bond between them was forged in bed. (When Paddy is cheated out of a rare night out with his wife because she has promised to keep watch with a pregnant friend who is fast approaching her time, his disappointment makes him angry, irrational, and wantonly irresponsible.) In both movies Zinnemann has cast Kerr opposite sexy, highly athletic American "personality" actors who communicate emotion in more straightforward and less delicate ways than she does. Robert Mitchum is a wonderfully relaxed performer who can look rumpled and foggy when the character he is playing hits an uncomfortable or unaccustomed feeling—as Paddy does when his son works up the courage to call him on his insensitivity to Ida's needs. Mitchum has done other memorable work, especially playing dangerously seductive men with frightening capabilities (*The Night of the Hunter*, *Cape Fear*), but Zinnemann gets him to do things in *The Sundowners* I have never seen him try before, like the way his whole face changes shape when one of the other men on the shearing team speaks admiringly of Ida, catching him off guard. You can see he hasn't thought much about how other people—men in particular—might perceive his wife, that he hasn't calculated her worth in the world's terms because he considers his own feelings about her private and exclusive.

Beefy Burt Lancaster looks tight and fit in his military garb in *From Here to Eternity*. Much of the pleasure of watching Lancaster at this stage in his career, in movies like this one and *The Crimson Pirate* and *The Rainmaker* and *Trapeze*, comes from the great shape he's in and his witty presentation of it. That is most obvious, of course, in something like the parodic swashbuckler *The Crimson Pirate*, where his delight in his own

FIGURE 15.3. FROM HERE TO ETERNITY (Columbia Pictures, 1953). Deborah Kerr and Burt Lancaster in the famous beach scene. (Courtesy Jerry Ohlinger Archives)

physicality is the movie's comic springboard. The fact that he looks like a walking erection is a great joke in *From Here to Eternity*, where he eyes Kerr with unmistakable lasciviousness the first time he sees her and where his character has mastered a crude but shrewd kind of sexual innuendo. He employs his whole body all the time in this role, like a dancer or a triathlete; he moves serenely, and he is beautiful in repose. When Warden gets smashed, his body stiffens and he drags it around as if it were made of cardboard. He is a cartoon of a drunken soldier; this is very inventive physical acting.

Of course, Lancaster's performance isn't primarily comic. What sticks with you—as with Mitchum's Paddy Carmody—is the amount of emotion he is able to get across in an almost completely physical way. You can recognize the source of Warden's tough-guy bravado and permanent state of physical readiness in Lancaster's forties film noir roles (like the fighter downed by love in the 1946 adaptation of Hemingway's *The Killers*). Warden's lineage goes back even farther, to the wisecracking macho posturing of those two hard nuts, Quirt and Flagg, in the much-filmed World War I classic *What Price Glory?* In *From Here to Eternity*, Lancaster and Zinnemann work on exposing the sensitive parts of this kind of man, whose home is the army. Zinnemann doesn't exactly stretch his star, the way he stretches Mitchum a few years later. The actor and the director find ways of releasing Warden's sensitivity in straight-arrow ways that seem perfectly in concert with his style—for instance, his befuddlement and exasperation when he finds himself so deeply in love with Karen that, rather than being contemptuous of her reputation for promiscuity, he's wracked by it; or his steady man-to-man admiration for the newcomer to the company, Prewitt, whose constitutional inability to compromise his principles earns him the unofficial post of the captain's whipping boy. Zinnemann was smart not to try to soften Lancaster, especially since Montgomery Clift (giving a legendary performance), representing the Actors Studio contingent, has the sensitive child-in-the-man role.

The third major male actor in *From Here to Eternity* is Frank Sinatra, as Prewitt's luckless buddy, Angelo Maggio. (He and Donna Reed carried off Oscars for their performances.) Watching Sinatra, who brings a kibitzing Hoboken energy and a touch of Damon Runyon to this touching clown role, you cannot help thinking of the scene in *The Godfather* where the Sinatra character, Johnny Fontane, played by Al Martino, begs Brando's Don Corleone to help get him the movie part he's been after to resuscitate his fading career (as, in fact, *From Here to Eternity* did for Sinatra)—a part he knows he'd be great in because the character is just "a guy like me." The beauty of Sinatra's acting here is that it is as easy and natural as his conversational singing style; his lines are mostly gags, and you wonder if he thought some of them up himself. This is the best kind of typecasting; it locates the area where the actor and the role overlap and then allows him to sink into the role so the performance deepens without your being aware of it. Sometime in the middle of the picture, Maggio gets himself arrested for sneaking off guard duty and the stockade sergeant, "Fatso" Judson (Ernest Borgnine), an old enemy from a barroom brawl, brutalizes him repeatedly. (One of the best examples of Zinnemann's hallmark restraint is his refusal to show us the beatings.) In one of the movie's best-known scenes, Maggio, having managed at last to escape from the stockade, dies in Prewitt's arms. This is Sinatra's big scene, and it's an extension of the loose, limpid acting he has been doing all along—but it's so startlingly good it knocks you out. The whispered, repeated warning to Prew—"Watch out for Fatso, watch out for Fatso"—is soft talk, bedtime talk, as if Angelo were merely drifting off to sleep. He tiptoes to his death, leaving a silence behind him—a commemorative moment to acknowledge the hole Maggio's departure leaves in the fabric of Zinnemann's terrific movie.

If Frank Sinatra's performance has a bebop rhythm, Ethel Waters's Berenice Sadie Brown in *The Member of the Wedding* has the lived-in tragic depth of gospel and blues and the built-in kick—the high of gospel and jazz. It could be the greatest performance ever given on screen by a singer in a nonmusical role. (The most serious contender would be Barbra Streisand in *The Way We Were*.) Waters must have been glorious as Berenice in the 1950 New York production, under Harold Clurman's direction, but this is one of those stage-to-screen translations—like Brando in *A Streetcar Named Desire*, Streisand in *Funny Girl*, or Lily Tomlin in *The Search for Signs of Intelligent Life in the Universe*—that you can feel expanding in the movie version because the performer has an innate sense for the camera and—especially in Waters's case—is such a phenomenal camera subject. Zinnemann and his superb cinematographer, Hal Mohr, capture her huge, jack-o'-lantern grin, her sashaying hunk of a body, which gives off tender waves of heat, and the transported glow of her face when she recounts some moving incident in her past to the two children in her charge, Frankie (Julie Harris) and her little cousin John Henry (Brandon de Wilde). At these moments she's like a parishioner at a revival meeting who finds God in the thick of a hymn: she throws back her head and smiles the most sublime smile you have ever seen.

As a singer in the twenties and thirties, Waters was famous for both her high-stepping razzmatazz approach to worldly-wise, frankly carnal numbers like "Birmingham Bertha" (in her first film, the 1929 *On With the Show*) and "Heat Wave" (which Irving Berlin wrote for her, for the 1933 revue *As Thousands Cheer*) and "Thief in the Night"—songs she glided and purred her way through—and for ballads she pledged a heart-felt commitment to, plunging her honey-and-smoked-cotton voice into, like Berlin's "Supper Time." Both sides of the black-Baptist coin—the earthiness and the born-to-trouble spirituality—are deeply seated in her Berenice. You can see both at once when Frankie, who is endlessly curi-ous about Berenice's romantic life, asks her if she plans to marry her friend T.T., and Berenice answers with respect for T.T.'s virtue—she calls him "a fine, upstanding man who has walked in a state of grace his whole life"—but admits, candidly, that "he don't make me shiver none." It is clearest, though, in the scene where she eulogizes her first husband, Ludie Maxwell Freeman, the love of her life, who died young. Phrasing Carson McCullers's magnificent poetic prose, setting it for her blues woman's range—she reaches for luminous high notes, then digs down raucously into the smoke at the bottom of her voice—she comes out with The Bal-lad of Ludie, which, if it had real music under it, might sound like "My Man's Gone Now" from *Porgy and Bess*, scooping the depths of a woman's sorrow. As Waters hits the climax of the speech—"Ludie died! Ludie died! Ludie Maxwell Freeman died!"—only the husk of a voice is left, and tears are pouring off her like sweat, yet she's smiling. (Though she doesn't say so, you feel that this is where God appears in the midst of Berenice's despair.) Then—logically—she begins to hum.

Scripture-quoting Berenice is the rock of Frankie's restless, bewil-dered, strangely burdened newly adolescent existence, though she isn't always adequate to the girl's needs. She gets some of Frankie's perceptions but not all of them, and her counsel, though it leaks through the worn layers of her sad decades of experience, isn't always what Frankie needs to hear at that particular agonized moment when her growing bones feel like they are coming right through her skin. What she provides, most cru-cially, is a safe haven for motherless Frankie. Berenice is watchful of Frankie's moods and alert to the signs that she is coming too close to the edge. When Frankie soars into her steam-powered, rhapsodic speech about the fantastic figure she envisions for herself, racing through the world alongside her brother and his bride (it is their wedding she longs to

231

FIGURE 15.4. THE MEMBER OF THE WEDDING (Columbia Pictures, 1952). A rare moment of calm for Julie Harris, Ethel Waters, and Brandon de Wilde. (Courtesy Museum of Modern Art/Film Stills Archive)

be a member of), Berenice is there to catch her as her adolescent energy turns in on her and to soothe her exasperated tears. Cradled in Waters's lap, her head tilted onto Waters's shoulder while John Henry clings on the other one, Harris's Frankie speaks wonderingly of the fleeting time: "This moment is passing, and it will never come again." She's right: this childhood shelter will shatter tomorrow, when tragedy strikes. Zinnemann captures the magic calm before the whole world cracks open. As the two children flank that immense black pearl of a face, which the camera has caught every hidden corner and slant of, Waters defines the moment, suspends it in time, with her *a cappella* rendition of the spiritual "His Eye Is on the Sparrow." After the final lyric glimmer of the song fades, she chuckles softly, "Frankie, you got the sharpest set of human bones I ever felt." Julie Harris's performance is the poetic center of this astonishing movie, but Ethel Waters provides its core of warmth.

Perhaps the most surprising piece of acting in any of Zinnemann's films is Audrey Hepburn's portrayal of Sister Luke in *The Nun's Story*. This remarkably understated and intelligent picture, highly praised on its release, is forgotten now, and Hepburn is remembered mostly for her elegant, fairy-princess presence in movies like *Roman Holiday*, *Breakfast at Tiffany's*, and *Charade*. But in *The Nun's Story*, Zinnemann liberates talents none of Hepburn's other roles—not even the blind woman who outwits a ruthless adversary in the thriller *Wait Until Dark*—makes visible. Working in the director's mode of exposing the feelings throbbing beneath well-laid surfaces—in this case, a surface provided by the vocation Sister Luke has selected, which strives to tamp down the private impulses of individuals—Hepburn gives a performance of extraordinary emotional clarity and precision. Sister Luke (or Gaby, as she is called before she enters the convent and adopts a new identity) is a young woman whose flaws, in the view of the order, are intellectual pride and independence of mind. The movie is ingenious in giving her vices that most of us would consider virtues. Though Zinnemann and the screenwriter, Robert Anderson, working from Kathryn C. Hulme's novel, present the order fairly and respectfully—certainly it would be difficult not to respond to the older nuns played with loving authority by Edith Evans, Peggy Ashcroft, and Mildred Dunnock—they constantly place us in a position of battling, as instinctively as Sister Luke does, against a vision that downgrades her distinctive qualities. The arc of Hepburn's performance is Sister Luke's movement through these battles to a greater self-awareness that tells her, in the final analysis, that her temperament is not suited for a nun's life. What the actress needs to do is to articulate both the struggle and the elements in her nature that make her decision to leave the order inevitable (though not obvious—Zinnemann isn't interested in the obvious.).

Hepburn accomplishes this task so quietly that it is almost impossible to separate out what the actress is doing from the way the director shapes her scenes, as in the sequence, for instance, where, assigned to assist a brilliant and tough-minded doctor (Peter Finch) in the Belgian Congo, she becomes aware of her sexuality and is baffled by it because her convent existence has not prepared her for confronting it. I don't mean to suggest that Zinnemann should take full credit for Hepburn's acting; she's splendid in this role. But her achievement is less obvious than other leading actors in his movies, like Marlon Brando and Montgomery Clift, Deborah Kerr, and Julie Harris, because the beauty of her acting is largely in her self-effacement—almost never a virtue of American stars (and rarely much fun to watch when they do practice it)—and in emotional expression so tiny and concentrated you can read it in the flicker of an eyelid. Subjected to the ritual haircut that accompanies the admission of postulants like herself into the convent, Sister Luke sits in profile with her eyes closed, and we understand what this attack on her vanity means to her when we see the stiffness in her neck and the flutter of resistance *under* her eyelids.

Looking at these performances in Fred Zinnemann's movies, and at the others I have only alluded to (and at still others I haven't mentioned, like Eva Marie Saint's in *A Hatful of Rain* or Lloyd Bridges's in *High Noon*), we can identify the kinds of emotional tension he favors and works toward, again and again. But in terms of actors, he is Hollywood's great democrat. Few filmmakers have gone so far with so many kinds of performers.

CHAPTER SIXTEEN

Mythic Figures:
Women and Co-Being in
Three Films by Fred Zinnemann

JOANNA E. RAPF

Sometimes a film, while avoiding any precise representation of historical or political reality, can incarnate in mythic figures, speaking in quite elementary language, the opposition between contemporary feelings, and can become very much more realistic than another film in which social and political matters are referred to much more precisely.

—Federico Fellini, *Fellini on Fellini*

There are a number of similarities between Italian director Federico Fellini and Fred Zinnemann besides their obvious status as *auteurs*. Both have been classified as neorealists or social realists concerned with revolutionary change, but their revolutions are nonviolent, focused not on external reality, but internal reality. Both men see art as discovering, supporting, and illuminating historical processes, but not in primarily political terms. Zinnemann says his films "deal with the dignity of human beings and have something to say about oppression, not necessarily in the political way but in a human way" (*American Film* 13). Behind both directors' work is a moral impulse—Zinnemann says "one of the crucial things today [is] trying to preserve our civilization" (*American Film* 12)— but they look to the inner struggles of individual human beings, those Fellini calls "mythic figures," to embody and reify the larger themes.

Myth is concerned with action based on a belief in equality, social justice, community, and great leadership.[1] In the three films with which this chapter is concerned, *The Member of the Wedding* (1952), *The Nun's Story* (1959), and *Julia* (1977), covering the roughly twenty-five years of Zinnemann's maturity as a director, his mythic figures are women. Asked why he chose to do *Julia*, for example, he cited two factors: one was that it was "the story of the friendship of two women," and the other was that it dealt with "the fact of conscience." He then went on to say:

I always find questions of conscience very photogenic. That kind of interior drama is to me very, very exciting because, among other things, I feel that the fact that somebody shoots a gun is of no interest. What I want to know is *why* he shoots it and what the consequences are. Which means that external action as such is less important than the inner motive through which you get to know what the person's about. (*American Film* 13)

Similarly, Zinnemann was excited about doing *The Member of the Wedding* because "in the stifling claustrophobia of that kitchen nothing ever happened. There was hardly any action: everything important took place in the souls of those people" (*Life* 112). In fact, external action can almost come as a surprise in a Zinnemann film, such as the violent protest against Nazi reprisals in Vienna where Julia is studying medicine or the attack on Sister Luke by the mental patient in the hospital in Brussels. The most external action we see in *The Member of the Wedding* is when Frankie hits a soldier over the head with a coke bottle. The important action in these mythic films about women is almost completely internal and surprisingly silent.

Martin Heidegger has observed that from birth on we experience ourselves as a being that is in the company of others. "The way we are— each of us—is already a being with others, a co-being."[2] It is only when we fundamentally understand each other to be fellow human beings that speech is possible. Language, therefore, is not a bridge that for the first time links separate beings; it is rather a testimony to the fact that we experience ourselves as part of each other to begin with, that *without* speaking, we feel ourselves to be members of a human *community*. In this respect, it is worth noting that some of the most eloquent moments in a Zinnemann film are silent expressions of this co-being, such as the close-ups of Berenice in *The Member of the Wedding* or the final exit of Gabrielle in *The Nun's Story*, both of which are discussed below. This sense of co-being and its resultant language are indispensable to the idea of myth with its action based on equality, social justice, *community*, and great leadership. When that sense of co-being is absent, as it is for Frankie as an "unjoined person" at the beginning of *The Member of the Wedding*, a person may fall into false individualism, as she adopts the affected name of "F. Jasmine," and language may drop away. This is described in Carson McCullers's novel at that climactic moment just before the outburst, described below, that ends Act II of the play:

> F. Jasmine felt the unsaid words stick in her throat and a choked sickness made her groan and knock her head against the door jamb. Finally she said in a high ragged voice: "This":
>
> Berenice waited, and when she did not speak again, she asked: "What on earth is wrong with you?"
>
> F. Jasmine could not speak the unknown words, so after a minute she knocked her head a last time on the door and then began to walk around the kitchen table. (McCullers 111)

Another result of the loss of a sense of co-being is a retreat from loss into a substitute for co-being: a crowd of nameless others in which the self drowns itself in its own namelessness. We see this in Sister Luke. Not only does Gabrielle give up her name to become a nun, but also her sense of self. "A nun," she is told, "is not a person who wishes or desires." To the degree that all three films under consideration here are based on autobiographical works, we can say that their characters' recognition of co-being, which is what their stories are all about, is what frees them to use language to create their own myths.

Although Zinnemann has been cited as a "fine woman's director," notably by Louis Giannetti (370), there has been very little written about him from a feminist perspective. In many ways, however, the strongest characters in *High Noon* (1952), to give one example, are the women, in spite of the fact that the center of the film remains the sheriff.[3] Carl Foreman had written the first draft of the script before a director ever came onto the project, and his script appealed to Zinnemann when he received the offer to direct, precisely because he saw it was something more than just another Western.[4] Its particular interest, he says, was that "it was a story of a man who must make a decision according to his *conscience*" (*Life* 96, italics mine), but *High Noon* is also the story of two women who make decisions according to their consciences, Amy Kane and Helen Ramirez. Where Amy's husband, the Gary Cooper character, Sheriff Will Kane, emerges from his crisis of conscience with both his ideals and his marriage intact, Amy and Helen, in their struggles of conscience, are forced into positions where they must give up significant aspects of their lives—Helen her economic base in terms of half ownership of the town store [the source both of her sense of security and self-worth], and Amy, her Quakerism, her categorical belief that killing is wrong [founded on the senseless deaths of her father and brother]. In the script, Helen is described as "intelligent, shrewd and strong-willed" and Amy as "young, attractive, intelligent, strong-willed."[5]

These repeated qualities of intelligence and a strong will are obviously ones that appeal to Zinnemann in his portrayal of women. In *The Member of the Wedding* there are two strong-willed, intelligent women, Frankie Addams and Berenice Sadie Brown. Frankie is in that turbulent time between childhood and womanhood when one feels so painfully that she no longer "belongs," that she is an "unjoined person." The story is about her yearning to be a "member of the wedding"—literally the wedding of her brother Jarvis to a woman named Janice—but allegorically it is "wedding" in a larger sense, meaning to become "joined." Berenice represents the other end of this journey through life, and in her we see the strength to endure as "joinings" fall away, in the death of her first husband, Ludie, and the loss of her stepbrother, Honey Camden Brown, who in the play hangs himself in jail but who is given a lesser fate in the novel and film: eight years on a chain gang [novel], ten years in prison [film]. Berenice cries out, "Lord, please look after Honey Camden—he's all the family I got left."[6] At the end, she is becoming an "unjoined" person; she has even lost her job with the Addams family, just as Frankie is becoming "joined." But her inner struggle to endure, her silent eloquence and wisdom, fill the screen in the deeply felt close-up of her face with which Zinnemann ends the film.

The Nun's Story is about Gabrielle Van der Mal, who becomes Sister Luke. Her character is established at the outset as she prepares to leave her home and become a nun. Initially we see her in an exterior shot, walking along the banks of the river in front of her house where we are shown from her point of view the reflection of buildings upside-down in the water, a representation, perhaps, of the change that is about to occur in her world. This is followed by an interior shot of Gabrielle looking out her second-story window. An anonymous voice-over narrator says, "He who shall lose his life for me shall find it," which establishes that the Hepburn character is about to commit herself to a religious order. We do not hear the voice-over again in the film, which, unlike *The Member of the Wedding* and *Julia*, is not told in flashback.[7] Gabrielle turns to the room and silently takes off her ring, a worldly possession, and places it with other such possessions on a table. There is no explanation of these objects, but a photograph in a heart suggests she is leaving a romantic tie. As with Frankie, her mother has died and she has been raised by her father, which psychologically may suggest that for both women their primary role model has been male rather than female. Her father is dubious of his daughter's decision to enter the convent. He says to her, "I can see you poor, I can see you chaste, but I can't see you, a strong-willed girl, obedient to those bells." And indeed, he knows his daughter better than she does at this point, for obedience is the one dictum of the Church she is unable to fulfill. At the end, with World War II raging around her, her father dead at the hands of the Nazis, she realizes she can no longer "forgive the enemy" as the teachings of Christ would have her do. "I am no longer a nun. . . . I simply can't obey."

There are two significant sequences at the end of the film. In the first, she meets with her Mother Superior to demand that she put before the Cardinal her request to leave the convent. The two sit in front of a glass wall, while outside the dark, rainy weather reflects the mood, and a single bare tree enduring the storm is an obvious metaphor of Sister Luke, who emotionally is already on the other side of that glass and alone. In a two-shot, Mother Emmanuel again stresses the heart of a nun's duty: "obedience without question, without inner murmuring." Since this is not possible for Sister Luke, Mother Emmanuel finally agrees to her request for release. The next shot is one of the most open of the film. Zinnemann likes to show ceilings and walls to suggest enclosure and entrapment, but in this shot Audrey Hepburn, as Sister Luke, now sits alone on a bench in the middle of the frame, no ceilings visible above her, no walls around her except that one glass one with the lone tree behind. The mise en scène perfectly reflects the character's sense of loss, aloneness, and vulnerability in a world which is no longer protected and enclosed.

The final shot of *The Nun's Story* is a famous one. It closes the film by allowing it to come full circle, as does *Julia* by returning to images with which it began. In *Julia* we return to the fishing scene and the voice-over narration of the old Lillian Hellman. In *The Nun's Story* we again see the Audrey Hepburn character taking off her ring, but this time she is giving up her cloistered life to re-enter the world. The order of the shots is therefore reversed, this time moving from interior to exterior. In one of the lengthy unedited shots for which Zinnemann is famous, we watch the Audrey Hepburn character open the door of the convent and walk slowly down an alley away from the camera, becoming smaller in the distance. At the end of the alley, she turns right, walks off screen, and the picture ends in silence.[8]

In order to become a nun, Gabrielle learns that she must wipe out all memory of her past life. Her decision to give up the convent means she returns not only to the external world but to memory. *Julia* is also about memory. In the last scene of the flashback in which the story of the friendship of the two women has been told, Dashiell Hammett says to Lillian, "I'll outlive you. Well, maybe not; you're stubborn." We then return to the present, and see a woman sitting in a boat fishing in the mist, her back to the camera in the same medium long shot with which the film began. As the film opened, Lillian's voice-over says, "I am old now" and "I want to remember." The flashback, the story of Julia, is that memory. Now the concluding voice-over tells us that Hammett did not outlive her. "But," she says, "he was right, I am stubborn" and "I haven't forgotten either of them." Georges Delerue's music then comes up and the final credits roll.

Significantly, *Julia* ends without any explanation of the effect that the friendship has had on Lillian Hellman, except that in real life we know that she goes on to become an enormously successful writer and a strong, self-sufficient woman. The films gives us reason to believe that Hellman became who she was in part because of Julia. In another case of an absent mother, Julia is raised by her rich grandparents and inherits a fortune that she eventually gives away in her fight against Nazi oppression and social injustice. Of the two friends, Julia is obviously the stronger. It is she who holds the rudder as they sail as young girls, it is she who boldly walks a log straddling the banks of a deep crevasse and tells Lillian, who is frightened to follow, that she should go the safe way underneath. Challenged, Lillian follows her friend and falls. Julia saves her life literally this time, and, it may be surmised, figuratively in the long run. In an era when

FIGURE 16.1. JULIA (Twentieth Century Fox, 1977). Lillian (Jane Fonda) and Julia (Vanessa Redgrave) meet for the last time. (Courtesy Museum of Modern Art/Film Stills Archive)

it was unusual for a woman to go to Oxford and study medicine, Julia does, and she writes angry letters back to her friend warning of the coming Nazi menace in Europe. Lillian's description of Julia at this period is eloquent: "There are women who reach a perfect time of life, when the face will never again be as good, the body never as graceful or powerful; it had happened that year to Julia." Julia eventually convinces Lillian to help the fight against the Nazis by carrying money into Germany. When they meet in Berlin at a little table in an enclosed and threatening cafe, Lillian learns her friend has lost her leg, had a baby, but continues her work with the underground, never doubting the rightness of her conviction that an individual has a duty to fight, as Zinnemann himself has said, "to preserve our civilization." She dies in that fight.

These three films about stubborn women, about mythic women, all end with at least one of their protagonists alone on the screen, but they do not, as Giannetti has suggested, end unhappily (354). In portraying loneliness Zinnemann is not portraying despair, but rather what Federico Fellini has called "the contrast between monologue and dialogue." Between individualism and the mythic state of co-being. Fellini writes that loneliness "permeates the very essence of our life today," and that films "should throw some light upon it and the forces that work against it." He goes on to say:

> When a film shows suffering in a concentrated and what I should call a microscopic image (the dimensions of history do not, after all, matter in art) and as far as it can, expresses the contrast between monologue and dialogue which is central to our life today and the source of so many of our troubles, it is dealing with a contemporary need and examining it in depth; in other words, it is using realism in the way which seems to me most suited to the realist movement. (*Fellini on Fellini* 62–63)

Zinnemann is again like Fellini in his preference for open endings. Fellini has written that in his films "the story never reaches its conclusion. . . . I have no intention of moralising, yet I feel that a film is the more moral if it doesn't offer the audience the solution found by the character whose story is told" (*Fellini on Fellini* 150). To give two famous examples, at the end of *La Strada* the camera pulls away to leave Anthony Quinn as Zampano crouched in his grief on the beach, while at the end of *La Dolce Vita* Marcello Mastroianni turns his back on the sea—and

also on the camera—and walks away towards the trees and the deraci-
nated, confining, uninspired social life represented by the back of the
frame.

These are unhappy endings, and they might aptly be described with
the title Giannetti applies to Zinnemann's mature works: "No Exit"
(354). But where Sartre's anxiety may be applicable to Fellini, it rarely fits
Zinnemann, who says, "I have always tried to offer an audience something positive in a film, to leave them looking up rather than looking
down" (Phillips 124). Giannetti is wrong to suggest that most of his
movies end "on a note of disintegration, loneliness, and shattered hope,"
although he is probably right in saying that those endings that might be
regarded as "happy" are "among the most equivocal of the American cinema" (365). Like Fellini, Zinnemann does not offer solutions.

In *The Member of the Wedding*, Frankie, who exits the screen before
the end of the film, is moving on with her life, gaining membership in a
larger club, the club of co-being, that will eventually involve reflecting on
life through the language of her writing. She has matured from the child-
ish "Frankie" and the artificial and fantasy-filled "F. Jasmine" to the more
assured and self-aware "Frances." In the novel, which was published first
in 1946, Carson McCullers writes of Frankie and her friend, Mary Littlejohn: "They read poets like Tennyson together; and Mary was going to be
a great painter and Frances a great poet" (150). Neither the play (1949)
nor the film (1953) contains this self-reflexive and literary reference,
although the play does include a discussion of Frankie as a playwright.
Jarvis's fiancée, Janice, comments: "Jarvis told me how you used to write
plays and act in them out here in the arbor," and she remarks as they are
leaving, "When you come visit us you must write beautiful plays, and
we'll all act in them" (Gassner 176, 199).

The film is not as self-reflexive of its author(s), and the close-up of
Berenice's face with which it concludes not only gives her inner life more
emphasis than it has in the other two versions of the story, but it makes
her character the emotional center of the work as a whole. Although the
film, like both *The Nun's Story* and *Julia*, begins with a voice-over narration—in this case taken verbatim from the opening of the novel: "It happened that green and crazy summer when Frankie was twelve years old . . .
and had become an unjoined person"—the voice-over drops out completely and the film's primary source switches from the novel to the play.
Oddly, Edward Anhalt has said that in doing the screenplay he worked
from the novel "on the theory that a novel is easier to adapt than a play."[9]

But the fact that the film follows the play so closely suggests that Zinnemann is correct in remembering that "the first draft script did not work" so we "decided to go forward with the play" (*Life* 112). However, the use of long durational shots, close-ups, and extreme close-ups brings us into the inner lives of the characters in a way that the limitations of space and time in the theater prevent. The close-up of Berenice's face, for example, as she describes Ludie's death to John Henry and Frankie fills the screen with her pain, and the pathos in both her eyes as they well with tears belies the fact that she is supposed to have a blue glass eye in one of them.

Giannetti is right to describe these lengthy takes as "unnerving" precisely because they do not "dissipate the tension by cutting to a variety of shots" (366). The most sustained example of this in *The Member of the Wedding* is at the close of what in the play is Act II. Frankie gradually becomes hysterical as she moves around the kitchen describing her fantasy of going away with Janice and Jarvis. The camera keeps her in the center of the frame and never cuts away from her for a different perspective or a reaction shot. As she tires, she collapses, crying, onto Berenice's lap. John Henry comes up and pushes on Frankie in jealousy. He also says, "I'm sick," which at this point in the action no one believes. The camera still holds on what is now a three-shot. There is the evocation of time passing as the camera gently dollies in, a visual sensation of the words Frankie is about to speak which can be conveyed by camera movement on film but is impossible to show on stage. As she begins to talk quietly, there is finally a cut. Now, in a masterfully composed shot, we see only a small part of Frankie's head in the lower right corner of the frame, which is dominated by an extreme close-up of Berenice's face as she reacts silently to the young girl's words:

> I wonder if you have ever thought about this? Here we are—right now. This very minute. Now, but while we're talking right now, this minute is passing. And it will never come again. Never in all the world. When it is gone, it is gone. No power on earth could bring it back again. (Gassner 197)

Zinnemann's technique here is a perfect illustration of Giannetti's remark that "the unedited shot can itself be a kind of spatial and temporal prison for which there's no escape" (366), and no film of his makes better use of this than *The Member of the Wedding*. But this moment is also one of joining, when the three of them share co-being after Frankie's haunting speech about time as they spontaneously and softly sing together the song Berenice hums to herself at the end of both the play and the film: "I sing because I'm happy." And this moment of joining is also a harbinger of the transition to the third part of all three versions of this story in which John Henry dies, Berenice experiences more loss, and Frankie discovers herself in community and can speak.

The Member of the Wedding is a brilliant example of what Zinnemann meant when he said that his films "deal with the dignity of human beings and have something to say about oppression, not necessarily in the political way but in a human way" (*American Film* 13). The film is more socially conscious than the play, although perhaps not more than the book, where there is time to develop Berenice's sense of entrapment as more extreme than Frankie's as she says, "I'm caught worse than you is."

> "Because I am black," said Berenice. "Because I am colored. Everybody is caught one way or another. But they done drawn completely extra bounds around all colored people. They done squeezed us off in one corner by ourself. So we caught that first way I was telling you, as all human beings is caught. And we caught as colored people also. (McCullers 113–14)

She goes on in this speech to talk about her stepbrother Honey sometimes feeling "like he just can't breathe no more" and that "sometimes it just about more than we can stand." Structural constraints prevent the development of this theme in the play, but we see it visually in the film. Honey is visibly hooked on drugs, a frustrated musician, and a victim of white prejudice. In doing the screenplay, Anhalt says, "we were all very gung-ho about the black situation at the time," and the film is very much the product of the emerging racial consciousness of the early 1950s rather than of the legacy of repression hanging on in the late 1940s after World War II. Consequently there is a strong undercurrent in the film which suggests that the entrapment these characters experience is social and political as well as personal; their struggles transcend the individual and become "mythic."

Toward the end of *The Member of the Wedding*, its mythic dimension is expressed both visually and verbally. Frankie has run away from home and stands alone in a dark alley. The illumination through the slats of the door to her left casts barlike streams of dark and light around the girl, enclosing her in a shadowy prison. A man walks towards her and we anticipate a confrontation, but he passes without interest, as if she were not even there. Off-screen we hear angry female voices and then we see an older woman kicking a younger woman out of the house. Her angry words resonate through the alley: "Get out, go someplace and die." There is no equivalent in either the novel or play. But cinematically the images and words serve to emphasize the contrast between Frankie's situation and this young woman's and what could be her plight if she continues on her flight from home. They are also, of course, another foreshadowing of John Henry's death (there are many in all versions of *The Member of the Wedding*), but more poignantly, they are a blatant summation of the final "unjoining" that must be the fate of all of us as we "get out," lose our co-being and our use of language in death. Frankie escapes from the confinement of the frame at the end, but Berenice remains trapped in its center with the fox fur given to her by her first husband Ludie draped sadly around her neck. Like Gabrielle in the penultimate sequence of *The Nun's Story*, she sits in the center of the frame, but unlike Gabrielle she is enclosed by the walls and ceiling around her. While Gabrielle's world is opening up, Berenice's is shutting down. She knows Frankie is moving on and that she will not see her very much in the future—"Your road is already strange to me"—but there is an acceptance of process here, and the figure of Berenice emanates the awesome strength of survival.

There is this same sense of survival, of enduring, in both *The Nun's Story* and *Julia*, which are similarly mythic in that their action consistently reaffirms "a belief in equality, social justice, community, and great leadership." We know Gabrielle, like Julia, has committed herself to a cause higher than herself, a *human* cause, and that in the immediate future she will go on to work in the underground to support the Resistance and fight Nazi oppression. And although Julia is dead, her story has been one of "great leadership," *human* survival, and the restoration and preservation of memory through the creative act, through image and language.

The rebellion of Frankie, the endurance of Berenice, the courage of disobedience enacted by Sister Like, the stubbornness of the Lillian Hellman character, and the remarkable strength, fight, and self-sacrifice of her friend, Julia, are in a remarkable way, qualities that seem to reflect Fred Zinnemann himself. He has said that Robert Flaherty was probably the greatest influence on him as a filmmaker, "particularly because he was always his own man" (Giannetti 356). Daniel Taradash, who did the screenplay of *From Here to Eternity*, has described Zinnemann as "stubborn, but only when he is right."[10] Taradash was responsible for bringing

Zinnemann onto *Eternity* as director because he had been so enormously impressed with his work on *Teresa* (1951) and the portrayal of the GIs in that film. At the time Zinnemann was doing *The Member of the Wedding* in Colusa, California, and according to Taradash, Stanley Kramer and company "bad-mouthed" the director, calling him "slow and difficult." This worried the president of Columbia Pictures, Harry Cohn, who didn't want to work with anyone who was "going to cause trouble." Zinnemann was also known as an "art house director," meaning he was good, but his films were not popular at the box office. But Taradash, whose interpretation of "slow and difficult" would be "stubborn and principled," obviously prevailed, and both he and Zinnemann ended up with Oscars. Today, Taradash describes the director as "a human treasure," a sentiment echoed by Paul Jarrico, a screenwriter on *The Search*, who has used the adjective "humanistic" to encompass Zinnemann's life and work. "He's concerned with people, he's a fine man, a fine director. And he's a progressive guy, and was sympathetic to all the blacklistees."[11]

To this day Jarrico considers *The Search* one of his finest credits, and stresses that "more than most directors, Fred respects the writer." The sentiment is echoed by Edward Anhalt, who goes on to say quite simply, "he's an awfully good director" and *The Search* is "a marvelous picture.[12] Jarrico uses the word *purity* to describe Zinnemann's style, stressing his command of the medium: "He knows his stuff." Zinnemann himself emphasizes working as a "team" with all members of the production, including the writers. But he also says that "having started life as a cameraman I am strongly oriented toward the visual aspect of storytelling" (*Life* 223). And in the Anhalt adaptation of *The Member of the Wedding*, this diminished the role of the screenwriter. The film sticks very closely to the play, and it works as a movie because of the way it is shot. Anhalt gives Zinnemann full credit for this: "The way it was shot was all Zinnemann's. I never write camera placement or movements. That's ridiculous."[13]

For Jarrico, *The Nun's Story* is the best example of Zinnemann's style: "it's so beautifully done." He refers specifically to the deliberate pacing. "The new crop of directors would call him 'old fashioned.' But he is extraordinary in terms of his expertise. With him, actors behave like real people. He's a wonderful technician, like Wyler and a few others of his generation." *The Nun's Story* was so well done there was a rumor "that Fred had become a Catholic in the making of it."[14]

Jarrico's praise of *The Nun's Story* corresponds, in some ways, with Zinnemann's own assessment of the film. Although he says that *The*

Member of the Wedding "has always been my favorite picture, perhaps because it is not entirely my own—or perhaps because of the equality of pure love that seems to radiate from it so strongly" (*Life* 115), *The Nun's Story* comes closest to articulating fully the central theme of his work (see Phillips 119). This theme was initially stated in the title of the film on which Jarrico worked: *The Search*. Zinnemann's films are about voyages of discovery, about the search for self and the means of enacting and preserving self. Phillips suggests that Zinnemann's central theme has to do with the "individual achieving a self-knowledge that enables him to find his place in the community in which he lives" (115). Except for the unfortunate use of the masculine pronoun, this is a good description of the self-discovery that comes with the experience of co-being and the restoration and preservation of civilization through memory, through action, through the images and language in the stories of the mythic figures who struggle with their lives and with their consciences in the three Zinnemann films discussed in this chapter.

When asked what is most important to him, as a man and as an artist, Federico Fellini once replied, "If you really want me to turn teacher, then condense it with these words: be what you are, that is discover yourself in order to love life. To me, life is beautiful, for all its tragedy and suffering, I like it, I am moved by it. And I do my best to share this way of feeling with others" (*Fellini on Fellini* 158). The same words might well have been said by Fred Zinnemann, who in commenting on *The Member of the Wedding* as his favorite film, reiterated that it is because the story is not just "about the great American disease, loneliness," but because "it is also full of enormous love" (*Life* 112).

NOTES

1. This argument is set out in detail in H. Mark Roelofs's *Ideology and Myth in American Politics: A Critique of a National Political Mind.*

2. *Being and Time.* Because the translations are from the German *Sein und Zeit,* 15th edition (Tübingen: Max Niemeyer Verlag, 1976 [original 1927]), references are to paragraph numbers in both editions to avoid difficulties with pagination. "Co-being" is treated by Heidegger in paragraphs 25–27; speech as sharing or taking part in joint being in paragraphs 34–35.

3. See Gwendolyn Foster's chapter, "The Women in *High Noon*: A Metanarrative of Difference," in this volume.

4. See my essay, "Myth, Ideology, and Feminism in *High Noon.*" *Journal of Popular Culture* 23 (Spring 1990): 75–80.

5. From the author's personal copy of the script of *High Noon*, p. 3, given to her by Carl Foreman.

6. These lines are in the film, from the script by Edward and Edna Anhalt, but not in the novel or play.

7. It is interesting to note that all three of the films under consideration here begin with voice-overs.

8. This silence was an issue. Franz Waxman, who did the score for the film, was, according to Zinnemann, anti-Catholic, and this came across in this music. He wrote an exultant theme for Hepburn's exit, which Zinnemann then removed. When Jack Warner objected by saying that "every Warner Brothers picture has music at the end," Zinnemann replied, "If you have festive music you are saying to the audience, 'Warner Brothers congratulates the nun on quitting the convent.' Is that what you want? If the music is heavy, the audience will be depressed; I don't see how you can win." The result, Zinnemann concludes, was that "Audrey was allowed to make her exit in silence" (*Life* 169).

9. Interview with the author, December 31, 1982.

10. Interview with the author, September 27, 1993.

11. Interview with the author, January 4, 1993.

12. December 31, 1982 interview.

13. December 31, 1982 interview.

14. January 4, 1993 interview.

WORKS CITED

Foreman, Carl. *High Noon.* Personal copy of the script.

Gassner, John, ed. *Best American Plays: Third Series—1945–1951.* New York: Crown Publishers, 1952.

Giannetti, Louis. "Films of Conscience: The Cinema of Fred Zinnemann." *Masters of the American Cinema.* Englewood, Cliffs, N.J.: Prentice-Hall, 1981. 354–74.

Heidegger, Martin. *Being and Time.* Trans. John Macquarrie and Edward Robinson. New York: Harper and Row, 1962.

Keel, Anna, and Christian Strich, eds. *Fellini on Fellini.* New York: Dell, 1977.

McCullers, Carson. *The Member of the Wedding.* New York: Bantam Books, 1950.

Phillips, Gene D. "Fred Zinnemann: Darkness at Noon," in *Major Film Directors of the American and British Cinema.* Bethlehem, Pa.: Lehigh University Press, 1990. 108–24.

Rapf, Joanna E. "Myth, Ideology, and Feminism in *High Noon.*" *Journal of Popular Culture* 23 (Spring 1990): 75–80.

Roelofs, H. Mark. *Ideology and Myth in American Politics: A Critique of a National Political Mind.* Boston: Little, Brown, 1976.

Zinnemann, Fred. "Fred Zinnemann." *American Film* 11.4 (January–February 1986): 12–13, 62, 66–67.

———. *A Life in the Movies: An Autobiography.* New York: Scribner's, 1992.

ZINNEMANN FILMOGRAPHY

As ASSISTANT CAMERAMAN

1927: *La Marche des machines* (dir. Eugène Deslaw), 1929: *Sprengbagger 1010* (dir. Karl Ludwig Achaz-Duisberg), *Ich Küsse Ihre Hand, Madame* (*I Kiss Your Hand, Madame*, dir. Robert Land), and *Menschen am Sonntag* (*People on Sunday*, dir. Robert Siodmak).

As ASSISTANT TO THE DIRECTOR

1930: *Main Trouble* (dir. Berthold Viertel), *The Spy* (dir. Berthold Viertel), 1932: *The Wiser Sex* (dir. Berthold Viertel), *The Man from Yesterday* (dir. Berthold Viertel), *The Kid from Spain* (dir. Leo McCarey; Zinnemann was assistant to dance director Busby Berkeley), 1935: *The Dark Angel* (dir. Sidney Franklin), *Peter Ibbetson* (dir. Henry Hathaway).

As DIRECTOR

SHORTS
(All made for MGM, except *Benjy*)

1938: *"A Friend Indeed"* (story about a blind man's dog). *"The Story of Dr. Carver"* (the life of black scientist George Washington Carver). *"That Mothers Might Live"* (Academy Award for Short Subject; about child bed fever). *"Tracking the Sleeping Death"* (about sleeping sickness). *"They Live Again"* (about insulin).

1939: *"Weather Wizards"* (about climatology). *"While America Sleeps"* (a look at the tactics of foreign spies). *"Help Wanted!"* (an expose of employment agencies). *"One Against the World"* (story of Dr. Ephraim MacDowell, the first to perform surgery). *"The Ash-Can Fleet"* (the story of a submarine). *"Forgotten Victory"* (how Russian wheat came to the Americas).

1940: *"The Old South"* (a look at several historical events that shaped the American cotton industry). *"Stuffie"* (a dog sacrifices its life). *"A Way in the Wilderness"* (the discovery of the cure for pellagra). *"The Great Meddler"* (about Henry Berg, who founded the American S.P.C.A).

1941: *"Forbidden Passage"* (about the smuggling of aliens into the United States during the war). *"Your Last Act"* (an account of highly unusual last wills and testaments). *"The Lady or the Tiger?"* (Frank R. Stockton's famous story).

1951: *Benjy.* The parents of a crippled boy (Lee Aaker) discover that the cause of his infirmity is scoliosis. Academy Award for Short Documentary. Sc: Stewart Stern. Ph: J. Peverell Marley. Ed: George Tomasini. With Lee Aaker, Marille Phelps, Adam Williams, and Neville Brand. Prod: The Orthopaedic Foundation of Los Angeles. Paramount. 30 mins.

FEATURE FILMS

The Wave (*Redes* or *Pescados,* 1934–1935). A Flaherty-influenced documentary about the lives of fishermen in the Gulf Coast, focusing on the efforts of a young fisherman (Silvio Hernández) to form a union. With Felipe Rojas (the foreman) and the people of Alvarado. Assistants to Zinnemann: Agustín Velázquez Chávez and Emilio Gómez Muriel. Script: Henwar Rodakiewicz. Editor: Gunther Von Fritsch. Music: Sylvestre Revueltas. Producer: Paul Strand for the Mexican Federal Department of Fine Arts. 60 mins.

Kid Glove Killer (1942). Meticulous lab work by criminologist Van Heflin leads to the identification of Special Prosecutor Lee Bowman, who is secretly a racketeer, as the murderer of a reform-minded mayor (Samuel S. Hinds). Not only do Zinnemann and his scriptwriters draw on their experience in the MGM "Crime Does Not Pay" series, but the characterizations have the kind of human touches that are typical of Zinnemann. With Van Heflin (Gordon McKay), Marsha Hunt (Jane Mitchell), Lee Bowman (Gerald I. Ladimer), Samuel S. Hinds (Mayor Daniels), Cliff Clark (Captain Lynch), Eddie Quillan (Eddie Wright), Ava Gardner (a car-hop waitress), John Litel, Catherine Lewis, and Nella Walker. Prod: Jack Chertok. Sc: Allen Rivkin and John C. Higgins (story by Higgins). Ph: Paul Vogel. Ed: Ralph Winters. Mus: David Snell. MGM. 74 mins.

Eyes in the Night (1942). Blind detective Edward Arnold and his seeing-eye dog uncover a Nazi spy ring. Zinnemann was amused when one reviewer summed up the film with this quip: "Dog Bites Axis." With Edward Arnold (Duncan Maclain), Ann Harding (Norma Lawry), Donna Reed (Barbara Lawry), Allen Jenkins (Marty), John Emery (Paul Gerente) Horace [Stephen] McNally (Gabriel Hoffman), Katherine Emery (Cheli Scott), Rosemary DeCamp (Vera Hoffman) Stanley C. Ridges (Hansen), Reginald Denny (Stephen Lawry), Barry Nelson (Busch), Steve Geray (Anderson), Erik Rolf (Boyd), Reginald Sheffield (Victor), Ivan Miller (Herman), Milburn Stone (Pete), Mantan Moreland (Alistair), Cliff Danielson (boy), Frances Rafferty (girl), Edward Kilroy (pilot), John Butler (driver), William Nye (Hugo), Frank Thomas (police lieutenant), Marie Windsor (actress), and "Friday" (Alsatian). Sc: Guy Trosper and Howard Emmett Rogers (based on Baynard Kendrick's novel *The Odor of Violets*). Ph: Robert Planck and Charles Lawton. Ed: Ralph Winters. Mus: Lennie Hayton. Art dir: Cedric Gibbons. Prod. Jack Chertok. MGM. 79 mins.

The Seventh Cross (1944). Set in Germany in 1936, this suspense film concerns an escaped political prisoner (Spencer Tracy), whose faith in mankind is restored by courageous individuals who risk their lives to help him. Zinnemann's first A-film, moodily photographed and well acted (especially by Tracy and by Hume Cronyn as a factory worker who comes to see Nazism for what it really is). With Spencer Tracy (George Heisler), Signe Hasso (Toni), Hume Cronyn (Paul Roeder), Jessica Tandy (Liasel Roeder), Agnes Moorehead (Madame Marelli), Ray Collins (Ernest Wallau; the film's narrator), Herbert Rudley (Franz Marnet), Felix Bressart (Poldi Schlamm), George Macready (Bruno Sauer), Katherine Locke (Mrs. Sauer), Steven Geray (Dr. Lowenstein), Paul Guilfoyle (Fiedler), Kurt Katch (Leo Hermann), Alexander Granach (Zillich), Karen Verne (Leni), Konstantin Shayne, George Suzanne, John Wengraf, George Zucco, Steven Muller, Eily Malyon, Paul E. Burns, Willliam Edmunds, Hugh Beaumont, William Tannen, William Challee, and Ludwig Donath. Sc: Helen Deutsch (from the Anna Seghers novel). Ph: Karl Freund (uncredited: additional ph by Robert Surtees). Art dir: Cedric Gibbons and Leonid Vasian. Ed: Thomas Richards. Mus: Roy Webb. Prod: Pandro S. Berman. MGM. 112 mins.

My Brother Talks to Horses (1947). The first of two pictures with child star Jackie "Butch" Jenkins that Zinnemann was forced to make as part of his MGM contract. He disliked both films ("the less said about them the better"). In *Horses* Jenkins's equine friends supply him with the names of the race winners. With Peter Lawford (John S. Penrose), Beverly Tyler (Martha), Edward Arnold (Mr. Bledsoe), Charles Ruggles (Richard Pennington Roeder), Spring Byington (Mrs. Penrose), O. Z. Whitehead, Paul Langton, Ernest Whitman, Irving Bacon, Lillian Yarbo, Howard Freeman, and Harry Hayden. Sc: Morton Thompson from his story, "Lewie, My Brother Who Talks to Horses." Ph: Harold Rosson. Ed. George White. Mus: Rudolph G. Kopp. Prod. Samuel Marx. MGM. 93 mins.

Little Mister Jim (1947). A little boy on a pre–World War II military base helps his father overcome a drinking problem brought on by personal tragedy. Some critics found the film's humor and pathos appealing, but Zinnemann had had enough. He turned down the next three scripts MGM gave him, and went on suspension. With "Butch" Jenkins (Little Jim Tucker), Frances Gifford (Mrs. Tucker), James Craig (Big Jim Tucker), Luana Patten (Missy Choosy), Chingwah Lee (Sui Jen), Laura LaPlante (Mrs. Glenson), Spring Byington, Henry O'Neill, Morris Ankrum, Celia Travers, Ruth Brady, Sharon McManus, Buz Buckley, Carol Nugent, and Jean Van. Sc: George Bruce. Ph: Lester White. Ed: Frank Hull. Mus: George Bassman. Prod: Orville O. Dull. MGM. 92 mins.

The Search (*Die Gezeichneten*, 1948). While his mother (Jarmila Novotna) searches for him, a young refugee (Ivan Jandl) is befriended and given a home by a GI (Montgomery Clift) stationed in occupied Germany. One of the first examples of "American neorealism," this film combines documentary elements (authentic Munich ruins, footage of actual war orphans) and fiction. Academy Award Nominations for Best Picture and Best Direction. With Montgomery Clift (Steve), Aline MacMahon (Mrs. Murray), Wendell Corey (Jerry Fisher), Jarmila Novotna (Mrs. Malik), Ivan Jandl (Karel Malik), Mary Patton (Mrs. Fisher), Ewart G. Morrison (Mr. Crookes), William Rogers, Leopold Borkowski, and Claude Gambier. Sc: Richard Schweizer and Lazar Wechsler (additional dialogue: Paul Jarrico and [uncredited] Clift). Ph: Emil Berna. Ed: Herman Haller. Mus: Robert Blum. Prod: Lazar Wechsler for Praesens Film. Swiss and MGM release. 105 mins.

Act of Violence (1949). A respected member of the community, Van Heflin is stalked by Robert Ryan, the only survivor from a group of prisoners of war whose plans for escape Heflin revealed to the Germans. A drama of conscience cast in film noir form, it is rich in atmospheric black and white photography. Zinnemann says that his visual imagination was getting liberated when he made the film. With Van Heflin (Frank Enley), Robert Ryan (Joe Parkson), Janet Leigh (Edith Enley), Mary Astor (Pat), Phyllis Thaxter (Ann Sturges), Barry Kroeger (Johnny), Nicholas Joy (Mr. Garvey), Harry Antrim (Fred Finney), Connie Gilchrist (Martha Finney), and Will Wright (Pop). Sc: Robert L. Richards (story by Collier Young). Ph: Robert Surtees. Ed: Conrad A. Nervig. Mus: Bronislau Kaper. Prod. William H. Wright. MGM. 82 mins.

The Men (1950). A drama about paraplegic war veterans, especially an embittered young man (Marlon Brando) who must learn to come to terms with his permanent disablement. Brando's film debut, and the first of three films that Zinnemann made with Stanley Kramer. With Marlon Brando (Ken "Bud" Wilochek), Teresa Wright (Ellie), Everett Sloane (Dr. Brock), Jack Webb (Norm), Richard Erdman (Leo), Arthur Jurado (Angel), Virginia Farmer (the head nurse), Ray Teal (man in bar), Dorothy Tree, Howard St. John, Nita Hunter, Patricia Joiner, John Miller, Cliff Clark, Marguerite Martin, Virginia Christine, Obie Parker, Paul Peltz, William Lea Jr., Tom Gillick, Ray Mitchell, Pete Simon, Randall Updyke III, Marshall Ball, and Carlo Lewis. Sc: Carl Foreman. Ph: Robert de Grasse. Ed: Harry Gerstad. Mus: Dimitri Tiomkin. Prod: Stanley Kramer. United Artists. 85 mins. Reissued in 1957 as *Battle Stripe*.

Teresa (1951). A psychological drama about a young GI (John Ericson) who nearly loses the Italian war bride he brings home (Pier Angeli) because of his own immaturity and dominating mother (Patricia Collinge). Italian and American cultures are subtly compared. Angeli gives an affecting performance in her film debut. With John Ericson (Philip Cass), Pier Angeli (Teresa), Patricia Collinge (Philip's mother), Ralph Meeker (Sgt. Dobbs), Richard Bishop (Philip's father), Rod Steiger (the army psychiatrist), Peggy Ann Garner (Susan, Philip's sister), Edward Binns (Sgt. Brown), Bill Maudlin (Philip's army friend), Ave Ninchi (Teresa's mother), Aldo Silvani (Teresa's father), Franco Interlenghi (Mario, Teresa's brother), Tommy Lewis, Edith Atwater, Lewis Cianelli, William King, Richard MacNamara, and Guido Martufi. Sc: Stewart

Stern (from Alfred Hayes's novel *The Girl on the Via Flaminia*). Ph: William J. Miller. Ed: Frank Sullivan. Mus: Louis Applebaum. Prod: Arthur M. Loew. MGM. 105 mins.

High Noon (1952). Classic, still controversial Western about a marshal (Gary Cooper) deserted by everyone except his new bride (Grace Kelly) when four outlaws show up to kill him. Interpreted by some as a political allegory about McCarthyism. Winner of four Academy Awards and the New York Film Critics Award for Best Picture and Best Direction. With Gary Cooper (Will Kane), Thomas Mitchell (Jonas Henderson), Lloyd Bridges (Harvey Pell), Katy Jurado (Helen Ramirez), Grace Kelly (Amy Kane), Otto Kruger (Judge Percy Mettrick), Lon Chaney, Jr. (Martin Howe, the former marshal), Ian MacDonald (Frank Miller), Howland Chamberlain (hotel clerk), Jack Elam (Charlie, the town drunk), Henry (Harry) Morgan (Sam Fuller), Eve McVeagh (Mildred Fuller), Harry Shannon (Cooper), Lee Van Cleef (Jack Colby), Robert Wilke (James Pierce), Sheb Wooley (Ben Miller), Tom London (Sam), Ted Stanhope (stationmaster), Larry Blake (Gillis), William Phillips (barber), Jeanne Blackford (Mrs. Henderson), and James Millican (baker). Sc: Carl Foreman (from John W. Cunningham's story, "The Tin Star"). Ph: Floyd Crosby. Ed: Elmo Williams and Harry Gerstad. Prod des: Rudolph Sternad. Mus: Dimitri Tiomkin. Song, "Do Not Forsake Me, Oh My Darlin'" (Theme from *High Noon*) by Tiomkin and Ned Washington, sung by Tex Ritter. Prod: Stanley Kramer. United Artists. 85 mins.

The Member of the Wedding (1952). A lonely twelve-year-old girl (Julie Harris) is so desperate to belong somewhere that she creates the fantasy that her brother and his bride will take her along on their honeymoon. Critics are divided over the film's effectiveness as a stage adaptation. Zinnemann has frequently cited it as his favorite of his films. With Julie Harris (Frankie Addams), Ethel Waters (Berenice Sadie Brown), Brandon de Wilde (John Henry), Arthur Franz (Jarvis, Frankie's brother), Nancy Gates (Janice), William Hansen (Mr. Addams, Frankie's father), James Edwards ("Honey," Berenice's foster brother), Harry Bolden (T. T. Williams), Dick Moore (drunk soldier), Charlcie Garrett, Danny Mummert, June Hedin, Ann Carter, and Harry Richards. Sc: Edward and Edna Anhalt (from the Carson McCullers play). Ed: William A. Lyon. Mus: Alex North. Ph: Hal Mohr. Prod: Stanley Kramer. Columbia. 91 mins.

From Here to Eternity (1953). An army private (Montgomery Clift) refuses to compromise his principles in this drama of military life in Hawaii that climaxes with the attack on Pearl Harbor. Zinnemann's most honored film: eight Academy Awards, three New York Film Critics Awards, including Best Picture and Best Direction. With Burt Lancaster (Sgt. Milton Warden), Montgomery Clift (Robert E. Lee "Prew" Prewitt), Deborah Kerr (Karen Holmes), Frank Sinatra (Angelo Maggio), Donna Reed (Alma "Lorene"), Philip Ober (Capt. Dana Holmes), Ernest Borgnine (Sgt. "Fatso" Judson), Mickey Shaughnessy (Sgt. Leva), Jack Warden (Corp. Buckley), John Dennis (Sgt. Ike Galovitch), Merle Travis (Sal Anderson), Tim Ryan (Sgt. Pete Karelsen), Arthur Keegan (Treadwell), Barbara Morrison (Mrs. Kipfer), Jean Willes (Annette), George Reeves (Sgt. Maylon Stark), and Harry Bellaver, Douglas Henderson, Don Dubbins, Claude Akins, Robert Wilke, John Cason, Kristine Miller, John Byrant, Joan Shawlee, Angela Stevens, Mary Carver, Vicki Bakken, Margaret Barstow, Delia Salvi, Willis Bouchey, Alvin Sargent, William Lundmark, Weaver Levy, and Tyler McVey. Sc: Daniel Taradash (from the novel by James Jones). Ph: Burnett Guffey. Ed: William E. Lyon. Mus: George Duning. Prod: Buddy Adler. Columbia. 118 mins.

Oklahoma! (1955). Film version of Rodgers and Hammerstein's 1943 smash Broadway musical about the romance of cow hand Gordon MacRae and farm girl Shirley Jones that is complicated by the dark presence of Rod Steiger. With Gordon MacRae (Curly), Shirley Jones (Laurey), Gloria Grahame (Ado Addie Carnes), Gene Nelson (Will Parker), Rod Steiger (Jud Fry), Charlotte Greenwood (Aunt Eller), James Whitmore (Judge Andrew Carnes), Eddie Albert (Ali Hakim, the Persian peddler), Barbara Lawrence (Gertie Cummings), Jay C. Flippen (Skidmore), James Mitchell (Curley in the Dream Ballet), Bambi Lynn (Laurey in the Dream Ballet), Roy Barcroft, Rory Mallinson, Jennie Workman, Marc Platt, Kelly Brown, Lizanne Truex, Jane Fischer, Virginia Bosler, and Evelyn Taylor. Sc: Sonya Levien and William Ludwig (adaptation of Rodgers and Hammerstein's musical based on the play *Green Grow the Lilacs* by Lynn Riggs). Ph: Robert Surtees. 2nd Unit ph: Floyd Crosby. Ed: Gene Ruggiero. Music supervised and conducted by Jay Blackton. Prod des: Oliver Smith. Chor: Agnes De Mille. Prod: Arthur Hornblow, Jr. for Magna. In Todd-AO. CinemaScope version (Twentieth Century-Fox release). 145 mins.

A Hatful of Rain (1957). Stark family drama about the efforts of a heroin addict (Don Murray) to hide the truth from his pregnant wife (Eva Marie

Saint) and visiting father (Lloyd Nolan). The film has not aged well, but Saint's performance, Herrmann's spare score, and MacDonald's black and white photography of New York locations are still effective. With Eva Marie Saint (Celia Pope), Don Murray (Johnny Pope, Jr.), Anthony Franciosa (Polo Pope), Lloyd Nolan (John Pope, Sr.), Henry Silva ("Mother"), Gerald O'Loughlin (Chuch), William Hickey (Apples), William Tannen, Herb Vigran, Michael Vale, Art Fleming, Tom Ahearne, Gordon B. Clark, William Bailey, Ralph Montgomery, Norman Willis, Emerson Treacy, Paul Kruger, Jason Johnson, Rex Lease, and Jay Jostyn. Sc: Michael Vincente Gazzo, Alfred Hayes, and (uncredited) Carl Foreman, from Gazzo's play. Ph: Joe MacDonald. Ed: Dorothy Spencer. Mus: Bernard Herrmann. Prod: Buddy Adler. CinemaScope. Twentieth Century-Fox. 109 mins.

The Nun's Story (1959). A young Belgian woman (Audrey Hepburn) joins a convent to become a nursing nun in the Congo, only to realize after years of an exhausting inner struggle that she simply cannot keep her vows. Nominated for eight Academy Awards, including Best Picture. Winner of the New York Film Critics Award for Best Actress and Best Director. Winner of the Golden Shell (Best Picture) at the 1959 San Sebastian Film Festival. With Audrey Hepburn (Gabrielle Van der Mal/Sister Luke), Peter Finch (Dr. Fortunati), Dame Edith Evans (Mother Emmanuel), Dame Peggy Ashcroft (Mother Mathilde), Dean Jagger (Dr. Hubert Van der Mal), Mildred Dunnock (Sister Margharita, Mistress of Postulants), Beatrice Straight (Mother Christophe), Patricia Collinge (Sister William), Rosalie Crutchley (Sister Eleanor, Mistress of Novices), Patricia Bosworth (Simone/ Sister Christine), Niall MacGinnis (Father Vermeuhlen), Colleen Dewhurst (Archangel Gabrielle, a schizophrenic patient), Dorothy Alison (Sister Aurelie), Ruth White (Mother Marcella), Eva Kotthaus (Sister Marie), Barbara O'Neill (Mother Katherine), Lionel Jeffries (Dr. Goovaerts), Margaret Phillips (Sister Pauline), Molly Urquhart (Sister Augustine), Stephen Murray (Chaplain), Orlando Martins (Kalulu), Errol John (Illunga), Jeanette Sterke (Louise), Richard O'Sullivan (Pierre), Diana Lambert (Lisa), Marina Wolkonsky (Marie), Penelope Horner (Jeannette Milonet), Ave Ninchi (Sister Bernard), Charles Lamb (Pascini), Ludovice Bonhomme (Bishop), Dara Gavin (Sister Ellen), and Elfrida Simbari (Sister Timothy). Sc: Robert Anderson, from the novel by Kathryn C. Hulme. Ph: Franz Planer. Mus: Franz Waxman. Prod Des: Alexander Trauner. Ed: Walter Thompson. Prod. Henry Blanke. Warner Bros. 149 mins.

The Sundowners (1960). In Australia of the 1920s a close-knit family of itinerant sheep drovers find themselves wanting different things: Robert Mitchum wants to continue living the life of a nomad, while Deborah Kerr and teenage son Michael Anderson, Jr. want to settle down on a farm of their own. Nominated for five Academy Awards, including Best Picture, Best Actress, and Best Director. With Deborah Kerr (Ida Carmody), Robert Mitchum (Paddy Carmody), Peter Ustinov (Rupe Venneker), Glynis Johns (Mrs. Gert Firth), Dina Merrill (Jean Halstead), Chips Rafferty (Quinlan), Michael Anderson, Jr. (Sean), Lola Brooks (Liz), Wylie Watson (Herb Johnson), John Meillon (Bluey), Ronald Fraser, Mervyn Johns, Molly Urquhart, Ewen Solon, Dick Bentley, Gerry Duggan, Peter Carver, Leonard Teale, Alastair Williamson, Ray Barrett, and Mercia Barden. Sc: Isobel Lennart from the novel by Jon Cleary. Ph: Jack Hildyard. Art dir: Michael Stringer. Ed: Jack Harris. Mus: Dimitri Tiomkin. Prod: Gerry Blattner. Warner Bros. 133 mins.

Behold a Pale Horse (1964). After twenty years of exile in France, aging guerilla leader Gregory Peck returns to Spain, deliberately walking into the trap set for him by arch enemy Anthony Quinn, a captain in the Guardia Civíl. Offers a compendium of Zinnemann themes and concerns, and two main characters—Peck and Sharif—struggling with their consciences. With Gregory Peck (Manuel Artiguez), Anthony Quinn (Capt. Viñolas), Omar Sharif (Father Francisco), Mildred Dunnock (Pilar), Raymond Pellegrin (Carlos, the informer), Paolo Stoppa (Pedro), Daniela Rocca (Rosanna, Viñolas's mistress), Rosalie Crutchley (Teresa, Viñolas's wife), Marietto Angeletti (Paco), Christian Marquand (Viñolas's lieutenant), Michel Lonsdale (news reporter), Molly Urquhart (nurse), Perette Pradier, Zia Mohyeddin, Claude Confortes, Jean-Paul Molinot, Laurence Badie, Alain Saury, Martin Benson, Jose-Luis Vilallonga, Jean-Claude Berck, Claude Berri, and Elisabeth Wiener. Sc: J. P. Miller from the novel *Killing a Mouse on Sunday* by Emeric Pressburger. Ph: Jean Badal. Prod des: Alexander Trauner. Ed: Walter Thompson. Mus: Maurice Jarre. Prod: Zinnemann for Highland-Brentwood/Columbia. 113 mins.

A Man for All Seasons (1966). When Sir Thomas More, Chancellor of England (Paul Scofield), finds that he cannot in good conscience sanction Henry VIII's divorce and new marriage, he resigns his office, but is subsequently imprisoned and executed. Vintage Zinnemann and winner of six Academy Awards, including Best Picture and Best Director, and the

New York Film Critics Award for Best Direction. With Paul Scofield (Thomas More), Wendy Hiller (Lady Alice), Leo McKern (Cromwell), Robert Shaw (Henry VIII), Orson Welles (Cardinal Wolsey), Susannah York (Margaret), Nigel Davenport (Duke of Norfolk), John Hurt (Richard Rich), Corin Redgrave (William Roper), Colin Blakely (Matthew), Vanessa Redgrave (Anne Boleyn), Cyril Luckham, Jack Gwillim, Thomas Heathcote, Yootha Joyce, Anthony Nicholls, John Nettleton, Eira Heath, Molly Urquhart, Paul Hardwick, Michael Latimer, Philip Brack, Martin Boddey, Eric Mason, Matt Zimmerrman, and Vernon Duke. Sc: Robert Bolt, from his play of the same name. Ph: Ted Moore. 2nd Unit Ph: Patrick Carey. Ed: Ralph Kemplen. Mus: Georges Delerue. Prod des: John Box. Prod: Zinnemann and William N. Graf for Highland/Columbia. 120 mins.

The Day of the Jackal (1973). A political thriller that pits brilliant French police investigator Michel Lonsdale against "The Jackal," an equally brilliant professional killer (Edward Fox) hired by a right-wing military organization to assassinate de Gaulle. The anonymous, amoral "Jackal" provides a fascinating contrast—and comparison—with other Zinnemann protagonists. With Edward Fox ("The Jackal"), Michel Lonsdale (Chief Inspector Claude Lebel), Delphine Seyrig (Colette de Montpelier), Terence Alexander (Lloyd), Michel Auclair (Col. Rolland), Eric Porter (Col. Rodin), Jean Martin (Wolenski), Denis Carey (Casson), Olga Georges-Picot (Denise), Cyril Cusak (Gozzi, the gunsmith), Alan Badel (the Minister), Maurice Denham (Gen. Colbert), Donald Sinden (Mallinson), Tony Britton (Inspector Thomas), Derek Jacobi (Caron, Lebel's assistant), Adrien Cayla-Legrand (de Gaulle), Ronald Pickup (forger/blackmailer), Vernon Dobtcheff (interrogator), Timothy West (Berthier), Jean Sorel (Lt.-Col. Bastien-Thiry), Barrie Ingham (Saint-Clair), Anton Rodgers (Bernard), David Swift (Monclair), Bernard Archard (English detective), Jacques Francois (Pascal), and Raymond Gerome (Flavigny). Sc: Kenneth Ross (from the novel by Frederick Forsyth). Ph: Jean Tournier. Ed: Ralph Kemplen. Prod des: Willy Holt. Mus: Georges Delerue. Prod: John Woolf, David Deutsch, and Julian Derode. Universal. 142 mins.

Julia (1977). Lillian Hellman (Jane Fonda) looks back on her relationships with Dashiell Hammett (Jason Robards, Jr.) and childhood friend Julia (Vanessa Redgrave), focusing on the dangerous mission she undertook in the early 1930s to help Julia in her effort against Nazism. The final meeting between the two women has been called "the most beautiful single scene Zinnemann has ever directed" (Neil Sinyard). Winner of three Academy Awards for Supporting Actor (Robards), Supporting Actress (Redgrave), and Adapted Screenplay. With Jane Fonda (Lillian Hellman), Vanessa Redgrave (Julia), Jason Robards, Jr. (Dashiell Hammett), Maximilian Schell (Johann), Hal Holbrook (Alan Campbell), Rosemary Murphy (Dorothy Parker), Meryl Streep (Anne Marie), Dora Doll (woman train passenger), Elisabeth Mortensen (young woman train passenger), John Glover (Sammy), Lisa Pelikan (young Julia), Susan Jones (young Lillian), Cathleen Nesbitt (Julia's grandmother), Maurice Denham (undertaker), Gerard Buhr (passport officer), Stefan Gryff (Hamlet), Lambert Wilson (young man on train), Phillip Siegel (little boy in hospital), Molly Urquhart (woman), Anthony Carrick (man in Berlin station), Jacques David (fat man), Jacqueline Staup (woman in green hat), Hans Verner (Vienna concierge), Christian De Tiliere (Paris concierge). Sc: Alvin Sargent (from the story by Hellman in *Pentimento*). Ph: Douglas Slocombe. 2nd unit ph: Paddy Carey and Guy Delattre. Ed: Walter Murch. Prod des: Gene Callahan, Willy Holt, and Carmen Dillon. Mus: Georges Delerue. Prod: Richard Roth. Twentieth Century-Fox. 117 mins.

Five Days One Summer (1982). During a climbing holiday in the Swiss Alps with her uncle (Sean Connery), who is also her lover, Betsy Brantley becomes increasingly shaken by events and the attraction she feels for their young guide (Lambert Wilson). With Sean Connery (Dr. Douglas Meredith), Betsy Brantley (Kate Meredith), Lambert Wilson (Johann Biari), Jennifer Hilary (Sarah Meredith), Isabel Dean (Kate's mother), Anna Massey (Jennifer Pierce), Sheila Reid (Gillian Pierce), Gerard Buhr (Brendel), George Claisse (Dieter), Kathy Marothy (Dieter's wife), Terry Kingley (Georg), and Emilie Lihou (old woman). Sc: Michael Austin (from "Maiden Maiden," the short story by Kay Boyle). Ph: Giuseppe Rotunno. 2nd unit ph: Norman Dyhrenfurth. Ed: Stuart Baird. Mus: Elmer Bernstein. Prod des: Willy Holt. Technical adviser: Norman Dyhrenfurth. Climbers: Martin Boysen, Paul Nunn, Paul Braithwaite, Rab Carrington, David Cuthbertson, Murray Hamilton, Wendy Leech, Ian Nicholson, and John Yates. Exec Prod: Peter Beale. Prod: Zinnemann. A Ladd Company Production. Warner Bros. 108 mins.

SELECTED
BIBLIOGRAPHY

□□
□□

As I See It. Producer: Tim Zinnemann. Editor: Walter Murch. Highland Films Production, 1997. 44 mins. [Tribute to Fred Zinnemann.]

Barson, Michael. "Fred Zinnemann." *The Illustrated Who's Who of Hollywood Directors. Volume 1: The Sound Era.* New York: Noonday Press. 476–78.

Buckley, Michael. "Fred Zinnemann." *Films in Review* 34.1 (1983): 25–40.

Dick, Bernard F., ed. *Columbia Pictures: Portrait of a Studio.* Lexington: University Press of Kentucky, 1992.

Drummond, Phillip. *High Noon.* BFI Film Classics. London: BFI Publishing, 1997.

Fitzpatrick, John. "Fred Zinnemann." *American Directors: Volume II.* Ed. Jean-Pierre Coursodon with Pierre Sauvage. New York: McGraw-Hill, 1983. 378–86.

"Fred Zinnemann *Sight and Sound* Dossier." *Sight and Sound.* Supplement [January 1996].

Fred Zinnemann Special Double Issue. *Film Criticism* 18–19 (Spring–Fall 1994).

French, Brandon. *On the Verge of Revolt: Women in American Films of the Fifties.* New York: Frederick Ungar, 1978.

Garbicz, Adam, and Jacek Klinowski. *Cinema: The Magic Vehicle. A Guide to Its Achievement. Volume One—The Cinema Through 1949.* New York: Schocken Books, 1983.

————. *Cinema: The Magic Vehicle. A Guide to Its Achievement. Volume Two— The Cinema in the Fifties.* New York: Schocken Books, 1983.

Giannetti, Louis. "Films of Conscience: The Cinema of Fred Zinnemann." *Masters of the American Cinema.* Englewood Cliffs, N.J.: Prentice-Hall, 1981. 354–74.

Girgus, Sam B. *Hollywood Renaissance: The Cinema of Democracy in the Era of Ford, Capra, and Kazan.* New York; Cambridge University Press, 1998.

Gow, Gordon. *Hollywood in the Fifties.* New York: A. S. Barnes, 1971.

————. "Individualism Against Machinery." Interview. *Films and Filming* 24.5 (February 1976): 12–17.

Griffith, Richard. *Fred Zinnemann* (Pamphlet). New York: Museum of Modern Art, 1958.

Hochman, Stanley, ed. "Fred Zinnemann." *American Film Directors: A Library of Film Criticism.* New York: Frederick Ungar, 1974. 522–30.

Horton, Robert. "Fred Zinnemann: Day of the Craftsman." *Film Comment* 33.5 (Sept.–Oct. 1997): 60–67.

Johnson, Albert. "The Tenth Muse in San Francisco, Part 3." *Sight and Sound* 25 (Autumn 1955): 102–104, 110.

Neve, Brian. "A Past Master of His Craft: An Interview with Fred Zinnemann." *Cineaste* 23.1 (1997): 15–19.

Phillips, Gene D. *Exiles in Hollywood: Major European Film Directors in America.* Bethlehem, Pa.: Lehigh University Press, 1998.

————. "Fred Zinnemann: Darkness at Noon." *Major Film Directors of the American and British Cinema.* Bethlehem, Pa.: Lehigh University Press, 1990. 108–24.

————. "Fred Zinnemann Talking to Gene Phillips." *Focus on Film* 14 (1973): 23–31.

Reid, John Howard. "A Man for All Movies: The Films of Fred Zinnemann." *Films and Filming* 13.8 (May 1967): 5–11.

Rohauer, Raymond. *A Tribute to Fred Zinnemann.* New York: The Gallery of Modern Art and Huntington Hartford Collection, 1967.

Sarris, Andrew. *The American Cinema: Directors and Directions, 1929–1968*. New York: E. P. Dutton, 1968.

———. "The Case for Fred Zinnemann." *The Village Voice,* November 16, 1982: 55, 122.

Schickel, Richard. *Movies: The History of an Art and Institution*. New York: Basic Books, 1964.

Shipman, David. *The Story of Cinema: A Complete Narrative History from the Beginning to the Present*. New York: St. Martin's Press, 1982. 701–705, 878–80.

Sinyard, Neil. "Spotlight on Fred Zinnemann." The National Film Theatre Booklet (London), October–December 1982. 34–37.

Stanbrook, Alan. "A Man for All Movies: The Films of Fred Zinnemann." *Films and Filming* 13.9 (June 1967): 11–15.

Toumarkine, Doris. "Fred Zinnemann." *World Film Directors: Volume One, 1890–1945*. Ed. John Wakeman. New York: H. W. Company, 1987. 1238–47.

———. "Zinnemann, Fred." *The Encyclopedia of Film*. Ed. James Monaco and the editors of Baseline. New York: Perigee, 1991. 594–95.

Welsh, James M. "Fred Zinnemann." *The International Dictionary of Films and Filmmakers, Volume II: Directors/Filmmakers*. Ed. Christopher Lyon. Chicago: St. James Press, 1984. 610–11.

Wolf, Matt. "Looking Back on a Career of Conscience." *The Valley News* (Hanover, N.H.), August 28, 1994: D5.

Zinnemann, Fred. "Conversation with Fred Zinnemann." Interview. By Arthur Nolletti Jr. *Film Criticism* 18–19 (Spring–Fall 1994): 7–29.

———. "Different Perspective." *Sight and Sound* 17.67 (Autumn 1948): 113.

———. "Fred Zinnemann." *American Film* 11.4 (January–February 1986): 12–13, 62, 66–67.

———. "*From Here to Eternity.*" *Sight and Sound* 57.1 (Winter 1987–1988): 20–25.

———. "Letter from Fred Zinnemann." *Film Criticism* 19.2 (Winter 1994–1995): 86–88.

———. *A Life in the Movies: An Autobiography.* New York: Scribner's, 1992.

———. "Remembering Robert Flaherty." *Action* (Directors Guild of America), May–June 1976. 24–27.

———. "Revelations." Interview. *Films and Filming* 10.12 (September 1964): 5–6.

———. "Zinnemann Talks Back." Interview with James R. Silke and Rory Guy. *Cinema* (Beverly Hills) 2.3 (October–November 1964): 20–22, 30.

CONTRIBUTORS

WHEELER WINSTON DIXON is Chairperson of the Film Studies program at the University of Nebraska, Lincoln. He is the author or editor of ten books, including *Re-Viewing British Cinema: 1900–1992*, *It Looks at You: The Returned Gaze of Cinema*, *The Films of Jean-Luc Godard*, *The Exploding Eye: A Re-Visionary History of the American Experimental Cinema*, and *The Transparency of Spectacle*. He is also a film and video maker whose works have been widely screened.

LINDA C. EHRLICH teaches film, theater, and Japanese language at Case Western Reserve University. She has written for such journals as *East-West Film Journal*, *Post Script*, *Literature/Film Quarterly*, *Cinema Journal*, and *Film Quarterly*, and is co-editor of *Cinematic Landscapes: Observations on the Visual Arts and Cinema of China and Japan*.

GWENDOLYN FOSTER teaches in the Department of English at the University of Nebraska, Lincoln. Her books include *Women Film Directors: An International Bio-Critical Dictionary*, *Women Filmmakers of the African and Asian Disaspora*, and an anthology on the films of Chantal Akerman. She also produced, directed, and wrote the screenplay for *Women Who Made the Movies*, and co-wrote the screenplay for the French-language feature, *Squatters*.

LOUIS GIANNETTI is Professor of English and Film at Case Western Reserve University. He is the author of the popular textbook, *Understanding Movies*, now in its eighth edition, *Godard and Others: Essays on Film Form*, *Masters of the American Cinema*, and *Flashback: A Brief History of Film* (with Scott Eyman). His daughter Francesca's nickname is "Frankie," after the heroine of *The Member of the Wedding*.

LLOYD MICHAELS is editor of *Film Criticism* and Professor of English at Allegheny College. He has published in numerous periodicals and references, including *Literature/Film Quarterly, Post Script, Film Quarterly*, and *University of Toronto Quarterly*, and is the author of *Elia Kazan: A Guide to References and Resources* and *The Phantom of the Cinema: Character in Modern Film*.

ARTHUR NOLLETTI JR. is Professor of English at Framingham State College where he teaches literature and film studies. His work has appeared in *Film Criticism, Jump Cut, Film Quarterly, Post Script*, and *The Journal of Popular Film*. He edited the Special Issue on Fred Zinnemann for *Film Criticism* and is co-editor of *Reframing Japanese Cinema: Authorship, Genre, History*.

MARTIN F. NORDEN teaches film at the University of Massachusetts at Amherst. He has written for *Journal of Film and Video, Wide Angle, Film & History, Journal of Popular Film and Television*, and various anthologies. He is the co-author of *Movies: A Language in Light* and author of *The Cinema of Isolation: A History of Physical Disability* and *John Barrymore: A Bio-Bibliography*.

STEPHEN PRINCE teaches in the Department of Communication Studies at Virginia Tech. He has published in numerous journals and is Book Editor of *Film Quarterly* and the author of *Visions of Empire: Political Imagery in Contemporary American Film* and *The Warrior's Camera: The Cinema of Akira Kurosawa*.

LEONARD QUART is Professor of Cinema at The College of Staten Island and the Graduate Center, CUNY. He is an editor of *Cineaste*, the co-author of *How the War Was Remembered: Hollywood & Vietnam*, and the author of the revised and expanded second edition of *American Film and Society Since 1945*.

JOANNA E. RAPF is Professor in the Department of English and the Program of Film and Video Studies at the University of Oklahoma. She writes in the areas of film history, theory, and criticism, and is the co-author of *Buster Keaton: A Bio-Bibliography*. Forthcoming is a book-length study of her grandfather, MGM producer, Harry Rapf.

CLAUDIA STERNBERG teaches English literature, film, and television at the Technical University Chemnitz (Germany). She is the author of *Written for the Screen: The American Motion-Picture Screenplay as Text* and the co-editor of *Many Voices—Many Cultures: Multicultural British Short Stories.* Forthcoming is a women's literary history.

JOEL N. SUPER received his Ph.D in English from the University of Illinois at Champaign-Urbana. His dissertation is on Fred Zinnemann.

STEVE VINEBERG teaches theater and film at Holy Cross, and writes regularly for *The Boston Phoenix, The Threepenny Review,* and *The Oxford American.* He reviews movies for "Fresh Air" on National Public Radio, and is the author of *Method Actors: Three Generations of an American Acting Style* and *No Surprises, Please: Movies in the Reagan Decade.*

INDEX

271